University of Plymouth
Charles Seale Hayne Library
Subject to status this item may be renewed
via your Primo account

http:/primo.plymouth.ac.uk
Tel: (01752) 588588

US Domestic and International Regimes of Security

This book maps the increasing convergence of US domestic and international security regimes, analyzing the trend towards global pacification in the name of 'security'.

The dream of liberal world peace after the Cold War is on the verge of collapsing into permanent global pacification – not only in the global south, but also in pockets of the 'Third World' within the territory of Western states. In this volume, the author explores the ways in which regimes of security have been extended into increasingly large aspects of social life and shows that their expansion has been driven by a constant broadening of the notion of 'war'.

Filling a gap in the literature, the book demonstrates how US security agencies have sought to develop indeterminate security capabilities aimed at distinguishing between legitimate and illegitimate flows of people and resources. This analysis of regimes of security is tied to a more general discussion about the persistence, or even multiplication, of illiberal forms of power within liberal governmentality.

This book will be of much interest to students of security studies, war and conflict studies and international relations in general.

Markus Kienscherf is Lecturer in Sociology at the John F Kennedy Institute for North American Studies, Freie Universität Berlin. His research interests include security studies, critical theory, criminology, and surveillance studies.

Routledge Critical Security Studies Series

Titles in this series include:

Securing Outer Space
Edited by Natalie Bormann and Michael Sheehan

Critique, Security and Power
The political limits to emancipatory approaches
Tara McCormack

Gender, Human Security and the United Nations
Security language as a political framework for women
Natalie Florea Hudson

The Struggle for the West
A divided and contested legacy
Christopher S. Browning and Marko Lehti

Gender and International Security
Feminist perspectives
Edited by Laura Sjoberg

Reimagining War in the 21st Century
From Clausewitz to network-centric warfare
Manabrata Guha

The New Spatiality of Security
Operational uncertainty and the US military in Iraq
Caroline M. Croser

Human Security as Statecraft
Structural conditions, articulations and unintended consequences
Nik Hynek

US Domestic and International Regimes of Security
Pacifying the globe, securing the homeland
Markus Kienscherf

US Domestic and International Regimes of Security

Pacifying the globe, securing the homeland

Markus Kienscherf

Routledge
Taylor & Francis Group

LONDON AND NEW YORK

First published 2013
by Routledge
2 Park Square, Milton Park, Abingdon, Oxon OX14 4RN

Simultaneously published in the USA and Canada
by Routledge
711 Third Avenue, New York, NY 10017

Routledge is an imprint of the Taylor & Francis Group, an informa business

British Library Cataloguing in Publication Data
A catalogue record for this book is available from the British Library

Library of Congress Cataloging-in-Publication Data
Kienscherf, Markus, 1979–
    US domestic and international regimes of security : pacifying the globe,
    securing the homeland / Markus Kienscherf.
    p. cm. – (Routledge critical security studies series)
    Includes bibliographical references and index.
    1. United States–Foreign relations–2001–2009. 2. United States–Foreign
    relations–2009– 3. Security, International–Government policy–United
    States. 4. National security–United States. I. Title. II. Title: United
    States domestic and international regimes of security.
    JZ1480.K545 2012
    355'.033573–dc23

                                                                    2012019650

ISBN: 978-0-415-52392-9 (hbk)
ISBN: 978-0-203-08106-8 (ebk)

Typeset in Times
by Wearset Ltd, Boldon, Tyne and Wear

Contents

Acknowledgments

This book is a completely revised version of my doctoral thesis, which I submitted to the Department of Political and Social Science, Freie Universität Berlin, on 19 October 2010. First and foremost, I wish to thank my supervisor Harald Wenzel for taking this project on board and for his enormous support and guidance throughout the course of my doctoral work. I should also thank my mentors, Michaela Hampf and Ursula Lehmkuhl, for giving me knowledgeable and aute advice on numerous occasions.

The Graduate School of North American Studies at Freie Universität Berlin provided an excellent setting for pursuing my research. I owe great thanks to its Managing Director, Katja Mertin, and its Program Assistant, Gabi Bodmeier, for all their indefatigable work in turning the School into such a congenial place of interdisciplinary scholarly inquiry. Thanks are also due to the School's faculty and my fellow students, as well as to the German Research Foundation (DFG) for funding the Graduate School and, by extension, also my own doctoral work.

This book has profited enormously from a range of critical comments. In particular, I wish to thank Frank Adloff, José Casanova, Sven Chojnacki, Irwin Collier, Sérgio Costa, Andreas Etges, Winfried Fluck, Stephen Graham, Derek Gregory, Ulla Haselstein, Margit Mayer and Don Pease. At this point, I would also like to thank the students who attended my undergraduate seminars on US counterinsurgency and security in everyday life, and whose questions and comments have helped me clarify many aspects of my research. Last, but not least, my thanks go to the four anonymous reviewers whose perceptive criticisms, comments and suggestions helped me forge a dissertation into a book. It goes without saying that all remaining errors and omissions are purely my own.

I have presented parts of this book at the following conferences: in June 2008 at 'Divided We Stand – United We Fall. Perspectives on Inclusion and Exclusion in America'; in May 2009 at 'The Complex' in Princeton; in June 2010 at 'War and the Body' in London; in September 2010 at 'Ordnance: War, Architecture and Space' in Cork; and in June 2011 at 'New Ways of War? Insurgencies, "Small Wars" and the Past and Future of Conflict' in Dublin. I would like to thank the organizers of these conferences for giving me a chance to present my work-in-progress.

Excerpts from Chapter 4, Chapter 5 and Chapter 6 have been previously published in 'Plugging Cultural Knowledge into the U.S. Military Machine: The Neo-Orientalist Logic of Counterinsurgency', *Topia – Canadian Journal of Cultural Studies*, 23–4: 121–43 and 'A Programme of Global Pacification: U.S. Counterinsurgency Doctrine and the Biopolitics of Human (In)Security', *Security Dialogue* 42 (6): 517–35.

Last, but by no means least, my thanks goes to Harald Weigl for his highly intelligent comments on numerous drafts; to Andrei Dumitrescu, Sebastian Iring and Steffen Rolke for helping me unwind; to Joe Clemoes, Mike Seelig and David Truby for their hospitality; and, most importantly, to Annika and Emma for their love.

Introduction

From 'defense' to 'security'

Security has become a veritable obsession in both the United States and Europe. Apparently, security is something we just cannot get enough of. Or, conversely, events and processes, which we need to be secured from, seem to be proliferating. Security is, after all, always contoured by insecurity and threat. The provision of security is but an attempt to identify, manage, contain and/or eliminate perceived insecurities. The main provider of security has been, and continues to be, the state. Indeed, the provision of security was, and is, one of the most important functions, if not the most important function, of the state. The most fundamental insecurities addressed by the state center around violence. Indeed, the state legitimizes its very existence through the protection of its citizens from both internal and external violence. The irony is, that states were themselves established through the use of violence and continue to use it in order to protect their populations. Historically, states emerged through the (often violent) production of a monopoly over the legitimate use of violence within a particular territory (Giddens 1987; Tilly 1992; Weber 1919). This monopoly is not set in stone, but has to be constantly (re)affirmed. Moreover, threats to life and limb are not the only insecurity states seek to contain and eliminate. States also derive their legitimacy from safeguarding the economic wellbeing of their population, especially by means of protecting private property. In liberal states in particular, the political principle of freedom, the right to own property and the provision of security are inextricably intertwined (see Neocleous 2008). Domestic threats to the bodies of citizens and their property fall under the category of criminality. Internally, the state aims to protect its population from criminality and, externally, from the territorial ambitions of other states. Crime control and foreign defense have thus been the two most significant fields of state intervention in the name of security. Traditionally, there has been a clear dividing line between domestic public safety (provided by the police) and foreign defense (provided by the armed forces), but this dividing line has become rather fuzzy.

In the United States, 'national security' replaced 'defense' after the end of World War II. 'National security' became institutionalized with the passage of the National Security Act of 1947. The Act was, above all, aimed at maintaining perpetual military and civil preparedness during peacetime, while signaling that this permanent mobilization would not endanger liberty and democratic principles. Indeed, the concept of security opens up a much more expansive semantic field and has more of a civilian and peaceful connotation than defense or war. But the shift from defense to security was about more than just semantics. It also marked a 'transformation in the way in which the international order is conceived, the rationalities through which it is apprehended, and the technologies through which it is maintained' (De Larrinaga and Doucet 2010b: 13). First of all, the National Security Act reorganized US 'technologies' for enforcing international order. Amongst other things, the Act and a 1949 amendment unified the armed forces, folding the Department of the Army, the Department of the Navy and the newly created Department of the Air Force into the Department of Defense. The Act also established the National Security Council as the central coordinating mechanism for US security policy, and set up the Central Intelligence Agency (CIA) as the first US peacetime intelligence organization. In short, the National Security Act established a centralized US national security apparatus to allow for better coordination of security policy across the military and civilian spheres. The creation of new technologies of security, and the reorganization of old ones, occurred in response to a fundamental shift in the way international security was problematized. Miguel de Larrinaga and Marc Doucet (2008, 2010b) argue that this shift occurred partly because during World War II, states realized that they were no longer able to effectively defend their territories and civilian populations against the threat of airpower. The increasing technological sophistication of airpower in general, and aerial bombardment in particular, made it possible to project military power far into an adversary's territory and thus also to directly target an adversary's infrastructure and population (2008: 523–24; 2010b: 13). In the face of the destructive capabilities of these new military technologies, traditional defense became both impossible and meaningless. The focus thus shifted from territorial defense towards efforts to manage power within an international system:

> The use of the word 'security' in relation to the international system, this externalization of a concept which had been historically deployed in relation to internal order, can be seen as a shift from understanding the interstate in terms of the logic of territorial defense to one in which the concern increasingly becomes the management of power within an international system projected at a global level.
>
> (De Larrinaga and Doucet 2010b: 13)

Yet, the shift from territorial defense to security marked not only the externalization of internal order maintenance, but also the internalization of external order building. Internal order came to be seen as vital for maintaining a permanent state of preparedness which, in turn, was perceived as pivotal for maintaining the international system. Furthermore, a steadily growing military apparatus tends to spill over into the civilian sphere or may even be deployed to secure the domestic order. Hence, the logic of security does not only signal the policing of international order but also the creeping militarization of maintaining domestic order.

Experiences with producing order abroad have long shaped the ways in which order is maintained at home. Drawing on Aimé Césaire's idea of a 'boomerang effect of colonization' (Césaire 1972: 5), Michel Foucault (2003) put it as follows:

> It should never be forgotten that while colonization, with its techniques and its political and juridical weapons, obviously transported European models to other continents, it also had a considerable boomerang effect on the mechanisms of power in the West, and the result was that the West could practice something resembling colonization, or an internal colonialism on itself.
>
> (Foucault 2003: 103)

The militarization of policing domestic order – 'the extension of military ideas of tracking, identification and targeting into the quotidian spaces and circulations of everyday life' (Graham 2010: xi) is indeed informed by 'experiments with styles of targeting and technology in colonial war-zones' (Graham 2010: xvi). In fact, 'the colonies were used (starting, in the case of Britain, with Ireland) as guinea pigs for experiments in governance that would not have been tolerated in the metropole. If the experiments succeeded, they might be reimported'. (Scott 2005: 401; see also Hindess 1998; Larner *et al.* 2007; Larner 2008).

Yet, instead of singular boomerang effects that brought mechanisms of power and violence designed for use in the periphery back to the metropolis, we now face an almost complete blurring of domestic policing and foreign warfighting. Arguably, under colonialism and the Cold War the division between inside/outside still held firm, although more research into this is surely needed: 'the policing of "life" applied on the inside of the state's territory; on the outside one waged war against biologically foreign "races" or against ideologically foreign "ways of life" such as fascism or communism' (Medovoi 2007: 65–6) – even if elements of these 'races' or 'ways of life' were also thought to have infiltrated the homeland. Today, insecurities and threats are, however, problematized as circulating below, across and beyond state borders. In response, rationalities and practices of domestic policing have become externalized, while rationalities and practices of foreign warfighting have become internalized. It seems as if the dream of post-Cold War liberal world peace has collapsed into a nightmare of permanent global pacification – not only in the global south, but also in pockets of the 'Third World' within the territory of Western states.

Threats to the global homeland

The terrorist attacks on the United States on 11 September 2001, are commonly seen as a major turning point in the ways in which security is understood and provided. Following 9/11, non-state war-making entities, such as insurgents, terrorists, pirates and mercenaries, have become a major global security concern. These groups are said to severely undermine states' monopoly over the means of violence, and are thus viewed as a threat to the very existence of the interstate system. In fact, some commentators even go as far as to declare that we are in the midst of a global conflict 'over humanity's new forms of social and political organization' (Bunker 2010: 24). Violent non-state actors are, moreover, thought to have close links to transnational criminal organizations. In fact, their funding is said to derive primarily from illegal activities, most notably drug trafficking (see Kan 2009). Changes in conflict, especially the shift from interstate wars to conflicts involving non-state groups, are thus viewed as inextricably intertwined with transnational circulations of crime. Indeed, contemporary threats are deemed to cut across the traditional division between domestic public safety and foreign defense, affecting individuals, populations and spaces at the local, national, regional and global level. In brief, contemporary insecurities are problematized as amorphous, interconnected and multi-scalar.

'Bad' circulations of violence, crime and illicit goods are also tied to 'good' circulations of capital, commodities, services, information and (to a much lesser extent) people, that are lumped together under the catch-all term of globalization. Indeed, the imagery used in problematizing circulations of violence is the same as that used in describing the processes and potentialities of global capitalism. The 'bad' circulations of violence and the 'good' circulations of globalization are now both frequently construed in terms of 'flows', 'networks', 'mobilities' and so on (Arquilla and Ronfeldt 2000, 2001; Arquilla 2007; Bakker *et al.* 2011; Milward and Raab 2006; Raab and Milward 2003).

This holds particularly true for discourses on terrorism which, following the attacks of 9/11, have invariably characterized Islamist terrorist organizations as local and regional networks that are loosely linked into a distributed global terrorist network (see Bauman and Galecki 2005; Downey and Murdock 2003; Ettlinger and Bosco 2004; Kilcullen 2005; Larner 2008; Sageman 2004, 2008). The prime exemplar of a distributed terrorist network of global reach is, of course, al-Qaeda – the organization behind the 9/11 attacks. A number of commentators have argued that, through ideological, personal, financial and operational links, different regional theaters of conflict are loosely tied to al- Qaeda's brand of global terror:

> Islamist movements appear to function through regional 'theaters of operation' where operatives cooperate, or conduct activities in neighboring countries. Evidence suggests that Islamist groups within theaters follow general ideological or strategic approaches aligned with Al Qaeda pronouncements, and share a common tactical style and operational lexicon. But there is no clear evidence that Al Qaeda directly controls jihad in each theater. Indeed, rather than a monolithic organization, the global jihad is a much more complex phenomenon.
>
> (Kilcullen 2005: 598)

Threats of violence in general, and the threat of terrorism in particular, are thus increasingly held to emanate from fluid, mobile and networked organizations that operate across different spatial scales. These insecurities are, moreover, deemed to cut across the traditional division between domestic public safety and foreign defense. As a consequence, these transversal threats are said to require equally transversal responses.

If, 'globalization and terrorism can be understood as based on the same political-economic imaginary' of networks and flows (Larner 2008), economic globalization and the US-led global war also have the same 'strategic field of intervention', namely the entire globe, (Walters 2004: 242) and operate according to the same biopolitical distinction between 'safe' and 'dangerous' global circulations:

> [Globalization and the war on terror] have precipitated the telling collapse of liberal society's traditional distinction between the internal and external enemy, as well as between the practices by which each is targeted: regulation and warfare, respectively. [...] If globalization is the name that implicitly designates the 'pacification' of populations in the name of world market integration, then 'the Global War on Terror' [...] should be understood as the territorially unbounded, politically malleable military strategy that this pacification actually demands.
>
> (Medovoi 2007: 53, 55)

Globalization can be understood as a set of rationalities and practices geared towards promoting the unfettered global circulation of capital, goods and services, while pacifying individuals, populations and states that are held to pose a threat to these circulations in order to eventually (re)integrate them into the global order. The global war on terror is aimed at eradicating circulations that are deemed to threaten both the global order and the US homeland. Rather than a traditional geo-strategic reaffirmation of US sovereignty and global hegemony, the war on terror is, above all, a biopolitical effort to weed out the 'bad' circulations of globalization and thus (re)produce a global capitalist order. As a consequence, the war on terror and the growing obsession over US homeland security do not so much mark a closing off of US borders and a reassertion of US sovereignty (which do however play a tactical role), as an attempt to deterritorialize US security, in order to manage insecurities across local, national, regional and global scales:

> The conception of homeland security goes hand in hand with a more flexible multifront mobile role for the armed forces abroad, as one department of a globalized police force. Advocates of homeland security argue for the need for more government, military, and intelligence coordination, for the armed forces to be involved in this country as well, and for the government through surveillance and policing to intrude into more areas of civil life at home. [...] Although homeland security may strive to cordon off the nation as

domestic space from external threats, it is actually about breaking down the boundaries between inside and outside, about seeing the homeland in a state of constant emergency from threats within and without.

(Kaplan 2003: 90)

We should, moreover, note that the global war on terror is not the first war on 'bad' circulations. As will become clearer in the course of this book, the US-led war on drugs,[1] which started under the Nixon administration, in many ways anticipated the global war on terror. Indeed, global wars on 'bad' circulations can be understood as inevitable consequences of attempts to regulate circulations globally. For instance, Moisés Naím, editor in chief of *Foreign Policy*, suggests that besides the war on terror, there are 'five other similar global wars that pit governments against agile, well-financed networks of highly dedicated individuals. These are the fights against the illegal international trade in drugs, arms, intellectual property, people, and money'. Naím argues that in some way or other, states have struggled with circulations of drugs, arms, illegal aliens, counterfeit goods and laundered money for centuries. Yet because of the growing speed, mobility and interconnectedness of global circulations, states now find it increasingly difficult to wage these 'five wars of globalization' (Naím 2003: 1). Indeed, the global promotion and management of 'good' circulations seems to require the permanent deployment of rationalities and practices that are geared towards identifying, locating, managing, containing and/or eliminating 'bad' circulations (see Grondin 2010; Hardt and Negri 2000, 2004; Medovoi 2007).

This book will analyze some of the concrete rationalities and practices of security by means of which the United States has sought to identify, locate, manage, contain and/or eliminate 'bad' circulations both domestically and globally. The book will thus seek to map the increasing convergence of US domestic and international security regimes, analyzing the trend towards global pacification in the name of 'security'.

There are very few genuinely interdisciplinary studies of the growing convergence of domestic and international regimes of security. This book aims to fill this gap. What is more, the existing literature has thus far primarily analyzed the expansion of security in terms of 'militarization'. Yet, not only has the production of domestic public safety been 'militarized', but foreign defense has also been increasingly 'civilianized'. What best describes efforts to respond to the contemporary security conjuncture are therefore neither notions of global policing nor ideas of conventional warfare, but the concept of pacification. In fact, contemporary regimes of security seek to control civilian populations through an ever-tighter articulation of civilian and military organizations, tactics and doctrines, aimed at identifying, tracking and targeting dangerous elements that supposedly hide among the circulations of everyday life. Potential and actual insurgents, terrorists and criminals are indistinguishable from ordinary civilians, while flows of contraband (such as illegal weapons and narcotics) are hidden amongst the licit circulations of global capitalism. Regimes of security are therefore not so much permeated by conventional doctrines of firepower-centered, high-tech warfare, as by forms of military doctrine that are focused on the lower end of the Pentagon's spectrum of conflict, namely Low Intensity Conflict (LIC) and Counterinsurgency (COIN) doctrine.

Counterinsurgency doctrine is of particular relevance here, because it seeks to combine regulation and violence into a comprehensive effort to pacify populations and spaces that are held to threaten both US national and global security. Since its formal promulgation in the 1960s, counterinsurgency has cut across distinctions between the military and civilian sphere as well as policing and warfighting, forming a concrete program for securing targeted populations and spaces in order to (re)integrate them into the international order. What is more, this book will show that in the 1960s and 1970s, practices of counterinsurgency-style pacification were re-imported to be used against risky populations and spaces in the American homeland.

This analysis also ties in with a more general discussion about the persistence, or even multiplication, of authoritarian forms of power within liberal rule. Liberal rule seeks to delimit the legitimate scope of governmental intervention through the promotion of individual liberty and autonomy, in order to promote socio-economic processes. Yet not everybody is considered to be equally capable of exercising their liberty, and some are even construed as threats to the very existence of the liberal order. Hence authoritarian forms of power and violence are redeployed within the field of liberal rule to target those spaces, populations and activities that are construed as internal and external threats to the free development of both domestic and global socio-economic processes.

Method

Security takes the form of specific responses to specific problems. Events and processes have to be problematized as insecurities; they have to be 'securitized' (Buzan *et al.* 1998), in order to become amenable to interventions in the name of security. What best fits the study of particular interventions in the name of security is a Foucauldian analytic of government. Government aims to intervene in and shape somebody else's conduct, or in Foucault's own words 'to structure the possible field of action of others' (Foucault 2000c: 341). Government consists of forms of knowledge, expertise and representations concerning the fields of intervention as well as the activities of intervention on the one hand, and technologies, techniques, instruments and tactics of intervention, on the other (see Dean 1999: 30–7; Rose and Miller 1992: 175–6; Miller and Rose 2008: 15–16). Government is characterized by the interrelations between rationalities or programs – 'deliberate and relatively systematic forms of thought' – and specific 'regimes of practices' (Dean 1999: 32). In short, government operates within the frame of what Foucault somewhat awkwardly termed 'governmentality' (Foucault 1991b).

The term *governmentalities of security* will be used to highlight the fact that security practices are always bound up with forms of knowledge and expertise (rationalities) both about the nature of insecurities and the ways in which they should be dealt with.

Yet, the analytic of governmentality has two significant shortcomings: first of all, the literature on governmentality tends to primarily concern itself with governmental rationalities and practices inside the state. This raises the question as to whether or not a concept that was originally developed for studying domestic power relations can be scaled up to the international domain. Yet, if we accept that with the aforementioned shift from 'defense' to 'security', mechanisms for maintaining domestic order have been externalized, we can also meaningfully speak of international or global governmentalities. Indeed, there is now a growing body of research into global governmentalities (for example Larner and Walters 2004a, 2004b; De Larrinaga and Doucet 2010a).

This leads to a second and closely related shortcoming: studies of governmentality tend to stress non-coercive liberal means for intervening in somebody else's actions, while sidelining the persistent threat and/or actual use of violence. This is most likely due to the fact that the concept has been developed, and continues to be primarily applied, in the context of studies of liberal governance. Drawing on Thomas Lemke's argument that governmentality constitutes a mode of power that cuts across 'the problematics of consensus and will on the one hand, and conquest and war on the other' (Lemke 2000: 4), this book will, however, draw out precisely the persistence of authoritarianism and violence within liberal governmentalities of security. This will be discussed in more detail in Chapter 1. For now, it will suffice to say that a 'will to divide appears as a core element within modern governmentality' (Walters 2004: 249). Liberal governmentalities of security are set to distinguish between those who can be governed liberally and those who must be governed coercively, or even be eliminated through the use of violence (see Hindess 2004).

At the most general level, governmentalities of security are mechanisms of power – rationalities and practices aimed at exerting power over others. Michel Foucault remarked that any analysis of power should:

> begin with its infinitesimal mechanisms, which have their own history, their own trajectory, their own techniques and tactics, and then look at how these mechanisms of power, which have their solidity and, in a sense, their own technology, have been and are invested, colonized, used, inflected, transformed, displaced, extended, and so on by increasingly general mechanisms and forms of overall domination.
>
> (Foucault 2003: 30)

This book will examine how particular rationalities and practices of security have come to be deployed across the inside/outside divide, how they have thereby increasingly blurred the dividing line between domestic public safety and foreign defense, and how they are being provisionally articulated into an overall strategy of global pacification.

Michel Foucault also showed that mechanisms of power tend to be neutral, politically invisible and independent of ideology (see Gordon 2000: xv; Foucault 2000d: 117). Using the example of the concentration camps, he demonstrates that mechanisms of power have their own specific, relatively autonomous history and are not characteristic of the political regimes that use them:

> The concentration camps? They're considered to be a British invention; but that doesn't mean or authorize the notion, that Britain was a totalitarian country. If there is one country that was not totalitarian in the history of Europe, it is undoubtedly Britain – but Britain invented concentration camps, which have been one of the chief instruments of totalitarian regimes. This is an example of a transposition of a technique of power. But I've never said, and I'm not inclined to think, that the existence of concentration camps in both democratic and totalitarian countries shows that there are no differences between those countries.
>
> (Foucault 2000a: 293)

Hence, an analysis of liberal mechanisms of power has to be aware of two points. First, although liberal societies have deployed and continue to use authoritarian or even totalitarian mechanisms of power, their political regimes cannot be characterized by the mechanisms they use. Second, mechanisms of power can be transposed not only from one society to another but also, within societies, from one particular domain to another. As mentioned above, mechanisms of power devised and deployed for imposing order on foreign populations have frequently boomeranged back into the domestic sphere.

Mechanisms of power operate within their own fields of knowledge – they comprise both regimes of practices and particular rationalities. The exercise of power is intertwined with calculations and tied to specific aims and objectives, but without being the result of the decisions of a clearly identifiable subject. Foucault's own words are quite instructive in this respect:

> [T]he rationality of power is characterized by tactics that are often quite explicit at the restricted level where they are inscribed (the local cynicism of power), tactics which, becoming connected to one another, but finding their base of support and their conditions elsewhere, end by forming comprehensive systems: the logic is perfectly clear, the aims decipherable, and yet it is often the case that no one is there to have invented them, and few who can be said to have formulated them: an implicit characteristic of the great anonymous, almost unspoken strategies which coordinate the loquacious tactics whose 'inventors' or decisionmakers are often without hypocrisy.
>
> (Foucault 1978: 95)

Foucault's reticence in identifying the decision-makers 'behind' the grand strategies of power is grounded in the epistemological assumption that the aims, effects, and logic of power are more accessible to analysis than the subjects and intentions 'behind' its exercise. Moreover, in Foucault's view, rationalities of power do not derive from transcendental reason but are immanent in practices. So, instead of evaluating the rationality of certain practices of power against a form of absolute reason, Foucault sought to understand how specific forms of rationality are inscribed in practices; how practices of power produce their own discursive fields in which their deployment is viewed as both rational and legitimate (Foucault 2000b: 230; Lemke 2000: 7–8).

A Foucauldian analytic is therefore better suited to drawing out the 'hows' of power rather than the 'whys' (De Larrinaga and Doucet 2010b: 11–12). This may be seen as a weakness. But it is also a particular strength of the Foucauldian perspective on power, because a Foucauldian approach does not presume 'to offer a way out of the power relation either in terms of the neutrality of social scientific knowledge in positivistic accounts, or, from a more critical standpoint, by providing knowledge that lays claim to emancipation' (De Larrinaga and Doucet 2010b: 12). In fact, any attempt to produce knowledge about power (this book not excluded) may ultimately end up reinforcing existing power relations. After all, power is always inextricably intertwined with the production of knowledge about its exercise, targets and limits.

Consequently, mechanisms of power in general, and governmentalities of security in particular, ought to be seen as: (1) at least relatively independent of grand ideological narratives; (2) historically specific and autonomous; (3) internally and externally transposable; and (4) tied to distinct forms of knowledge. This impinges on this study in a number of ways.

First, this book will analyze how rationalities and practices of foreign intervention came to be transposed to the domestic sphere, and vice versa. So, which particular rationalities and practices of imposing order on foreign populations and spaces have been transferred to the domestic sphere? And, conversely, which particular mechanisms for maintaining domestic order have been transferred to the international domain? How have these rationalities and practices circulated across and beyond the inside/outside divide and the concomitant dividing line between policing and warfighting? In response to what diagnoses and analyses of insecurity and threat have these transpositions occurred? And to what extent has the distribution of specific governmentalities of security across the inside/outside divide been articulated into more general global strategies of power and domination?

Second, governmentalities of security will be treated as relatively independent of any grand ideological narratives. That is to say, too much of a focus on totalizing ideological narratives does not necessarily yield useful insights into the highly localized development and deployment of rationalities and practices that always produce their own localized legitimacy. Practices of security are frequently deployed according to much more pragmatic, instrumental rationalities informed by notions of effectiveness, efficiency and expedience. This is what Foucault (1978: 95) called the 'local cynicism of power' – a pragmatic getting-the-job-done attitude on the part of local practitioners. Yet governmentalities of security are never wholly independent of grand ideological narratives, because such narratives are frequently used to justify their design and deployment. In fact, the production of legitimacy is an important part of the operational logic of governmentalities of security. And attempts to legitimize liberal security draw as much on an instrumental logic of effectiveness as on grand narratives about the rule of law, peace and freedom.

Third, an analysis of governmentalities of security deployed by and in the United States will not provide any grounds for a more general characterization of the US political regime. Through an in-depth analysis of the discursive fields in which they are embedded, this book will merely problematize and critique the actual socio-political effects produced by the development, deployment and extension of specific rationalities and practices of security across different domains. These discursive fields are primarily drawn from the US context due to the fact that the US has been, and continues to be, a global hegemony as well as the greatest military power the world has ever seen. Moreover, we should also note that only very few of the analyzed practices were invented by, and in, the United States. More often than not, they were appropriated and transposed from other contexts, such as French experiences with counter-revolutionary warfare, the British tradition of imperial policing and the general history of colonial and imperial domination.

The book

Governmentalities of security never operate in isolation; they are always embedded in larger ensembles and operate within particular domains. This book will analyze rationalities and practices of security in terms of how they configure space, how they are organized and how their deployment is legitimized. Of course, these domains are inextricably intertwined but for analytical purposes, space, organization, and legitimacy will be treated as distinct domains of security that will be analyzed in separate chapters.

Chapter 1 draws out the conceptual and theoretical issues at stake in analyzing and critiquing security beyond the inside/outside binary. First, the chapter discusses what Giorgio Agamben's notion of a permanent state of exception and Michel Foucault's deconstruction of sovereignty can contribute to a critique of security. Second, liberal governmentalities of security are shown to center on a biopolitical distinction, or 'triage', between circulations that need to be promoted and those that need to be contained or even eliminated. In order to do so, liberal security relies both on a sliding scale of risk and a binary opposition between 'friend' and 'enemy'. Actual practices of targeting are then adjusted accordingly, ranging from seemingly benevolent (albeit often highly disciplinary) assistance, to the use of lethal force. Third, the chapter shows that in the face of an increasing blurring of war and peace as well as law and emergency, 'pacification' is much better suited to critiquing a transversal logic of security than concepts of 'militarization' or 'war'. Last but not least, the chapter addresses the question as to who or what drives the proliferation and increasing circulation of governmentalities of security across and beyond the inside/outside binary.

This is followed by two historical chapters, which deal with the international and the domestic sphere of security respectively. Chapter 2 summarizes a particular international governmentality of security that, as shown in later chapters, epitomizes the erosion of the boundaries between policing and warfighting and the civilian and the military spheres, as well as security and development. Since its promulgation in the 1960s, US counterinsurgency doctrine has been devised and deployed as a concrete program for pacifying at-risk and risky populations and spaces. This chapter sketches the rise of counterinsurgency doctrine in the US under the Kennedy administration, its demise in the aftermath of the Vietnam War, and its current renaissance in response to the vicissitudes of the global war on terror. Moreover, US attempts to develop counterinsurgency capabilities are situated in the broader context of major transformations in warfare, most notably the emergence of what some military analysts call fourth-generation warfare and the rise of non-state warmaking entities.

Chapter 3 provides a brief historical overview of major developments in US domestic policing. It outlines how, in the 1960s and 1970s, the federal government became increasingly involved in the hitherto predominately local affair of crime control. This general realignment of policing has been spurred by the declaration of the wars on crime and drugs, which also served to justify a general clampdown on domestic dissent. Moreover, the chapter shows that the primary targets of an increasingly para-militarized police have been particular populations (mainly poor people of color) and particular spaces (primarily deprived inner-city neighborhoods). Last but not least, the chapter argues that many of the mechanisms for identifying and targeting risky populations and spaces at home are informed by practices of expeditionary pacification.

The next three chapters focus on the domestic, as well as international, deployment of governmentalities of securities within the domains of space, organization, and legitimacy, respectively. Chapter 4 maps out the domestic and international expansion of what will be called geographies of security. Geographies of security are complex assemblages geared towards controlling and managing circulations in space. Above all, they are shown to hinge on a distinction between those people and goods whose mobility must be facilitated and those that need to be interdicted. Geographies of security range from seemingly benign attempts to empower local residents to defend themselves against 'criminal invasions', to a veritable archipelago of prisons and detention centers that provide the spaces for permanently warehousing those populations who are seen as irredeemable threats to the liberal order.

Chapter 5 analyzes how security agencies in the United States have sought to redraw organizational boundaries in response to a security environment in which global and domestic insecurities are held to be increasingly intertwined. It sketches how security experts have problematized major shifts in the security environment, most notably the rise of violent non-state actors, and points out some of the organizational reforms they have proposed in response to these changes. The chapter, moreover, provides some concrete examples of how US security agencies have recently been reorganized.

Chapter 6 examines the role of legitimacy in the design and deployment of governmentalities of security. This chapter argues that governmentalities of security produce their legitimacy by purporting to protect 'safe' circulations, while containing and/or eliminating 'dangerous' ones. It, moreover, shows that governmentalities of security also serve to (re)produce the legitimacy and the sovereignty of the intervening state as well as the legitimacy and sovereignty of the states targeted by interventions. However, the (re)production of legitimacy and sovereignty is not an end in itself, but merely serves to enforce a global capitalist order where 'good' circulations are being fostered and 'bad' ones are being eliminated.

The Conclusion highlights some of the wider socio-political implications of the colonization of ever increasing aspects of political, social, economic and cultural life by the logic of security.

The 'reality' of insecurity

Perfect security is impossible. There will always be new insecurities and threats. And some individuals and groups will always seek to subvert or bypass existing security provisions. In fact, security and insecurity feed upon each other. But while governmentalities of security are ultimately doomed to fail because some dangerous elements will always elude identification, tracking and targeting, their very failure also drives their constant expansion, fine-tuning, overhauling and re-organization. This book is a critique of current efforts to permanently adapt to problematizations of insecurity.

However, lest the book is accused of downplaying or even ignoring the 'real' existence of threats, it should be stressed that there is indeed a host of formidable global problems. Yet the tendency towards articulating these problems as interconnected global insecurities that call for ever increasing pacification efforts, is not necessarily the best of way of addressing these problems. On the contrary, the continuous securitization of global challenges may be part of the problem rather than the solution.

In their discussion of governmentality, Peter Miller and Nikolas Rose (2008) express the relations between problems and solutions very succinctly:

> There was little point, or so it seemed from the perspective of government, in identifying a problem unless one simultaneously set out some measures to rectify it. The solidity and separateness of 'problems' and 'solutions' are thus attenuated. Or, to put it differently, the activity of problematizing is intrinsically linked to devising ways to remedy it. So, if a particular diagnosis or tool appears to fit a particular 'problem', this is because they have been made so that they fit each other. For to presume to govern seemed to require one to propose techniques to intervene – or to be dismissed as a mere critic or philosopher. In short, to become governmental, thought has to become technical.
>
> (Miller and Rose 2008: 15)

Governmentalities of security always fit specific solutions to particular diagnoses and vice versa. For instance, there was no inevitability in framing the 9/11 attacks as an act of war that called for a global war on terror. The terror attacks might as well have been cast as a problem of domestic terrorism – they were, after all, launched from within the United States – calling for a purely domestic law enforcement solution. This book will, however, not propose any alternative solutions to the manifold problems we face. Rather, it will merely problematize problematizations of insecurity as well as the solutions devised to counter them, because its author does not 'presume to govern' and would happily be 'dismissed as mere critic or philosopher'.

1 Liberal security and the biopolitics of global pacification

Security beyond the inside/outside divide

A number of commentators have suggested that the terrorist attacks on the World Trade Center and the Pentagon, on 11 September 2001, highlighted both the permeability of US borders and their vulnerability to attack. Judith Butler (2004: 20), for example, suggested that these attacks spelled the end of American First Worldism. She explained this as follows:

> It is the loss of the prerogative, only and always, to be the one who transgresses the sovereign boundaries of other states, but never to be in a position of having one's own boundaries transgressed. The United States was supposed to be the place that could not be attacked, where life was safe from violence initiated from abroad, where the only violence we knew was the kind that we inflicted on ourselves.
>
> (Butler 2004: 39)

Yet, the 9/11 attacks were not actually launched from outside the United States, though they were probably planned abroad and the attackers had logistical, financial as well as ideological support from abroad. Rather, they were launched from within US territory, as the attackers had boarded domestic flights in Boston, Dulles and Newark, before they hijacked the planes and crashed them into the Twin Towers and the Pentagon. Indeed, the fact that the 9/11 attacks were, on the one hand, probably instigated from abroad and, on the other, carried out by means of the domestic transportation infrastructure points up the growing impossibility to clearly define threats as either domestic or foreign. Following the attacks, politicians and security professionals, as well as academics, therefore immediately asked themselves how to respond to threats that cut across any neat divide between domestic public safety and foreign defense.

The political stakes are enormous, because many of the proposed and implemented responses are deeply authoritarian and undemocratic. So, how are these problematizations of threat and the prescribed solutions to be problematized? How can these governmentalities of security be critiqued, challenged and resisted? Or, how can we secure both ourselves and others from the proliferation of increasingly authoritarian governmentalities of security?

According to Israeli architect and writer Eyal Weizman (2007), the very logic of security already entails the dissolution of the boundaries between inside and outside and the concomitant blurring of the lines between policing and warfighting:

> The logic of 'security' [...] presupposes that the danger is already inside, presented by a population in which subversive elements exist. The relation that 'security' implies between 'inside' and 'outside', as well as between military and police action, is ambiguous. [...] If defence engages directly with the concept of war, security engages with the temporarily ill-defined and spatially amorphous 'conflict' not only between societies, but within them as well.
>
> (Weizman 2007: 106–7)

Three interrelated processes are thus at play in the logic of security: a merging of policing and warfighting, a shift from 'war' to 'conflict' and an overall blurring of the lines between 'inside' and 'outside'. So, if we want to critically engage with the now almost ubiquitous logic of security, we will have to closely interrogate these three processes.

Yet, the scholarly analysis of security still tends to follow a strict disciplinary division of labor: domestic security is studied by sociologists and criminologists, and international security by international relations (IR) scholars. Or, as Didier Bigo (2008: 15) – one of the notable exceptions to this rule – put it, '[t]he structuring of academic knowledge has blocked analysis by reproducing the mapping of state borders onto organizational divisions' (see also Neocleous 2011: 192; Walker 1990, 1993). By and large, the study of security is still guided by the mythical dichotomy between an internally pacified state territory where security is enforced by the police, on the one hand, and the anarchic sphere of international relations where at least a semblance of security is provided by the military, on the other. However, the myth of a clearly delineated division between inside and outside conceals more than it reveals, because governmentalities of security no longer operate within these neatly demarcated boundaries.

Governmentalities of security always serve as specific 'solutions' to shifting problematizations of insecurity and their more general impact on questions of identity and social and political boundaries, as well as on sovereignty (Buzan and Hansen 2009: 5; see also Walker 1990, 1993, 1997; Williams 1998, 2005, 2007). As will be shown in this book, in the United States problematizations of insecurity, and 'solutions' devised to tackle them, began to traverse the clear-cut distinction between domestic public safety and foreign defense well before the 9/11 attacks. Thus, if we want to move the study of security beyond the mythical inside/outside dichotomy, we will have to map out how problematizations of threats, and the rationalities and practices designed and deployed in response to these threats, have increasingly cut across the divide between domestic public safety and foreign defense.

A permanent state of exception?

Above all, the dichotomy between the domain of pacified political communities and the anarchic sphere of relations between such communities is anchored in the principle of state sovereignty. The principle of state sovereignty establishes the boundaries between 'life inside and outside a centered political community' (Walker 1993: 62). In *Homo Sacer*, Italian philosopher Giorgio Agamben (1995) shows that sovereignty constantly (re)draws the boundaries between who belongs to a given political community and who is (often violently) excluded from political life. Agamben traces the concept of sovereignty across two theoretical positions: conservative German philosopher Carl Schmitt's statist perspective on sovereignty as the capability to declare exceptions to given legal norms, on the one hand (Schmitt 1985: 5); and Walter Benjamin's radical (or even eschatological) position that states of exceptions have been rendered normal and permanent, on the other (Benjamin 1999: 253–64; see also Neal 2004: 374). Agamben (1995, 2005) argues that in contemporary liberal democracies, the state of exception occupies a zone of indistinction between violence and law. It is both outside the normal legal order and an integral part of it, and thus forms the conditions of possibility for deciding who is to be included in, and who is to be excluded from, a given political order. Agamben deploys the rather paradoxical Roman concept of homo sacer (the sacred man) defined as a human being, 'who may be killed yet not sacrificed', to critique modern liberal democracy (Agamben 1995: 8). Drawing on the distinction between zoē (political life) and bios (bare life) he argues that:

> [i]f anything characterizes modern democracy as opposed to classical democracy, then it is that modern democracy presents itself from the beginning as a vindication and liberation of zoē, and that it is constantly trying to transform its own bare life into a way of life and to find, so to speak, the bios of the zoē.
>
> (Agamben 2005: 9)

Liberal democracies aim to exclude bare life, but at the same also seek to include and pacify it, turning it into political life. The homo sacer emerges as a human being who is reduced to bare life – neither outside nor inside the legal order, that is to say, as a subject who occupies the zone of indistinction that characterizes a permanent state of exception. 'Homo sacer' thus denotes the illiberal subject positions produced by the liberal distinction between those who are included in a given legal order, and those who are seen as threats and who must therefore be excluded (but always through means of exclusion that are at the same time forms of inclusion). Supposed risks to liberalism are located both inside and outside liberal society. The illiberal governmental techniques brought to bear upon these risks are, in turn, aimed at both including and excluding them. For example, incarceration is a form of exclusion from society by means of including prisoners in exceptional spaces that are at same time within and outside state territory. And failed states often become the targets of outside intervention aimed at including them in the increasingly global networks of liberal governance, by often violently excluding the dangerous elements supposed to emanate from them.

The 9/11 attacks have ushered in a 'global war on terror' that is waged through a whole panoply of 'exceptional' security measures. Besides two conventional wars that turned into protracted counterinsurgency conflicts, there has been an expansion of border controls and surveillance, a ratcheting-up of law-enforcement and intelligence-gathering (including domestic spying), a general shift of power to the executive, the so-called 'extraordinary rendition' of suspected terrorists, the rise of extraterritorial detention centers, such as Guantánamo Bay, and so on and so forth. Moreover, since the 'war on terror' is supposed to end only when 'every terrorist group of global reach has been found, stopped, and defeated', as President George W. Bush (2001; cited in Neocleous 2008: 40) declared in his 'Address to the Nation' on 20 September 2001, the state of exception is thought to have become permanent. Indeed, many critical commentators agree that the overall expansion of security measures in the wake of 9/11 amounts to what, following Benjamin, Agamben (1995, 2005) calls a permanent state of exception (see for example, Amoore 2008; Bigo 2002; De Goede 2008; Gregory 2006; Jabri 2006; Mbembe and Meintjes 2003; Watson 2005; Ericson 2008; Aradau and van Munster 2007, 2008). This prompts the question as to whether the 9/11 attacks have led to a new era of permanent exception, or whether the responses to 9/11 have merely 'uncovered the mask of liberal democracy' (Bigo and Tsoukala 2008: 3).

In *Critique of Security*, Mark Neocleous (2008) argues that the term 'state of exception' should be replaced by 'state of emergency' because exception still implies a clear division between the normality of the rule of law and the exceptionality of emergency powers (see also Neocleous 2006a, 2006b, 2007). He rather suggests that 'far from being outside the rule of law, emergency powers emerge from it. They are part and parcel of the political technology of security and thus central to political administration' (Neocleous 2008: 72). Emergency powers have long played a pivotal role in producing both the internal order of liberal societies and the stability of the overall Western-dominated international system. In fact, Neocleous demonstrates that in liberal thought and practice, security and liberty have always been wrapped up in one another. Emergency powers have been the chief technology for producing liberal order both domestically and internationally.

For Agamben, a permanent state of exception is not just a conjunctural consequence of 9/11 either, but rather the culmination of a complex process that began much earlier: 'World War I (and the years following it) appear as a laboratory for testing and honing the functional mechanisms and apparatuses of the state of exception as a paradigm of government' (Agamben 2005: 7). Moreover, 'the functional mechanisms and apparatuses of the state of exception' are nothing but governmentalities of security that have been expanded to such an extent that the state of exception has become permanent. And a permanent state of exception, in turn, requires the constant preparedness and fine-tuning of governmentalities of security. Agamben (2005: 14) maintains that 'in conformity with a continuing tendency in all of the Western democracies, the declaration of the state of exception has gradually been replaced by an unprecedented generalization of the paradigm of security as the normal technique of government'. Agamben thus explicitly connects the normalization of the state of exception with the proliferation of governmentalities of security.

In the field of international relations, Barry Buzan and Ole Wæver, as well as other members of what has since become known as the Copenhagen School, have also sought to analyze security in terms of the state of exception. In an attempt to draw out the discursive and performative dimension of security, Buzan and Wæver developed the concept of securitization (Buzan and Hansen 2009: 212–21). Securitization denotes the performance of security, the process of rhetorically framing an issue as an existential threat that warrants an exceptional response:

> The way to study securitization is to study discourse and political constellations: When does an argument with this particular rhetorical and semiotic structure achieve sufficient effect to make an audience tolerate violations of rules that would otherwise have to be obeyed? If by means of an argument about the priority and urgency of an existential threat the securitizing actor has managed to break free of procedures or rules he or she would otherwise be bound by, we are witnessing an act of securitization.
>
> (Buzan *et al.* 1998: 25; cited in Buzan and Hansen 2009: 214)

The discursive force of acts of securitization establishes links between securitizing actors and referent objects (Buzan and Hansen 2009: 214). Securitizing actors are 'actors who securitize issues by declaring something – a referent object – existentially threatened', whereas referent objects are 'things that are seen to be existentially threatened and that have a legitimate claim to survival' (Buzan *et al.* 1998: 36; cited in Buzan and Hansen 2009: 214).

Governmentalities of security are, thus, not just responses to objectively given threats. Rather, the very framing of issues as threats ought to be seen as immanent to the rationalities and practices designed and deployed to counter them.

That said, the framework of securitization has been criticized for its failure to conceptualize 'effects of power that are continuous rather than exceptional' (Bigo 2002: 73; cited in Buzan and Hansen 2009: 217; see also Huysmans 2006, 2011). The framework of securitization highlights particularly dramatic declarations of the state of exception, while neglecting the creeping inscription of emergency powers into everyday life through the proliferation of security routines. Since it is based on 'a sharp distinction between the exceptional and the banal, the political and the everyday, the routine and the creative' (Huysmans 2011: 375; see also Bigo 2002: 73), the framework of securitization cannot account for the fact that declarations of the state of exception have been 'replaced by an unprecedented generalization of the paradigm of security as the normal technique of government' (Agamben 2005: 14). Because of its essentially decisionist and exceptionalist focus, the framework of securitization 'implies an elitist vision of politics' and may ultimately merely reinforce the very dividing practices of sovereignty (Huysmans 2011: 375).

In order to gain a critical purchase on rationalities and practices of security, we have to attend to the normality and ordinariness of security routines. We have to examine how security plays out beyond the dazzling spectacle of sovereignty and the concomitant dichotomies between the normal and the exceptional, and the inside and the outside. In short, we have to look at what Bigo (2002, 2008; Bigo and Tsoukala 2008) calls 'the governmentality of unease'.

Processes of securitization allow for the definition and prioritization of threats and the resultant mobilization and allocation of resources needed to deal with them. Processes of securitization are thus immanent to decentralized routines of government. In other words, if we want to understand the transversal character of governmentalities of security we have to discard the perspective of state sovereignty and elite politics and perhaps even, as Michel Foucault (2000d: 122) put it, 'need to cut off the king's head' in political theory.

Political power as war and/or government

Michel Foucault – more than any other thinker – sought to critically interrogate, and ultimately move beyond, the problematic of state sovereignty (Neal 2004; Pasquino 1993). He attempted to decenter a juridical-sovereign notion of centralized political power, replacing it by a conception of power as continuous struggle.

In his 1975–1976 lectures at the Collège de France, Michel Foucault addressed the issue as to whether war can serve as a conceptual matrix for analyzing power relations:

> If we have to avoid reducing the analysis of power to the schemata proposed by the juridical constitution of sovereignty, and if we have to think of power in terms of relations of force, do we therefore have to interpret it in terms of the general form of war? Can war serve as an analyzer of power relations?
>
> (Foucault 2003: 266)

At the time of the lectures, Foucault was working on the first volume of *The History of Sexuality*, in which he set out to examine 'a certain form of knowledge regarding sex, not in terms of repression or law, but in terms of power' (Foulcault 1978: 92). The peculiar conception of power Foucault deployed in his analysis of sexuality is indeed underpinned by a bellicose grammar. Power is seen as the effect of highly mobile and unstable societal force relations: 'it is the name that one attributes to a complex strategical situation in a particular society' (Foucault 1978: 93). Foucault maintained that power is relational and depends on points of resistance that are inscribed in relations of power as an irreducible opposite. Accordingly, power is the expression of a veritable social battlefield where numerous mobile forces deploy local tactics that may, or may not, be stratified into institutions and centers of power. Apparatuses and institutions are therefore nothing but the effects of strategic codifications of local tactics deployed within a field of societal force relations.

When Foucault (2003: 15) went as far as to invert von Clausewitz's (1976: 99) famous dictum that war is 'a continuation of political intercourse, carried on with other means', in order to think of the problematic of political power as the 'continuation of war by other means', he sought to draw out the war-like force relations – 'the distant roar of battle' (Foucault 1991a: 308) – that persist even within internally pacified societies. In his early writings on political power, Foucault thus sought to (re)inscribe the supposed features of relations between states – contingency, war and violence – into the apparently domesticated domain of internally pacified societies.

Yet, it seems as if Foucault looked into the abyss of politics as permanent warfare, and pulled back (see Hansen 2000). For, in his later work, he sought to move both beyond the juridical-sovereign conception of power and his own bellicose notion of power, in order to study political power in terms of *government* (Dean 1999). In Foucault's own words:

> The relationship proper to power would therefore be sought not on the side of violence or of struggle, nor on that of voluntary contracts (all of which can, at best, only be instruments of power) but, rather, in the area of that singular mode of action, neither warlike nor juridical, which is government.
>
> (Foucault 2000c: 341)

In the now burgeoning academic field of 'governmentality studies' (Merlingen 2008: 272), government is held 'to shape conduct by working through desires, aspirations, interests and beliefs for definite but shifting ends and with a diverse set of relatively unpredictable consequences, effects and outcomes' (Dean 1999: 266–7). However, the exclusive focus on the consensual aspects of government, or power more generally, misses the fact that relations of government continue to be shaped both by the threat and the actual use of violence. Indeed, Foucault's (see 2000c: 220) later opposition between violence (which turns subjects into objects who are condemned to passivity) and power (which acts upon subjects who have the capacity to (re)act) fails to account for security practices, such as counterinsurgency operations that aim to combine relations of consent with the use of violence (see also Hansen 2000: 152–3; Jabri 2006: 54). For, as Vivienne Jabri writes:

> [V]iolence is imbricated in relations of power, is a mode of control, a technology of governmentality. When the population of Iraq is targeted through aerial bombardment, the consequence goes beyond injury and seeks the pacification of the Middle East as a political region.
>
> (Jabri 2006: 54)

Although, in his later writings, Foucault sought to distinguish between power and violence, we should note that both potential and actual violence continues to be part and parcel of governmental relations, and may even provide the very conditions of possibility for shaping the actions of others.

Liberal government

Foucauldian readings of liberalism stress both the differences and overlaps between two specific political rationalities: the so-called 'science of police' (Polizeiwissenschaft) and liberalism. The science of police, which covered a much broader field than what we now understand by the term police, was based on an attempt 'to promote the happiness of society by deploying state and non-state agencies to regulate all forms of behaviour' (Hindess 2005: 394). The science of police envisioned a practice of government that 'does not limit its action on the governed to the general form of laws: it works by the means of specific, detailed regulation and decree' (Gordon 1991: 10; see also Dean 2000; Knemayer 1980). As Foucault put it:

> From the seventeenth century 'police' begins to refer to the set of means by which the state's forces can be increased while preserving the state in good order. In other words, 'police' will be the calculation and technique that will make it possible to establish a mobile, yet stable and controllable relationship between the state's internal order and the development of its forces.
>
> (Foucault 2007: 313)

Liberalism, on the other hand, is concerned about governing too much. 'Liberal political reason sees individual liberty as a limit, if not to the legitimate reach of the state then certainly to its effectiveness' (Hindess 2005: 394). As Mitchell Dean observes:

> [L]iberalism emerges as a critique of a theory and practice of rule that regards 'good police, security, and public order' as conditions to be achieved by a comprehensive set of regulations based on a transparent and detailed knowledge of the population to be governed.
>
> (Dean 2000: 42)

However, attempts to promote order in and through the production of knowledge about populations and their activities persist in modern liberal societies. Although liberalism marks a shift from a 'police conception of order as a visible grid of communication' to a concern with promoting 'the necessarily opaque, dense, autonomous character of the processes of population', the unfolding of these autonomous processes still has to be protected and secured (Gordon 1991: 20). According to Foucault (2007: 34, 44–9), under liberal rule the free circulation of goods, information and people correlates with the spread of what he calls 'mechanisms of security' (see also Gordon 1991: 21).

Liberalism emerged as an epistemico-political critique of the presumption that the processes of the population can be fully knowable. But, on the other hand, liberalism still tries to grasp the opaque nature of these processes, in order to make sure that they unfold according to that nature. Mechanisms of security are liberalism's answer to the intractable problem of the ultimately unknowable processes of the population that must nonetheless be regulated and controlled.

Yet the circulation of people, goods, and information has probably never merely occurred within clearly demarcated territorial boundaries. And, nowadays, the processes of the population have become even more transnational. As a consequence, under globalization, efforts to promote and secure these processes at the global level have been stepped up. Globalization can thus be understood as an attempt to externalize the rationalities and practices of liberal rule in order to regulate and secure the socio-economic processes of the population on a planetary scale.

Liberalism ushers in a new form of policing based on 'a knowledge of economics, social, and other processes outside the formal sphere of the state rather than on a transparent knowledge of the minutiae of activities, things, and humans' (Dean 2000: 42). Liberalism thereby demarcates the social from the political, while at the same time constantly intervening in the social in an attempt to monitor, know, and regulate societal processes, so that they can unfold according to what is posited – by the very attempts at knowing them – as their immanently natural course. This knowledge is produced above all by the various social sciences – notably sociology and economics – that seek to understand society on its own grounds. Zygmunt Bauman (2002: 2), for instance, suggested that since its inception, the discipline of sociology tried to position itself as the intelligence branch of the modern nation-state, helping it manage its territory and population more effectively. Under liberalism, the social constitutes the prime 'field of governmental security in its widest sense' (Gordon 1991: 35). Moreover, the processes of globalization also project the social onto the global level, giving rise to a global society that needs to be policed. In short, the rationalities and practices of liberal government are concerned with making societal processes intelligible, in order to intervene in, guide and secure these processes – not only domestically but also globally.

Colin Gordon suggests that liberal security does not merely consist of 'closed circuits of control'. Rather, liberal security is 'inherently open-ended' and 'transactional', giving rise to 'a zone of (partially) open interplay between the exercise of power and everything that escapes its grasp'. Liberal security is therefore in a relation of mutual supposition with everything that eludes it. However, the '(partially) open interplay between the exercise of power and everything that escapes its grasp' (Gordon 1991: 36) also feeds into the constant (re)adjustment and expansion of mechanisms of security. In fact, mechanisms of security depend as much, if not more, on what escapes them than on what they capture. Indeed, a Foucauldian reading of security shows up the intricate links between freedom, security and danger. Mechanisms of security thrive on the insecurity and fear provoked by elusive flows, because insecurity and fear can be re-channelled into the expansion of security mechanisms. Security 'involves organizing or (anyway) allowing the development of ever-wider circuits' (Foucault 2007: 45).

Or, as Michael Dillon (2007: 34) pointed out, 'the operation and proliferation of mechanisms of security continually inflated the concern with security'. The ultimate impossibility of perfect security thus feeds the constant extension of security into ever more aspects of global socio-political life.

Liberal security is also in a relation of mutual supposition with freedom:

> I think it is this freedom of circulation, in the broad sense of the term; it is in terms of this option of circulation, that we should understand the word freedom, and understand it as one of the facets, aspects, or dimensions of the deployment of apparatuses of security.
>
> (Foucault 2007: 48–9)

In liberal regimes, freedom is above all the freedom to circulate, to exchange and to come into contact. Liberal governmentalities of security, in turn, are responses to the problem of 'allowing circulations to take place, of controlling them, sifting the good and the bad, ensuring that things are always in movement [...] but in such a way that the inherent dangers of this circulation are canceled out' (Foucault 2007: 67). Contrary to the common assumption of a tension, or balance between security and liberty, liberal security ought to be seen as inextricably intertwined with freedom (see Neocleous 2008: 11–38).

Liberal governmentality emerged from a critique of an excess of government that was said to stifle the vital processes of the population. It seeks to delimit the legitimate scope of government through the promotion of individual liberty and autonomy in order to more effectively regulate and promote socio-economic processes – not only domestically, but also on a global scale (see Dean 2000, 2002; Gordon 1991; Hindess 2000, 2004, 2005).

Liberalism and its others

Yet not everybody is considered to be equally capable of exercising his or her liberty, and some are even construed as threats to the very existence of the liberal order. This is why authoritarian mechanisms of power persist within liberal regimes.

Broadly speaking, most accounts of liberalism tend to discount the persistence of authoritarian or even violent practices within liberal rule. This is partly due to liberalism's supposed apolitical conception of the political. According to Karl Schmitt's (1996: 70; cited in Mouffe 2005: 110) poignant, but ultimately misguided, critique of liberalism, 'no liberal politics, only a liberal critique of politics' exists. For Schmitt, the political signifies, above all, the relations between friend and enemy, and liberal thought is said to be incapable of grasping the antagonistic and oftentimes violent dynamic of the formation of collective identities. Since liberal thought is too preoccupied with the dangers of excessive governmental interference, it thus 'cannot but remain blind to the specificity of the political in its dimension of conflict/decision' (Mouffe 2005: 2).

However, even if liberal thought remains blind to conflict, coercion and strug-gle, liberal governmental practice has no such qualms, because liberal rule rests on a distinction between those who can be governed liberally, those who must be ruled in a more authoritarian manner, and those who must even be violently excluded from liberal life (Hindess 2004: 28; Corva 2008: 177). This is, in fact, the location of sovereignty within the decentered field of liberal governmental-ity. The sovereign decision on the state of exception no longer occupies a clearly identifiable central position. Rather, sovereignty has become decentered: it now pervades the entire social field; manifest in all the multiform and variegated gov-ernmentalities of security that are geared towards distinguishing between 'safe' and 'dangerous' lives.

The two most fundamental illiberal assemblages of liberalism are 'the appli-cation of the military apparatus (the strategy of warfare) and the application of the criminal justice apparatus (the strategy of policing citizens)' (Corva 2008: 177). The main purpose of these increasingly intertwined assemblages is to target those illiberal individuals, populations and spaces that supposedly threaten the smooth unfolding of the processes of liberal life.

Now we have reached a point where we can specify the role of the state of exception within liberal governmentality. For, rather than a permanent state of exception, we face a much more uneven proliferation of emergency powers that do not affect everyone to the same extent. In fact, emergency powers target particular individuals, populations and spaces. 'There is, hence, a "profile" to the state of exception and its experience. [...] Those targeted by exceptional measures are members of particular racial and cultural communities' (Jabri 2006: 53). The per-manent state of exception is thus nothing but the sum total of governmentalities of security which are overwhelmingly directed at illiberal individuals, populations and spaces; that is to say, at those individuals, populations and spaces that are con-strued as threats to the smooth unfolding of socio-economic processes.

There is, however, more than just a binary opposition between liberal and illiberal life, or between what Agamben (1995) calls zoē (political life) and bios (bare life), at play here. Or to be more precise, Carl Schmitt's conception of the political as a spatial division between 'friend' and 'enemy' is mapped upon a temporal scale of development, and vice versa (Walker 1993: 152).

In his article on the persistence of authoritarian features in liberal rule, Mitch-ell Dean (2000: 48) lays out five '(fluid) categories of liberal subjects of govern-ment grouped according to their capacities for autonomy:

1   Group A: Includes those who are capable of fully 'exercising liberal autonomy'.
2   Group B: Consists of 'those who need assistance to maintain capacities for autonomy' (e.g., welfare recipients, etc).
3   Group C: Have the potential for acting autonomously but need further train-ing and education.
4   Group D: Includes all those who 'are for one reason or another not yet or no longer able to exercise their own autonomy or act in their own best interests'.

5   Group E: Encompasses all 'those who disrupt or simply get in the way of the establishment and maintenance of a liberal legal and political order within national states or internationally'.

In fact, both domestic and international stages of personal as well as collective politico-economic development depend on locating individuals, populations and spaces on a hierarchy of liberal life, with those said to possess the full capacity of living liberal lives at the top and those considered to pose a threat to liberal life at the bottom. Indeed, hierarchies of liberal development always tend to slide into the much cruder division between friend and enemy. Hence, governmentalities of security hinge both on a sliding scale of risk and a distinction between risk-free and risky individuals, populations and spaces.

Biopolitics and the pacification of illiberal life

Liberal governmentalities of security are ultimately aimed at life itself. They seek to promote certain forms of life while securing them against those forms of life that are construed as threats to (liberal) life. Liberal security thus operates within the overall strategic frame of what Foucault (1978) called biopolitics – a form of power aimed at making life live. Yet, biopolitics is not just directed at mere biological life, but at the promotion of forms of *economic* life that are seen as conducive to the (re)production of a liberal capitalist order. According to Foucault (2008: 106), political economy serves as 'the major form of knowledge' by means of which liberalism judges the value of human lives (see also Kiersey 2010: 67). Thus, the aforementioned sliding scale of illiberality and the concomitant distinction between liberal and illiberal life, inevitably entail a verdict on whether a subject is enterprising and self-prudential enough to pass the test of the market, or whether he or she even poses a threat to the market. Hence, the biopolitical pacification of illiberal life is always geared towards (re) producing a capitalist order.

The relevance of Michel Foucault's idea of biopolitics to critical analyses of 'the liberal problematic of security' has been amply demonstrated (Evans 2010: 414; see also Cairo 2006; Dillon and Neal 2008; Dillon and Reid 2001, 2009; De Larrinaga and Doucet 2008, 2010a; Duffield 2007, 2010; Edkins *et al.* 2004; Neal 2006; Reid 2005, 2006). Mark Duffield (2008: 146) for instance, argues that security and development have merged into a potentially global strategy for the management of at-risk and risky populations – a biopolitical containment strategy 'that seek[s] to restrict or manage the circulation of incomplete and hence potentially threatening life' (see also Duffield 2003, 2005, 2007, 2008, 2010). And he even goes as far as to assert that 'liberal practices of development traditionally associated with NGOs have been rediscovered as essentially civilian forms of counterinsurgency' (Duffield 2008: 157; see also Slim 2004). The attempt to contain and/or eliminate circulations of risky life is also one of the major objectives of the global pacification efforts that, according to Michael Dillon and Julian Reid (2009), characterize 'the liberal way of war'. In fact,

Duffield's (2010) 'liberal way of development' easily bleeds into Dillon and Reid's (2009) 'liberal way of war', and vice versa. While the liberal way of development seeks to foster 'adaptive patterns of household and communal self-reliance in the global south', the liberal way of war is aimed at securing global life itself from those 'patterns of self-reliance' that are viewed as a threat to global (liberal) life (Duffield 2010: 55–6, 68; Dillon and Reid 2009). Indeed, the liberal way of war is inextricably intertwined with 'the liberal way of rule' and its biopolitical 'commitment to making life live' (Dillon and Reid 2009: 11). Following Dillon and Reid (2009: 89–90), governmentalities of security can be broadly characterized as a form of triage: they aim to single out troublesome individuals, populations and spaces for 'treatment' and administer forms of 'treatment' that are often violent or even lethal.

But governmentalities of security seek to promote and secure 'adaptive patterns of communal self-reliance' (Duffield 2010: 55–6) not just in the global south, but also in pockets of the Third World held to be located within Western cities. Indeed, domestic pacification campaigns waged against the poor, most notably against poor people of color, are nothing but a domestic manifestation of the linkage between the liberal way of development and the liberal way of war. In *Punishing the Poor*, Loïc Wacquant (2009b: 1–37) shows how the management of rising social insecurity and the increasingly para-militarized police crackdown on dispossessed individuals, populations and spaces has merged into a 'new government of social insecurity':

> The activation of disciplinary programs applied to the unemployed, the indigent, single mothers and others 'on assistance' so as to push them onto the peripheral sectors of the employment markets, on the one side, and the deployment of an extended police and penal net with a reinforced mesh in the dispossessed districts of the metropolis, on the other side, are two components of a single apparatus for the management of poverty that aims at effecting the authoritarian rectification of the behaviors of populations recalcitrant to the emerging economic and symbolic order.
>
> (Wacquant 2009b: 14)

What Wacquant lays out is nothing but the domestic deployment of governmentalities of security, aimed at promoting certain forms of life that are deemed safe while securing liberal life itself from those lives that are seen as dangerous. Moreover, Wacquant's (2009b: 11, 14) 'new government of insecurity' also entails a form of triage that singles out particular populations (the unemployed, single mothers, delinquents, etc.) and individuals thought to belong to these troublesome populations, as well as specific spaces ('dispossessed districts of the metropolis'). This triage aims to either reintegrate troublesome populations into liberal life through disciplinary workfare programs, or to exclude them from liberal life through the erection of material as well as symbolic barriers (see also Wacquant 2001b, 2008, 2009a). Indeed, the domestic US (in)security-welfare nexus, mapped by Loïc Wacquant, is just one aspect of a global liberal (in)security-development nexus geared towards pacifying un- and underdeveloped life (Hettne 2010; Stern and Ojendal 2010).

Global (counter)insurgencies and the logic of militarization

The blurring of the lines between domestic and expeditionary pacification are contoured by a constant broadening of the notion of war to encompass an ever wider array of 'emergency situations' that seem further and further removed from traditional ideas of interstate conflict.

In 1991, military historian Martin van Creveld (1991: 197) predicted that, 'In the future, war will not be waged by armies but by groups whom we today call terrorists, guerrillas, bandits, and robbers, but who will undoubtedly hit on more formal titles to describe themselves'. Since 9/11, numerous commentators across the political spectrum have asserted that the West is embroiled in a protracted global conflict against violent non-state actors. This conflict has been assigned a spate of different labels. The initial Bush administration response was to declare a global war on terror. Since then, the rhetoric has been toned down a bit. But Pentagon officials and security pundits still claim that the United States and its allies are engaged in what is now called a 'long war', a 'global counterinsurgency', or a potentially endless series of 'global contingency operations' (see Berger and Borer 2007; Cassidy 2006a, 2006b, 2008; Kilcullen 2005, 2009, 2010; Wilson and Kamen 2009). There have also been numerous attempts to conceptualize more general shifts in the nature of war: concepts such as 'revolution in military affairs', 'netwar', 'epochal war', 'non-trinitarian war', 'postmodern war', 'unrestricted warfare', 'hybrid wars', 'fourth-generation wars', etc. All seek to come to grips with what is seen as an across-the-board transformation of war (Bunker 2011b: 730–1; see also Arquilla and Ronfeldt 2000; Arquilla and Ronfeldt 2001; Gray 1997; Hammes 2006; Hoffman 2007a; Quiao and Xiangsui 1999; van Creveld 1991, 2006). Security consultant, Robert J. Bunker (2010: 24), even goes as far as to state that Western nation states are in the midst of a loosely connected series of 'societal conflicts' 'over humanity's new forms of social and political organization' (see also Sullivan and Bunker 2011).

A number of security experts and academics maintain that Western nation states are now faced by opponents that differ radically from conventional state competitors. These commentators view the rise of new, non-state, war-making entities – exemplified not only by al Qaeda and Iraqi or Afghan insurgents, but also by drug cartels and so-called Third Generation Gangs[1] – as a direct threat to the international state system (see Bunker 2005, 2010, 2011b; Bunker and Begert 2008; Bunker and Sullivan 2010, 2011; Kan 2009; Manwaring 2005, 2008; Sullivan 2005; Sullivan and Bunker 2011; van Creveld 1991, 2008). Michael Hardt and Antonio Negri (2004: 5 emphasis in the original), moreover, suggest that we are in the midst of 'a *general global state of war* that erodes the distinction between war and peace such that we can no longer imagine or even hope for real peace'. In a similar vein, critical development scholar, Mark Duffield (2008: 146), argues that the current global security environment is marked by a biopolitical conflict over human life itself, or in his own words, 'a global civil war between "developed" and "underdeveloped" species-life'. In spite of their theoretical, political and ideological differences, most of these commentators thus agree that the global security conjuncture cannot be understood in terms of conventional interstate conflict, but ought to be seen as a loosely connected string of local, national, regional as well as global (counter)insurgencies. In this context, traditional distinctions between combatants and non-combatants, war and peace, military and police operations, victory and defeat, are no longer applicable.

Military theorist Carl von Clausewitz (1976: 83) famously described war as 'an act of force to compel our enemy to do our will'. But in contemporary unconventional warfare, the use of force is just one particular channel for imposing one's will on the enemy. In what Thomas X. Hammes (2006: 207–8) calls 'fourth-generation warfare' (4GW), which he describes as 'an evolved form of insurgency', war has shifted from the industrial-scale destruction of one's opponent's armed forces to undermining the political will of enemy decision- makers through both violent and non-violent means. In fact, war can no longer be clearly distinguished from non-violent forms of imposing one's will on others. Likewise, the traditional divide between crime and war, and the concomitant division between domestic public safety and foreign defense, has become increasingly fuzzy. Thus, what Anthony Giddens (1987) called the internal pacification of society has bled into the defense against external threats, and vice versa. Indeed, as Hardt and Negri (2004: 7) suggest: 'war seems to have seeped back and flooded the entire social field'.

The domestic consequences of the shift from traditional notions of interstate war to the far more ambiguous idea of conflict are often described, in a rather one-dimensional manner, in terms of 'militarization'. In his comprehensive historical account of the impact of militarization on the United States, Michael Sherry (Sherry 1995) suggests that many aspects of American socio-political life have been shaped by both the reality and imagery of war. He argues that since the 1930s, the United States has been in the grip of a process of militarization, which has eluded the control of individual decision-makers; sweeping them along, rather than being directed by them. Moreover, comparing it to industrialization, Sherry maintains that militarization did not originate in the US, and that it affected other nations as well, despite the fact that from World War II onwards the United States has been at the cutting edge of this process (Sherry 1995: 498–9). Above all, Sherry seeks to highlight how the metaphor of war has been deployed in framing a host of internal problems. This metaphorical use of war by both conservatives and liberals has been geared to the construction of national unity in the face of various highly divisive issues (Sherry 1995: 445–62). Metaphorical warfare can thus be seen as one particular form of domestic pacification. Susan Sontag puts it quite succinctly:

> The transformation of war-making into an occasion for mass ideological mobilization has made the notion of war useful as a metaphor for all sorts of

ameliorative campaigns. [...] Abuse of the military metaphor may be inevitable in a capitalist society [...] that increasingly restricts the scope and credibility of appeals to ethical principle, in which it is thought foolish not to subject one's actions to the calculus of self-interest and profitability. [...] In all-out war, expenditure is all-out, unprudent – war being defined as emergency in which no sacrifice is excessive.

(Sontag 1989: 10–11; cited in Sherry 1995: 458)

However, militarization is about more than just the use of the metaphor of war for 'ideological mobilization'.

In *Cities under Siege,* geographer Stephen Graham (2010) compellingly demonstrates how military doctrines, technologies, and expertise have slowly but steadily colonized ever more aspects of social, political and cultural life. In his view, 'a wide range of policy debates, urban landscapes, and circuits of urban infrastructure, as well as whole realms of popular and urban culture' have been permeated by a military rationality and increasingly militarized practices (Graham 2010: xiv).

Yet, in response to intractable unconventional wars in Iraq and Afghanistan, Western military forces have also scrambled to develop so-called community-oriented and population-centered doctrines that are explicitly designed to make them more police-like (see Sewall 2007; Kilcullen 2005, 2009; Ucko 2009). In fact, we are faced by processes that increasingly cut across the traditional divide between policing and warfighting. Counterinsurgency doctrine, for example, aims to turn soldiers and marines into armed relief workers, spin doctors and even social scientists. At the same time, domestic policing has been progressively militarized and the armed forces now play a growing role in controlling civilian populations not only abroad but also, to an ever larger extent, at home. Furthermore, there is the rise of what Graham (2010: 89–152) calls 'ubiquitous borders' – borders that no longer serve only to demarcate a national territory, but also increasingly separate an imaginary, predominately white middle-class, homeland from the Third World within.

Graham's observation that what he calls militarization ultimately amounts to 'the extension of military ideas of tracking, identification and targeting into the quotidian spaces and circulations of everyday life', is more than apt (Graham 2010: xi). Indeed, governmentalities of security center on identifying, tracking and targeting risky elements supposed to hide amongst 'the circulations of everyday life'. Potential and actual insurgents, terrorists and dangerous criminals are indistinguishable from ordinary civilians; while flows of contraband, such as illegal weapons and narcotics, are hidden amongst the licit circulations of global capitalism. Identifying and locating these risky elements poses significant, probably even insurmountable, challenges to both civilian and military agencies – both in organizational terms and in terms of their knowledge requirements. But it is not only risky spaces, populations and activities that require to be identified, tracked and targeted. Spaces, populations and activities that are construed to be at risk of various social ills (such as poverty, disease, crime and violence) are also supposed to be identified, to become the targets of all sorts of more or less benevolent (albeit often highly coercive) social campaigns. What is more, *at-risk* individuals, populations, spaces and activities frequently bleed into *risky* ones.

The proliferation of tracking and targeting ties in with a general trend towards 'targeted governance' (Valverde 2003; Valverde and Mopas 2004). Targeted governance does not necessarily mean less government; nor is it based on a more benign configuration of political power:

> Liberalism has been defined as arising out of a concern not to govern too much. But the neoliberal strategies for the governance of security could be seen as suggesting that liberalism is perhaps only a fear of governing too much all at once. 'Targeting' does not necessarily mean governing less. There are always more targets; and there are endless ways of fiddling with existing 'smart' weapons, smart drugs, and targeted social programmes. The logic of targeted governance is in its own way as endless, as utopian, as the better-known logic of totalitarian control.
>
> (Valverde and Mopas 2004: 247–8)

These risk-based and 'targeted' forms of governance are not only aimed at a potentially endless series of targets, but also deploy a variety of rationalities and practices to identify, track and ultimately 'hit' these targets.

Liberal governmentalities of security can be understood as a targeted form of governance directed at particular individuals, populations and spaces both at home and abroad. But despite the prevalence of a military logic of tracking and targeting, these governmentalities of security cannot be adequately analyzed in terms of a unidirectional flow of doctrines, tactics and technologies from the military to civilian agencies, such as the police.

Another more subtle variant of the militarization argument is provided by Vivienne Jabri, who adopts Foucault's pre-governmentality argument that we should use war as an analyzer of power relations. Jabri suggests that a grammar of war provides a more critical perspective on the vicissitudes of the war on terror than the grammar of security and securitization because, for her, the analytic of war is better suited to 'highlight[ing] the workings of power and their imbrications with violence' (Jabri 2006: 51). Indeed, Jabri's notion of a 'matrix of war' which she loosely defines as an ensemble of 'both discursive and institutional practices, technologies that target bodies and populations, enacted in a complex array of locations', can be a rather powerful critical concept (Jabri 2006: 55). Yet, the very idea of war has become increasingly problematic, as Jabri herself admits. For, if the state of war has become permanent and if, therefore, the boundaries between war and peace, domestic public safety and foreign defense, policing and warfighting, etc. have become blurred, the very idea of war becomes meaningless and loses its critical edge. Or, to put it differently, how can we return to a state of peace, when we are no longer able to tell peace from war?

Neocleous (2008: 71–5), moreover, shows that the same holds true for the rule of law: how can we hope to return to the normality of the rule of law, when 'exceptional' emergency powers are part and parcel of the 'normal' legal order. Neither peace nor law can thus offer a vantage point from which to critically interrogate a security environment in which war and peace, as well as the state of exception and the rule of law, are completely wrapped up in one another.

Are we not faced with what Rudyard Kipling (1899), in the context of nineteenth-century imperialism, called 'savage wars of peace' – spatially and temporally indeterminate pacification campaigns that target particular individuals, populations and spaces both domestically and globally, and which have become increasingly indistinguishable from ordinary modes of government? Allen Feldman (2004) refers to these conflicts as 'securocratic wars of public safety':

> These wars are not exclusively focused on territorial conquest, or on an easily locatable or identifiable enemy with its own respective goals of territorial appropriation. Rather, they are focused on countering imputed territorial contamination and transgression – 'terrorist', demographic and biological infiltration. These campaigns are not structured by time-limited political goals but are temporally open-ended.
>
> (Feldman 2004: 331)

Securocratic wars of public safety are nothing but spatially and temporally indeterminate programs of pacification, implemented through governmentalities of security that target particular individuals, populations and spaces.

Mark Neocleous (2011: 194, 204) suggests 'that critical theory really needs to re-appropriate the term "pacification" to help grasp the nature of security politics', because the concept 'carries a powerful theoretical charge, linking as it does the military to the police, the foreign to the domestic, the colonial to the homeland'. The term 'pacification' and the set of practices it signifies, date back to early European attempts to subdue recalcitrant colonial populations (Neocleous 2011: 198–201). The term entered the US politico-military lexicon during the Vietnam War, but has been rarely used since the United States' defeat in Indochina. However, even if the term itself is now no longer in fashion, we will see that rationalities and practices of pacification continue to be deployed in attempts to fabricate liberal order both at home and abroad. Liberal pacification aims to produce and reproduce more pliable populations, while trying to eradicate those who are deemed recalcitrant to liberal rule. Indeed, pacification is a 'political technology for organizing everyday life through the production and re-organization of the ideal citizen-subjects of capitalism' (Neocleous 2011: 198); that is to say, pacification is one of the prime political technologies for conducting the biopolitical triage between liberal and illiberal life that characterizes both global and domestic liberal rule (Dillon and Reid 2009: 89–90). Liberal rationalities and practices of pacification thus seek to fabricate and reinforce a liberal capitalist order both at home and abroad, through a combination of government and violence.

In short, an analytic of pacification provides us with a more useful critical 'grammar' than war, because it helps us not only draw out the relations between power and violence, but also understand the routine processes of liberal order-building that now occur across and beyond territorial borders.

Governmentalities and agents of liberal security

But who or what is the driving force behind the convergence of domestic public safety and foreign defense into spatially and temporally indeterminate pacification efforts? Are these processes driven by pivotal events, such as 9/11, that just force political decision-makers, security professionals and the public to respond to objectively given changes in the global security environment? Or, have they been brought about by dark conspiratorial forces, such as some variant of the military–industrial complex in cahoots with neoconservative politicians?

As will become clearer in the course of this book, the attacks of 9/11 did not single-handedly transform the US approach to domestic and international security. Rather, the US response to 9/11 shone the spotlight on certain authoritarian processes that have long played a crucial part in US government in particular, and in liberal regimes in general. Indeed, the logic of security and the routine use of emergency powers are inextricably intertwined with liberal modes of governance. More specifically, Matt Coleman (2005), for instance, has pointed out that the PATRIOT Act and the Enhanced Border Security Act (which were rammed through Congress after 9/11) built on prior immigration control and crime fighting measures, such as the 1986 Immigration and Reform Control Act, the 1994 Violent Crime Control and Law Enforcement Act and the 1996 Immigrant Responsibility and Illegal Immigration Reform Act (IRIIRA). Coleman suggests that the 'exceptional' post-9/11 legislation was indeed 'part of a long-standing geopolitical frontier regime rooted in congressional immigration law' (Coleman 2005: 194).

If we have to be wary of the significance attributed to the events of 9/11, we have to be even more suspicious of what Pierre Bourdieu (1990: 71) called the 'functionalism of the worst case', that is to say, any account that considers historical developments as the inevitable unfolding of deliberate strategies of domination (see Wacquant 2009b: xx). In fact, the convergence of domestic public safety and foreign defense into programs of global pacification has not been the result of a comprehensive strategy on the part of political and military elites. And, if there is an overarching strategy at work, it is not so much the driving force behind these processes, as the effect of provisional articulations of specific problematizations, rationalities and practices of in(security). According to Didier Bigo and Anastassia Tsoukala (2008: 8), what is at stake here is 'a process of consolidation of different insecurities constructed as if they were unified and global'. Thus, if we want to understand the emergence of biopolitical programs of global pacification, we must attend both to the active production, prioritization and articulation of categories of threat and the design and deployment of responses to these threats. But who has the capacity to problematize phenomena as threats and to prescribe 'solutions' to these problematizations?

Didier Bigo (2008: 16, 23) suggests that there is an increasingly transnational 'field of the professionals of the management of unease' whose agents have the 'capacity [...] to produce statements on unease and present solutions to facilitate the management of unease'. This field comprises a mosaic of different institutions, agencies, organizations and individuals, such as the military, the police, border guards, private security firms, security consultants, academics, etc., that all share a preoccupation with (in)security (Bigo 2008: 19–22, 39). The 'field of the professionals of the management of unease' is constantly shifting due to struggles between different agencies over conceptions of (in)security and their attempts to impose particular definitions of (in)security and specific prioritizations of threats upon other, adjacent and/or overlapping fields, such as the sphere of politics or the news media (Bigo 2008: 22–31). Yet, the field of (in)security has a certain coherence, because the sum total of what its actors do produces a field effect that delimits what they can do (Bigo 2008: 26). This is absolutely crucial: a coherent field demarcated by clear, albeit constantly shifting, boundaries emerges through the sum total of the actions of agents located within the field, while this overall field effect, in turn, sets the parameters within which these actions can occur in the first place. Thus, the field of the professionals of the management of unease is both the cause and effect of governmentalities of security. In brief, the 'field of (in)security' is contoured by the shared rationalities and practices designed and deployed by its agents – governmentalities that span 'four previously unconnected conceptual worlds – internal security, external security, war and conflict, and crime and delinquency' (Bigo 2008: 23–31, 30). And an analysis of these rationalities and practices, or governmentalities, is what makes a coherent field of (in)security intelligible in the first place.

We will now take a much more in-depth look at the empirical relations between rationalities concerning the referent objects and targets of security and the regimes of practices designed and deployed to secure particular referent objects and target specific threats. We will examine how governmentalities of security aim to identify and target at-risk and risky individuals, populations and spaces; how they configure and reconfigure spatial and organizational boundaries; how they are legitimated vis-à-vis domestic and global audiences and, above all, how their effects provide the conditions of intelligibility of a coherent field of security professionals, as well as an overall biopolitical strategy of global pacification. In short, we will look at how governmentalities of security seek to respond to specific problematizations of insecurity, and how they are provisionally articulated into wider institutional and strategic regimes.

2 Expeditionary pacification

Introduction

Following the 9/11 attacks, the United States and its allies scrambled to respond to what were seen as increasingly global circulations of insecurity. These circulations were, above all, thought to emerge from the world's ungoverned spaces and were viewed as putting the very stability of the international state system at risk. A number of policymakers and military top brass, as well as civilian academics from both the United States and allied nations – most notably the United Kingdom – stressed that these threats called for more 'population-centered' and 'community-oriented' military strategies (see for example, Gompert *et al.* 2009; Kilcullen 2005, 2009, 2010; Long 2006; Nagl 2005; Ucko 2009). One prominent and widely publicized response was a shift in US military strategy, from conventional firepower-centered warfare towards counterinsurgency (COIN) and stability operations, even though this strategic realignment met with a lot of resistance from within the US military establishment and still remains contested (Ucko 2009).

US and allied forces' difficulties in effectively pacifying and stabilizing post-invasion Iraq and Afghanistan brought counterinsurgency and stability operations, which had fallen into doctrinal oblivion since the end of the Vietnam War, back onto the top of the Pentagon's agenda in 2004/2005. The renaissance of counterinsurgency started under the Bush administration but gained additional momentum under President Obama. In his speech about the new Afghanistan strategy on 1 December 2009, Obama (2009) stressed that the United States was engaged in a protracted unconventional conflict with al-Qaeda that 'extends well beyond Afghanistan and Pakistan':

> [U]nlike the great power conflicts and clear lines of division that defined the twentieth century, our effort will involve disorderly regions, failed states, diffuse enemies. So as a result, America will have to show our strength in the way that we end wars and prevent conflict – not just how we wage wars. We'll have to be nimble and precise in our use of military power. Where al Qaeda and its allies attempt to establish a foothold – whether in Somalia or Yemen or elsewhere – they must be confronted by growing pressure and strong partnerships.
>
> (Obama 2009)

The new long-term commitment to dealing with 'disorderly regions, failed states, diffuse enemies' is also enshrined in the 2010 'Quadrennial Defense Review' (QDR) (Department of Defense 2010a). The QDR asserts that 'the changing international environment will continue to put pressure on the modern state system, likely increasing the frequency and severity of the challenges associated with chronically fragile states' (Department of Defense 2010a: 32).

Indeed, numerous policymakers: members of the armed forces, Pentagon officials and civilian academics, touted counterinsurgency as an effective response to global circulations of threat emanating from failing states. A global counterinsurgency strategy was frequently pitched not only as an instrument for defeating Iraqi or Afghan insurgents, but also as a panacea for fighting global terrorism.

In 2006, a new *Counterinsurgency Field Manual* (Department of the Army 2007) was published with a lot of media fanfare – the first manual exclusively dedicated to counterinsurgency since the 1980s. The new manual defines insurgency as 'an organized, protracted politico-military struggle designed to weaken the control and legitimacy of an established government, occupying power, or other political authority while increasing insurgent control'. Counterinsurgency, in turn, is defined as 'military, paramilitary, political, economic, psychological, and civic actions taken by a government to defeat insurgency' (Department of the Army 2007: 2).

Counterinsurgency [COIN] ought to be understood as a rationality and practice of security geared towards pacifying ungoverned spaces and populations that more often than not tend to be located in the post-colonial global south. This pacification effort hinges on providing security to the local population while (re) building the politico-economic infrastructure that would ultimately enable the so-called host-nation to govern itself. Moreover, the provision of security and development is supposed to occur against the backdrop of an overall battle over perceptions, to be waged through effective information operations (IO)[1] (Department of the Army 2007).

But the idea of counterinsurgency doctrine is much older than the war on terror. In fact, a US counterinsurgency doctrine was first promulgated in response to what was then seen as communist destabilization efforts in the Third World. If we want to understand the role of counterinsurgency doctrine in the war on terror, we thus have to first examine its Cold-War history.

The rise of counterinsurgency doctrine

> We are opposed around the world by a monolithic and ruthless conspiracy that relies primarily on covert means for expanding its sphere of influence – on infiltration instead of invasion, on subversion instead of elections, on intimidation instead of free choice, on guerrillas by night instead of armies by day.
>
> (Kennedy 1961: 336)

Shortly after his inauguration in 1961, President John F. Kennedy took a personal lead in pushing for the development of a comprehensive US counterinsurgency strategy (Blaufarb 1977: 52–5; McClintock 1992: 161–5; see Shafer 1988: 20–4). Roger Hilsman (1967: 413; cited in Blaufarb 1977: 52), who was a key aide and foreign policy advisor to Kennedy, wrote that one of the first questions the newly elected president put to his aides was, 'What are we doing about guer- rilla warfare?' Kennedy's desire to develop US counterguerrilla capabilities seemed to have been a direct response to Soviet premier Nikita Khrushchev's remarks about wars of liberation in the Third World: 'Is there a likelihood of such wars recurring? Yes there is. [...] The communists support just wars of this kind wholeheartedly and they march in the van of the peoples fighting for libera- tion' (cited in Blaufarb 1977: 53). Khrushchev's incendiary language chimed with a series of events that seemed to be connected to a wider Soviet strategy of fomenting unrest in the Third World: uprisings, rebellions and insurgencies in Laos, South Vietnam, Cuba, Colombia, Venezuela and Algeria, even if the latter was not influenced by Communism, fuelled Kennedy's fears about a Communist conspiracy in the global south (Blaufarb 1977: 53).

However, a sweeping Soviet conspiracy to foment unrest in the Third World was probably an example of American hysteria, rather than actual fact. Accord- ing to Douglas Blaufarb (1977: 18), 'The Soviet Union by the late fifties had no voice in determining the policies of the Vietnamese Communists or of Castro and his group, to cite the two insurgencies which caused most concern in Wash- ington'. What is more, Khrushchev's reference to wars of liberation was more likely meant to address Chinese criticisms about mounting Soviet reticence in providing support to national liberation movements (Blaufarb 1977: 54). However, according to Arthur Schlesinger Jr. (1965: 282; cited in Blaufarb 1977: 18) the 'bellicose confidence' of Khrushchev's remarks made 'a conspicu- ous impression' upon the newly elected president and galvanized him into action.

National Security Action Memorandum (NSAM) 2 (United States Govern- ment 1961a), written and signed by Special Assistant to the President for National Security Affairs, McGeorge Bundy, on 3 February 1961, was the first formal step towards a US counterinsurgency strategy. The document 'request[ed] that the Secretary of Defense, in consultation with other interested agencies, should examine means for placing more emphasis on the development of counter-guerrilla forces' (United States Government 1961a). NSAM 2 led to a flurry of activities at all levels of the national security apparatus: seminars and courses on counterinsurgency; major efforts at bureaucratic re-structuring; and the frenetic formulation of new policies and doctrines.

In March 1961, Kennedy established an interagency group, headed by Richard Bissell, a deputy director of the CIA. This group was tasked with looking into the bureaucratic reforms needed for establishing a permanent coun- terinsurgency capability. The Bissell committee report 'called for the creation of a high-level interagency committee to monitor and guide the foreign affairs com- munity in its counterinsurgency efforts and to provide a forum for the develop- ment of doctrine' (Blaufarb 1977: 67). President Kennedy gave his approval, which was circulated in the form of National Security Action Memorandum 124

(United States Government 1962a) on 18 January 1962. NSAM 124 called for the establishment of the so-called 'Special Group (Counterinsurgency)', which came to include the following high-ranking members of the administration: The Attorney General, the Deputy Under Secretary of State for Political Affairs, the Deputy Secretary of Defense, the Chairman of the Joint Chiefs of Staff, the Director of Central Intelligence, the Special Assistant to the President for National Security Affairs, the Administrator of the Agency for International Development and the Director of the United States Information Agency. NSAM 124 inscribed the significance of counterinsurgency into the highest levels of government and thus laid the institutional groundwork for a comprehensive US counterinsurgency strategy. The document centered on the assumption that what it so oxymoronically called 'subversive insurgency'[2] required a hitherto unprecedented degree of interdepartmental cooperation and the formulation, as well as implementation, of programs beyond the traditional remits of individual government agencies. Moreover, the fact that the Administrator of the Agency for International Development (AID) came to be included in a group whose other members were mostly drawn from the national security apparatus, points to the pivotal role of development efforts in counterinsurgency.

Security, development and the management of modernization

In *Deadly Paradigms*, Michael Shafer (1988) argues that counterinsurgency doctrine has never been fully applied in practice:

> Counterinsurgency is inapplicable as well as unapplied. It misconstrues American relations with insurgency-threatened governments, the constraints facing leaders of those governments, and the relationship between governments and their subjects, as well as between them and the insurgents. [...] Worse, misassessments of government-population relations and the sources of insurgency may produce inappropriate prescriptions, some of which aggravate the very problems they are designed to alleviate.
>
> (Shafer 1988: 6)

As a consequence, counterinsurgency programs have often resulted in abysmal failure. Although there are examples of successful *avant-la-lettre* US counterinsurgency efforts, such as the Greek Civil War (1947–1949) and the uprising in the Philippines (1946–1957), these either succeeded in spite of US involvement, as in the Philippines, or because American prescriptions were ignored, as in Greece (Blaufarb 1977: 22–51; see also Shafer 1988: 6). According to Shafer (1988: 7), the misjudgment of what counterinsurgency programs can actually achieve was due to 'the systematic and distorting impact of a coherent set of widely shared and unchallenged assumptions concerning the sources, nature, direction, and potential consequences of political change in the Third World'. These assumptions hinged on a view of 'the Third World state as beleaguered modernizer and the United States as manager of modernization' (Shafer 1988: 6).

After the end of World War II, and during the period of decolonization, many social scientists espoused what came to be known as modernization theory. They assumed that political change in the Third World was the effect of an initial contact with modernity which, due to the clear superiority of modern ideas and institutions, gave rise to 'a modernized local elite [...] making modernization a self-sustaining process by which the modern center sought to penetrate and absorb the passive, traditional periphery' (Shafer 1988: 57).

The process of modernization was, above all, associated with the rise of nationalism and the emergence of nation-states. Western educated elites were considered the prime agents of this process, because they were expected to act as 'the creators of the new nation and not merely of the new state' (Shils 1958: 6; cited in Shafer 1988: 58). According to Rupert Emerson (1960: 188; cited in Shafer 1988: 58), 'Nationalism wherever it manifests itself is in essence a response to the forces which in recent centuries have revolutionized the West and have penetrated in successive waves to the farthest corners of the world.' Now it was up to Western-educated third world elites to respond to the challenges of 'how to build a single coherent society from the multiplicity of "traditional societies"' (Ake 1967: 486; cited in Shafer 1988: 58).

But the processes of modernization did not unfold in the orderly fashion envisaged by Western social scientists. By the mid-1960s Third World elites were confronted with severe bouts of political instability (Shafer 1988: 59). But rather than reassessing their theoretical claims, modernization theorists now asserted that development would have occurred as expected, if it had not been blocked by a combination of internal and external threats. Political instability was now considered to be the consequence of a breakdown of modernization (Eisenstadt 1964: 578; Shafer 1988: 59). Shafer (1988: 59) argues that '[t]he "breakdown of modernization" literature stresses the overwhelming forces released by modernization and the comparatively underwhelming nature of still shaky new regimes'. One of the most influential proponents of the breakdown of modernization hypothesis was Samuel Huntington (1968: 4, 35) – of current *Clash of Civilizations* fame or, rather, notoriety – who argued that by destroying traditional organizations and social structures, modernization had generated new needs and desires on the part of the population. These new needs and desires, in turn, led to a rise in political demands and participation that threatened to overwhelm the fledgling institutions of new states and thereby gave rise to political instability. Thus, political instability was regarded as the consequence of a democratic excess that could not be accommodated by fledgling state structures.

Since Third World populations had been culturally uprooted by the onslaught of modernization and the concomitant destruction of traditional organizations, they were considered to be 'naturally susceptible to the temptations of revolutionary agitation' (Olson 1963: 532–3; cited in Shafer 1988: 61). Insurgencies in the Third World were identified as security threats that cut across the divide between inside and outside. Guerrillas were regarded as disgruntled members of the population, recruited and mobilized through outside agitation.

The discourse of modernization thus provided the intellectual support for a strategy geared towards securing young Third World nations from both internal and external threats. Many of the tenets of modernization theory came to be reiterated in the formulation of counterinsurgency doctrine. In September 1962, US counterinsurgency strategy was promulgated in a document entitled 'United States Overseas Internal Defense Policy' (United States Government 1962b). This document declared that the Third World was shaped by two major forces:

> The principal forces at work throughout the undeveloped world are: (1) the stresses and strains of the developmental process brought about by the revolutionary break with the traditional past and uneven progress toward new and more modern forms of political, social, and economic organization; and (2) the contest between communism and the Free World for primary influence over the direction and outcome of the developmental process.
>
> (United States Government 1962b: 4)

And it goes on to cite the following causes of insurgency:

> Insurgency is grounded in the allegiances and attitudes of the people. Its origins are domestic, and its support must remain so. The causes of insurgency therefore stem from the inadequacies of the local government to requite or remove popular or group dissatisfactions. It is during the interim, between the shattering of the old mold and its consolidation into a viable modern state of popularly accepted and supported institutional strength, that a modernizing state is vulnerable to subversion and insurgency.
>
> (United States Government 1962b: 5)

So, only the provision of security would allow development to proceed in an orderly fashion. As Shafer puts it:

> Development policies seek to ameliorate the overwhelming demands unleashed by social mobilization, and security policies attempt to bolster the underwhelming capabilities of new states that they may manage disruptions while forging ahead with modernization. Without security, so the argument goes, development is impossible; without good government and economic progress, efforts to maintain it will be bootless.
>
> (Shafer 1988: 79)

In the early 1960s, counterinsurgency doctrine was formulated to enable the US to manage the process of modernization by assisting friendly Third World governments in controlling their populations through a combination of security and development. What Mark Duffield (2001: 16) describes as 'a noticeable convergence between development and security' is, thus, not just a recent phenomenon, but was already an integral part of 1960s US counterinsurgency strategy.

Security and development were supposed to be fused into a coherent pacification strategy by articulating hitherto distinct US governmental capabilities. According to the 'United States Overseas Internal Defense Policy' (United States Government 1962b), successful counterinsurgency campaigns depended on a 'blend of civil and military capabilities':

> Anticipating, preventing and defeating communist-directed insurgency requires a blend of civil and military capabilities and actions to which each U.S. agency at the Country Team level must contribute. [...] Success will depend on the accurate information, a careful evaluation thereof and on a unified concept of operations based on a comprehensive plan tailored to the local situation in which civil and military measures interact and reinforce each other.
>
> (United States Government 1962b: 10–11)

This blend of military and civilian capabilities could only come to fruition through the increasing cooperation between distinct agencies from the Country Team level: representatives of different agencies tasked with dealing with the situation in a specific country, all the way up to the highest echelons of US government.

Mao and fourth-generation warfare

In *The Sling and the Stone*, retired Marine Corps colonel Thomas Hammes (2006) asserts that the second half of the twentieth century witnessed the rise of a new form of war, which he calls fourth-generation warfare (4GW). Fourth-generation warfare differs markedly from earlier forms of warfare in that 'it does not attempt to win by defeating the enemy's military forces' but rather aims to destroy the enemy's will to fight (Hammes 2006: 2, 31). Hammes (2006: 31) argues that war has evolved in step with the ability 'to project power over much longer ranges'. First- and second-generation warfare sought to destroy the enemy's armed forces, while third-generation warfare aimed to destroy the enemy's command, control systems and logistics (Hammes 2006: 2, 31). And, 'fourth-generation warfare now uses all available networks – political, economic, social, and military – to convince the enemy's political decision-makers that their strategic goals are either unachievable or too costly for the perceived benefit' (Hammes 2006: 31).

However, in contrast to earlier military innovations, 4GW was not developed in the West, but in the context of wars of liberation in the global south. It emerged as a weapon of the weak, designed to prevail against far superior Western states. Indeed, Hammes (2006) traces the evolution of 4GW from its origins in Mao Tse-tung's concept of guerrilla warfare over Ho Chi Minh, and Vo Nguyen's modification of the latter to the first and second Intifada and the current transnational terrorist activities of al-Qaeda.

So, what is this peculiar asymmetrical form of warfare all about? And why has it confronted superiorly equipped and much better trained Western armies with such intractable problems? At this point, it is worthwhile to briefly look at Mao's strategy of guerrilla warfare, which according to Hammes, marked the birth of 4GW.

Mao's strategy relied on two key principles. First, guerrillas must rely on mobility, alertness and flexibility, and try to avoid all direct confrontation with superior enemy forces: they 'must move with the fluidity of water and the ease of the blowing wind' (Mao 1961: 103–4) Second, guerrilla forces were thought to depend above all on the support of the population. For Mao, guerrilla victory pivoted on the political mobilization of the people:

> Our job is not merely to recite our political program to the people [...]. [We must] transform the political mobilization for the war into a regular movement. This is a matter of the first magnitude on which the victory primarily depends.
>
> (Mao 1954: 77; see also 1961: 92–3)

In short, Mao, ultimately, sought to wrest control over the population from the government.

Most Western analysts break Mao's strategy down into three distinct but overlapping phases: during phase one, the population is stirred up, mobilized and ultimately organized through propaganda and agitation; while '[m]ilitary action is limited to selected, politically motivated assassinations', or armed propaganda (Hammes 2006: 53). The main purpose of this phase is to politicize the population and build a lasting politico-military structure. Once the insurgents have consolidated political control in certain areas they move into phase two, which marks the start of guerrilla operations proper. This phase relies on 'the establishment of base areas, usually in some remote and inaccessible zone' where the guerilla movement acts as a quasi-government, 'collects taxes, establishes training camps, hospitals, and depots, and builds reserve supplies of food and ammunition' (Blaufarb 1977: 4). Military operations are primarily geared towards obtaining arms and other equipment and 'wear[ing] down government forces' (Hammes 2006: 52). This phase tends to be the most protracted and difficult one for the guerrillas and the government alike. In phase three, the insurgents launch a broad offensive against government forces by regular military units led by battle-hardened ex-guerrillas. This is when guerrilla operations cease and conventional warfare begins. Now the ultimate goal becomes to replace the central government (see Blaufarb 1977: 3–12; Mao 1978; Hammes 2006: 50–3).

The first two phases only serve to 'change the "correlation of forces" between the government and the insurgents. Once these have shifted in their favor the insurgents are ready to move to phase three, the final destruction of the government by conventional forces' (Hammes 2006: 52). However, the distinction between the phases is not as clear-cut as it might seem. Insurgents can always revert back to earlier phases if they realize that the 'correlation of forces' is not yet stacked in their favor.

But Mao also understood that this struggle did not stop at China's borders and that international public opinion was a crucial frontline element of any revolutionary war:

> He expanded his ideas to state that to maximize political power insurgents must project it beyond their borders. Through propaganda, they must attack their enemy by undermining the political will of that enemy's people, allies, and sponsors. The insurgents must further mobilize neutral political opinion to pressure the enemy's major political allies into withdrawing support. The final task of the insurgent propagandist was to generate material and economic support for the movement from friendly and neutral countries.
>
> (Hammes 2006: 53)

Hammes (2006: 53) further suggests that 'Mao counted heavily on political maneuvering to change the "correlation of forces" both internal and external to China [...] [and] had also developed long-term, effective strategic, operational, and tactical approaches to achieve that shift in forces'.[3]

Mao did not single-handedly create a new form of war – guerrilla warfare had existed well before Mao gave clear expression to what he saw as its key principles (for earlier instances of guerrilla warfare see Laqueur 1978). But what he did do was to 'provide a strategic concept that moved guerrilla warfare from a subordinate effort to support a conventional army to a war-winning approach' (Hammes 2006: 51). This is where Mao can indeed be considered a real innovator: he was the first to argue that a war can be won by guerrilla forces alone.[4]

Mao's strategic innovation was to show, in both theory and practice, that the political mobilization of the population combined with a protracted unconventional politico-military conflict, and a focus on both domestic and international propaganda, could enable guerrillas to defeat far superior forces. However, Mao's guerrilla strategy was still rather state-centered. For him, the formation of a guerrilla movement was not only geared towards subverting and defeating the state, but also towards replacing it. The guerrilla organization, formed in the first phase of his strategy and consolidated and territorialized in the second, was bound to become a full-fledged conventional counter-state army in the third, and turn into just another state upon victory.

This is what the Kennedy administration saw itself confronted with, militarily and politically. Highly politically motivated guerrillas with decentralized command structures, who were hiding amongst the civilians, were thought to threaten the stability of fledgling Third World nations. Indeed, The Kennedy administration perceived guerrilla warfare as a major threat to US interests in the Third World.

According to Shafer (1988: 21), 'the president read – and ordered his advisors to read – Mao, Giap and other architects of revolutionary theory'. This obsession with Mao stemmed from the fact that revolutionary theory and modernization theory were both underpinned by similar assumptions about the Third World. In fact, US counterinsurgents found their intellectual mirror image in revolutionary doctrine (Shafer 1988: 108). Theories of insurgency and counterinsurgency clustered around a similar conceptualization of modernization. On the one hand, this conceptualization postulated the inexorable onslaught of progress and modernity; and, on the other, considered these historical forces as something that could be externally managed. In both cases the management of modernization hinged on the population. Populations were regarded as the raw material shaped by the forces of modernization. And in order to channel these historical forces in a desired direction, one 'only' had to mobilize populations according to one's own ideological program of modernization. Through the management of populations one could thus (supposedly) act on, and regulate, the process of modernization itself. Counterinsurgency, therefore, became a 'universal countertactic' (Shafer 1988: 110), geared towards countering revolutionary attempts to manage the modernization process through establishing and exerting control over Third World populations.

In 1966, one Lieutenant Colonel McCuen (1966: 78; cited in Shafer 1988: 110) wrote that 'the most logical solution [...] does lie in developing a counter-revolutionary strategy which applies revolutionary strategy and principles in reverse to defeat the enemy with his own weapons on his own battlefield'. Indeed, the Kennedy administration pressed the US military to establish permanent counter-revolutionary capabilities. This would have ultimately entailed nothing short of a revolution in the overall organization and strategic orientation of the US armed forces.

The military contribution

In terms of scope and resources, the military saw the most extensive counterinsurgency programs, some of which even predated the establishment of the aforementioned Special Group (CI). But what were these capabilities? First of all, there was the buildup and expansion of the Special Forces. The so-called Green Berets became Kennedy's pet unit[5] and the 'symbol of the president's favor was the green beret, which he insisted be restored to the unit after the army command, enforcing a general policy against highly visible insignia, had taken it away' (McClintock 1992: 180; see also Blaufarb 1977: 76). Kennedy was obsessed with the Special Forces and took a strong personal interest in their training and equipment. His advisor and speechwriter, Theodore Sorenson, (1965: 632; cited in McClintock 1992: 180) remarked that his obsession even extended to what footgear his pet unit was to wear: the president 'personally supervised the selection of equipment – the replacement of heavy noisy combat boots with sneakers, for example, and when the sneakers proved vulnerable to bamboo spikes, their reinforcement with flexible steel inner soles'. In early 1961, Kennedy launched a program to expand the Special Forces – their numbers were to be doubled, their resources increased and their headquarters at Fort Bragg came to be commanded by a general. The commander of Fort Bragg Special Warfare Center, William P. Yarborough, was promptly promoted to the rank of Brigadier General (Blaufarb 1977: 76, 79; see McClintock 1992: 180).

The Special Forces were originally 'conceived as a permanent version of the improvised guerrilla units of the OSS [Organization of Strategic Services] during World War II' (Blaufarb 1977: 76), but now – in a rather strange and ironic reversal – their brief was extended to include counterinsurgency capabilities:

> [T]heir role was the generation of resistance forces behind the lines of an enemy, and they sought men with special language and other useful talents – particularly a liking for personal combat. In the new version, their role was broadened to include advice, training, and leadership for friendly counterguerrilla forces – somewhat the reverse of the original mission but not, in fact, inconsistent with the requirement that guerrillas be fought with guerrilla-style tactics.
>
> (Blaufarb 1977: 76)

Indeed, the buildup of the Special Forces was guided by the assumption that only guerrilla tactics would be able to defeat guerrillas.

Yet, some of the tactics that were adopted by the US military in the context of counterinsurgency operations often militated against the overarching goal of winning the support of the population, because they were rarely applied within a broader political strategy:

> The tactics of guerrilla-counterguerrilla warfare were nominally to have been part, and only a part, of an integrated political strategy. In counterinsurgency war, though, a strategy of establishing governmental control and winning hearts and minds was not always well served by unconventional tactics.
>
> (McClintock 1992: 42)

McClintock further suggests that, '[i]t is significant that the army's Special Forces – elite practitioners of violence, not diplomatic civil affairs officers – were the crux of the counterinsurgency realignment'. McClintock somewhat overstates the role of the Special Forces, but he has a valid point in arguing that '[a]lthough much has been made of the president's conflicts with the military over counterinsurgency, there appears to have been little dissent over the pivotal role of the Special Warfare establishment in the new policy' (McClintock 1992: 181).

But there were also other counterinsurgency-related programs. In 1961, the White House also pushed the armed forces to develop a comprehensive military civic action program. On 18 December 1961, NSAM 119 (United States Government 1961b) was issued to express the president's concern 'that we may be missing an opportunity this year to develop methods for supporting whatever contribution military forces can make to economic and social development in less-developed countries'. NSAM 119 defined civic action as the use of military forces 'on projects useful to the populace at all levels in such fields as training, public works, agriculture, transportation, communication, health, sanitation, and others helpful to economic development' (United States Government 1961b). In short, military civic action sought to harness the civilian skills and resources of the armed forces to infrastructure and public works programs aimed at improving the life of Third World populations.

Blaufarb (1977) observes that '[f]ar too much emphasis during these years was placed on military civic action as a kind of panacea and all-purpose preventative to insurgency'. He holds that military civic action is not without its merits as long as it is used for training and equipping the security forces of a beleaguered regime, because 'it helps to improve the relations of the military with the communities among which they have to move in order to master an insurgency'. Yet, the direct performance of military civic action by US forces would be out of the question, unless they were directly involved in combat operations. And even then, military civic action would only be a 'means to improve relationships with the surrounding population' and 'not a substitute for a national development program' (Blaufarb 1997: 77).

Both the Special Forces buildup and the focus on military civic action point to a key dilemma in the military's response to counterinsurgency. This dilemma lay in the crucial difference between supporting a host-nation's counterinsurgency efforts in terms of training, advice, and equipment, and the direct involvement of US forces in combat operations. Military civic action was primarily conducted through the Military Aid Program, which already existed and was merely expanded in response to counterinsurgency requirements (see Blaufarb 1977: 78). The US military civic action program was supposed to help threatened regimes build their own civic action capabilities, rather than operate as a tool for US combat forces on the ground. On the other hand, due to their small numbers, the brief of the Special Forces was restricted to providing training and advice to foreign forces as well as to a support role in limited combat operations. The moment US involvement required a large-scale deployment of combat units, regular military forces would have to step in (Blaufarb 1977: 79).

Indeed, US counterinsurgency strategy sought to avoid the deployment of regular combat forces in counterinsurgency operations. The 'United States Overseas Internal Defense Policy' (United States Government 1962b), stated that:

> The scale of U.S. involvement at the level of force should be as limited as the achievement of its objectives permit and only ancillary to the indigenous effort. It is important for the U.S. to remain in the background, and where possible, to limit its support to training, advice, and material, lest it prejudice the local government effort and expose the U.S. unnecessarily to charges of intervention and colonialism.
>
> (United States Government 1962b: 10)

The purpose and scope of the document itself only included 'the range and measures to assist vulnerable regimes in preventing and defeating subversion and insurgency', short of the 'tactical employment of US Armed Forces in combat operations' (United States Government 1962b: 1). Moreover, the president himself stated on numerous occasions that such conflicts should be fought by indigenous forces.

Yet, the administration clearly assumed that the deployment of combat troops in counterinsurgency conflicts would at some point be inevitable. And such a deployment would require a more far-reaching counterinsurgency capability than a few thousand Green Berets and a military civic action program. According to Blaufarb (1977), the question for the military command became: '[w]ould certain units be singled out for specialization in counterinsurgency warfare, or would all be required to add this to their other conventional missions?' The Chiefs of Staff decided on the latter – counterinsurgency was added to the conventional mission of the armed forces (Blaufarb 1977: 80). This is illustrated by the 1963 *Counterguerrilla Operations Field Manual (FM 31–16)* (Department of the Army 1963). On the one hand, the manual stressed that the civilian population should not be treated too harshly in order to prevent them from defecting to the guerrillas:

> Government forces must determine which elements of the civilian population are supporting the guerrillas. Since this may be difficult initially, strict controls may be necessary and have sometimes proved effective. Harsh measures against entire populations, however, may influence mass defections and encourage support for the guerrilla forces. The civil population must be apprised of the reasons for actions taken against it and must be made to understand that such measures are of a temporary nature and will be discontinued when cooperation is effected.
>
> (Department of the Army 1963: 20)

But on the same page, *FM 31–16* also unequivocally declared that counterguerrilla operations necessitate aggressive offensive action to very much the same extent as in conventional wars:

> An area confronted with a serious guerrilla menace must be considered a combat area. Units in such areas must maintain the same alert and aggressive attitudes as forward troops in conventional war. A 'rear area' psychology makes it easier for guerrilla forces to employ one of their most potent weapons, surprise. Purely defensive measures only allow the guerrilla force to grow and become strong. They are justified only when the strength of the friendly forces available does not permit offensive action. Even limited offensive operations are preferable to a purely passive attitude. Offensive action should be continuous and aggressive.
>
> (Deaprtment of the Army 1963: 20)

By and large, the field manual treated guerrilla war as a largely conventional mode of conflict that required certain unconventional skills and resources in exchange for a few conventional warfighting capabilities. For instance, the manual briefly mentioned the importance of police operations, population control and security measures, which were more or less added to the regular mission of the armed forces; whereas, on the other hand, it prescribed for the use of tanks and artillery to be adjusted to the unconventional requirements of counter-guerrilla operations and for certain units, such as anti-tank platoons, to be stripped down and assigned other duties (Department of the Army 1963: 37–48, 84–5, 88–91, 83). Counterguerrilla doctrine was thus reductive in that it required 'a reversion to a simpler form of combat [...] and the abandonment of the doctrine of concentration of force in favor of the deployment of numerous platoon-sized units on constant patrol' (Blaufarb 1977: 81). On the other hand, the implementation of the doctrine was additive, 'It left the combat division unchanged in organization and equipment but required it to fight in the counterinsurgency mode, when required, in addition to other missions' (Blaufarb 1977: 81). As a consequence, counterinsurgency was a mere plug-in – something that was added to the already existing mission of the armed forces. The military thus failed to implement the far-reaching organizational reforms needed to counter a 4GW enemy. The failure to develop a designated counterinsurgency force was to have an enormous impact on how US forces fought the Vietnam War and, by implication, also on the fortunes of US counterinsurgency doctrine itself.

Vietnam and the 'end' of US counterinsurgency doctrine

Arguably, US counterinsurgency doctrine did not live up to its promises, and as the United States became increasingly embroiled in the Vietnam War, interest in the doctrine quickly declined. Indeed, many commentators suggest that Vietnam marked the failure of the doctrine. The relevant literature cites a number of inter-related reasons for this failure:

1   An inadequate implementation of an otherwise more or less sound doctrine because of (a) a failure on the part of the US military to recognize and adapt to the unconventional nature of the conflict, and (b) a lack of effective inter-agency cooperation on the ground.
2   The attempt to prop up a regime that proved to be completely unviable.
3   Inherent limitation of the doctrine itself, especially in terms of its disregard of the local socio-political context of insurgencies.[6]

Hammes (2006) contends that the US lost because it did not understand the true nature of the war it was fighting. Indeed, there are many indications that the US armed forces saw the conflict in overwhelmingly conventional terms, concentrating on the regular North Vietnamese army rather than on the Vietcong guerrillas. This, for example, was the view of Colonel Harry Summers (1982) whose 1982 book *On Strategy: A Critical Analysis of the Vietnam War* 'was widely acclaimed in political, military, and academic circles as a clear, accurate strategic assessment of the U.S.–Vietnamese War' (Hammes 2006: 57). Summers contended that:

It is indicative of our strategic failure in Vietnam that almost a decade after our involvement the true nature of the Vietnam War is still in question. There are still those who would attempt to fit it into the revolutionary war mold and who blame our defeat on our failure to implement counterinsurgency doctrine. This point of view requires an acceptance of the North Vietnamese contention that the [...] North Vietnamese regular forces were an extension of the guerrilla effort, a point of view not borne out by the facts.

(Summers 1982: 83)

There is, in fact, an ongoing debate about whether the Vietnam War was a conventional war with some unconventional features, or a largely unconventional conflict. Over the last few years, there has been a flurry of revisionist publications on counterinsurgency and the lessons of the Vietnam War, written mainly by career officers, who are too young to have fought in Vietnam. John A. Nagl's *Eating Soup with a Knife* (Nagl 2005) is a significant contribution to this body of literature and is cited in almost all recent publications on counterinsurgency, including the current field manual. Nagl compares the learning processes of the British army in Malaya and US forces in Vietnam, in order to find out why the British army did become an effective learning organization able to pacify Malaya, while US forces did not make this adaptation, and ultimately failed in Vietnam. Like Hammes, Nagl argues that US forces lost the Vietnam War, because they clung to the precepts of conventional warfare and thus failed to become a genuine learning organization capable of adapting to the vicissitudes of insurgency warfare.

However, Nagl (2005: 128–68) also discusses a number of tactical innovations, most of which were devised and implemented by civilian agencies and often poorly coordinated with the military. What is more, the moment control of these programs passed from a civilian agency (such as the CIA or the State Department) to the military, they were frequently watered down and lost their innovative edge. For instance, in the early 1960s, the CIA developed and implemented the so-called Civilian Irregular Defense Group (CIDG) program (Nagl 2005: 128–9). This program was geared towards pacifying villages by arming and organizing the rural population. Nagl argues that 'CIDG worked well until control was transferred to MACV [Military Assistance Command Vietnam], which changed the program to emphasize offensive operations rather than village security' (Nagl 2005: 128; see also Hunt 1995). Another example of, in Nagl's view (Nagl 2005: 164–6), a rather successful counterinsurgency initiative is the Civil Operations and Revolutionary Development Support program (CORDS), which was in effect from 1967 to 1971. CORDS was a genuine inter-agency effort including staff from the CIA, USIA, AID, the State Department, the White House and all military services (Nagl 2005: 165; see also Hunt 1995). The program sent armed civil-military advisory teams into 250 districts and 44 provinces, in order to conduct a massive pacification effort. CORDS was headed by Robert Komer, a member of the National Security Council, who reported directly to the Commander: US Military Assistance Command Vietnam (COMUSMACV).[7] Nagl (2005: 166) suggests that the success of CORDS owed more to 'Komer's personal characteristics and ability to gain the ear of the president than [to] the army's willingness to adapt to the demands of counterinsurgency warfare'. Ultimately, as Komer himself (cited in Nagl 2005: 166) put it: 'The greatest problem with pacification was that it wasn't tried seriously until too late, or if not too late certainly very late in the day'.

In Nagl's view, US efforts in Vietnam were doomed because the US military relied too much on the – more often than not indiscriminate – use of firepower, which alienated a population whose hearts and minds US forces should have tried to win. At the same time, many high-ranking officers dismissed the pacification effort as 'the other war'. This was, moreover, compounded by bureaucratic constraints and the lack of proper inter-agency coordination.

As former members of the US military, both Hammes and Nagl[8] thus attribute the US defeat in Vietnam to the inability of the US military to adapt to the unconventional nature of the war.

While not denying that the military's emphasis on conventional warfare played a crucial role in the United States' defeat in Vietnam, Douglas A. Blaufarb (1977) and Michael Shafer (1988) also highlight some of the inherent limitations of counterinsurgency doctrine. Blaufarb, a former CIA operative, who has firsthand experience of counterinsurgency operations, focuses on the organizational challenges that counterinsurgency campaigns invariably present. He holds that first of all, 'involvement in counterinsurgency in any depth immediately confronts us with very difficult obstacles internal to our government and growing out of the nature of permanent bureaucracies' (Blaufarb 1977: 298). These obstacles derive from the fact that counterinsurgency 'cuts across the norms and hierarchies of the concerned agencies in several ways' (Blaufarb 1977: 298). Consequently, it compels agencies to assume roles that are beyond their normal remits, and, if an effective coordinating mechanism is put in place, 'it short-circuits normal command channels in favor of a new, temporary command structure that grievously flouts institutional loyalties and prerogatives' (Blaufarb 1977: 298). But, besides confronting US military and civilian agencies with almost insurmountable problems, a pacification program must also cope with the specific problems of the regime it is trying to prop up. Regimes that are not overly blessed with legitimacy often tend to be more vulnerable to insurgency in the first place. And imposing reform on a threatened regime from the outside – when need be with the help of superior firepower – is no panacea for generating legitimacy (the same holds true for current COIN efforts in Afghanistan). The Diem regime is a case in point, because it was in dire need of both reform and legitimacy:

> It should be starkly clear by now that counterinsurgency places unique demands upon a threatened regime, and that the governments which have most need of the courage, understanding, and the cohesion required are the least likely to muster these essential qualities. That, more likely than not, is why they have become targets of insurgency and why their defensive efforts will fail to the point that they require outside help.
>
> (Blaufarb 1977: 310)

For Blaufarb, counterinsurgency doctrine is thus an 'ambiguous heritage' (Blaufarb 1977: 310) – an instrument one has to reluctantly wield now and then – but also 'a lesson of the limits of American power' (Blaufarb 1977: 311).

Shafer's (1988) analysis of the intellectual limitations of counterinsurgency arrives at a similar conclusion:

> In each case, the insurgency was defined as an illegitimate challenge to a legitimate government struggling to manage both the trauma of modernization and the subversive efforts to exploit it. Thus, policymakers prescribed assistance to improve threatened governments' performance in three areas: physical control of territory and populations; penetration of authority into the periphery; and promotion of economic and social development. But this pat assessment obscured the issues critical to outside power contemplating intervention in support of an insurgency-threatened ally: the constraints on leverage; intragovernmental limits on reform; and the nature of relations between government and populace and, conversely, insurgents and populace.
>
> (Shafer 1988: 281)

Counterinsurgency efforts were thus severely hampered by the problematic of legitimacy, that is to say, the lack of legitimacy of both the host-nation government and the counterinsurgent forces that were more often than not seen as foreign occupiers, bent on propping up a corrupt regime. In Chapter 6, we will examine how the problematic of legitimacy has shaped, and continues to shape, contemporary counterinsurgency campaigns.

In short, from its formal inception in the early 1960s to its post-Vietnam demise, US counterinsurgents were pitted against adversaries who tended to be more innovative and adaptive than the US government and military. Above all, insurgents were in a much better position to win the support of the populace than corrupt regimes supported by the largely conventional and indiscriminate use of US firepower.

Interlude: counterinsurgency between Vietnam and the war on terror

Interest in counterinsurgency waned after Vietnam. Although there were still classes on counterinsurgency at a number of academies, and soldiers still received some counterinsurgency-related training, there was no longer any high-level political and public interest in the doctrine. Under the Reagan administration, however, the fortunes of counterinsurgency were on the rise again and culminated in what came to be known as Low Intensity Conflict doctrine. Deriving its name from the Pentagon's spectrum of conflict and its division into low, medium, and high, Low Intensity Conflict (LIC) doctrine was in fact just a conventionalization and simplification of counterinsurgency (Klare and Kornbluh 1988: 6; Klare 1988). This is how Michael T. Klare and Peter Kornbluh summarize LIC doctrine:

LIC begins with counterinsurgency, and extends to a wide variety of other politico-military operations, both overt and covert. For US policy-makers and war planners, however, low-intensity conflict has come to mean far more than a specialized category of armed struggle; it represents a strategic reorientation of the US military establishment, and a renewed commitment to employ force against Third World revolutionary movements and governments.

(1988: 3)

Klare and Kornbluh also mention that LIC was so broadly defined as to include 'drug interdiction in Bolivia, occupation of Beirut, invasion of Granada, and 1986 air strikes on Libya' (Klare and Kornbluh 1988: 7).

According to McClintock (1992), the 1980s also saw a revival of Special Operations in a bid to reverse the restrictions put on the CIA and the Special Forces by the Carter administration and Congress during the mid- to late 1970s. Special Operations became a key component of LIC doctrine:

The 1980s revival made the special operations forces concept the center-piece of 'low-intensity' operations. The patchwork strategy of the 1960s, combining the commitment of huge conventional forces, guerrilla opera-tions, and 'nation-building' development programs [was scrapped] as too expensive, too slow, and too politically costly.

(McClintock 1992: 344)

The formulation of LIC doctrine can thus be read as an attempt to do counter-revolution on the cheap without getting involved in any protracted conflict – pro-viding 'security' without bothering too much about nation-building and development.

After the end of the Cold War, the US military's obsession with conventional high-tech warfare continued unabated. And during the 1991 Gulf War, this type of warfare was celebrated on prime-time TV in real time. The first Gulf War gave us the spectacular impression that technology can resurrect the clear bound-aries between civilians and soldiers through the precision-targeting capabilities of so-called 'intelligent' munitions. Indeed, the successful implementation of high-tech warfare in the 1991 Gulf War prompted military planners to concen-trate on the field where the US reigned supreme – technology – while neglecting the actual challenge of intelligent adversaries bent on subverting US technolo-gical dominance through the creative modification and adaptation of insurgency.

Counterinsurgency revamped

Only well after the attacks on 9/11 and the ongoing failure to pacify both Afghan-istan and Iraq, did the US military respond to the tactical and strategic innovations designed and implemented by so-called asymmetrical opponents. Between 2003 and 2006, many military analysts revisited 1960s counterinsurgency doctrine and embarked on revisionist scholarship about US failure in Vietnam. Hammes's and Nagl's books, alongside many other publications, ought to be seen as part of an effort within the armed forces to break with conventional thinking, in order to pave the way for a general overhaul of the US military. This effort culminated in the publication of the new *Counterinsurgency Field Manual* (Department of the Army 2007).

General David Howell Petraeus[9] was one of the most well known architects both behind the promulgation of the new doctrine and its application during the 'surge' in Iraq. Petraeus served as Commanding General of the Multi-National Force in Iraq from 26 January 2007 to 15 September 2008, and has been widely acclaimed for leaving Iraq a safer place (see Filkins 2008).

However, the new *Counterinsurgency Field Manual* (Department of the Army 2007) bears not only the imprint of General Petraeus and other high-ranking military leaders; but, in line with its demands that the army should become an adaptive organization capable of responding to fresh ideas coming from the bottom up, it was also heavily influenced by the experiences of more junior officers.

Both the manual and a number of earlier studies of counterinsurgency, constantly reiterate the need for turning the US military into an effective learning organization (Department of the Army 2007; Downie 1998; Nagl 2005). The US armed forces are enjoined to learn how to adapt to the demands of the inherent contingency, complexity and ambiguity of insurgencies. The authors of the *Counterinsurgency Field Manual* (Department of the Army 2007: lii) put this quite succinctly, 'In COIN, the side that learns faster and adapts more rapidly – the better learning organization – usually wins.'

The manual also emphasizes that the success of counterinsurgency operations depends on obtaining the support of a majority of the population: 'at its core, COIN is a struggle for the population's support' (Department of the Army 2007: 51). To achieve this, soldiers and marines are said to require a thorough understanding of the host-nation's culture and society. Cultural anthropologist, Montgomery McFate (2005b): co-author of the field manual's chapter on intelligence, regular contributor to military publications and chief scientific consultant with the Army's Human Terrain System, famously declared that:

> Understanding foreign cultures and societies has become a national security priority. The more unconventional the adversary, the more we need to understand their society and underlying cultural dynamics. To defeat non-Western opponents who are transnational in scope, non-hierarchical in structure, clandestine in their approach, and operate outside of the context of nation-states, we need to improve our capacity to understand foreign cultures and societies.
>
> (McFate 2005b: 47)

This knowledge about the enemy should also be produced in and through operations on the ground:

> Intelligence in COIN is about people. U.S. forces must understand the people of the host nation, the insurgents, and the host-nation government. Commanders and planners require insight into cultures, perceptions, values, beliefs, interests and decision-making processes of individuals and groups. [...] Intelligence and operations feed each other. Effective intelligence drives effective operations. Effective operations produce information, which generates more intelligence. [...] All operations have an intelligence component. All soldiers and Marines collect information whenever they interact with the populace.
>
> (Department of the Army 2007: 80)

Tactical operations on the ground are thus supposed to provide fresh information that is fed back into the design and planning of operations. But this feedback loop between operations, tactics and intelligence requires significant changes in the organization of the military. The bottom-up flow of information calls for a decentralization of command in order to allow junior officers, who interact with the population on a more regular basis than the higher echelons of military command, to make their voices heard (Department of the Army 2007: 47 this will be discussed in more detail in Chapter 5).

Successful counterinsurgency operations are, moreover, said to require not only organizational changes within the armed forces, but also an integration of civilian and military activities. The main objectives of counterinsurgency: winning popular support and providing security and development, create the demand for a 'comprehensive strategy employing all aspects of national power' (Department of the Army 2007: 53). The manual lists the following counterinsurgency participants: US military forces, multinational (including host-nation) forces, US government agencies, other government agencies, Nongovernmental Organizations (NGOs), Intergovernmental Organizations (IGOs), multinational corporations and contractors, as well as host-nation civil authorities. All these different agencies and organizations are supposed to work under the military umbrella of what the manual refers to as 'unity of effort' (Department of the Army 2007: 60–7, 57–88). The fact that the manual dedicates a whole chapter to the integration of military and civilian efforts is clearly indicative of the ambiguity of counterinsurgency operations. In fact, counterinsurgency efforts always cut across the military/civilian divide, and thus presuppose a network of actors.

It is noteworthy that the blurring of the boundaries between the civilian and military sphere is already reflected in the process of doctrine formation, notably in the pivotal role of the social sciences in crafting and implementing current doctrine – a role that will be discussed in more detail in Chapter 5. The *Counterinsurgency Field Manual* was indeed shaped by a host of different actors, including members of the armed forces, civilian academics, private consultants and journalists. In the introduction of the University of Chicago Press Edition of the manual, Sarah Sewall (2007: xxxiii), director of Harvard's Carr Center for Human Rights Policy, writes how she 'joined with General David Petraeus and the US Army Combined Arms Center to cosponsor the doctrine revision

workshop, "Developing a New U.S. Counterinsurgency Doctrine"' (see also
Carr Center for Human Rights Policy 2006):

> In an unprecedented collaboration, a human rights center partnered with the
> armed forces to help revise the doctrine. Representatives from nongovern-
> mental human rights organizations raised sensitive issues about detainee
> treatment and escalation of force. The response was unequivocal and
> untainted by parallel controversies in Washington and in the field. Military
> leadership pledged that the doctrine would fully embrace the Geneva Con-
> ventions and highlight the risks inherent in COIN. Military leaders insisted
> that no matter how challenging the mission, Americans would do it as well
> as it can possibly be done. A touch of idealism, buttressed by extraordinary
> faith in the U.S. Soldier and Marine, coursed through the workshop and
> materialized in the manual.
>
> (Sewall 2007: xxxiii)

A number of critics dismissed the manual's endorsement of human rights as
mere window dressing and decried the complicity of humanitarians in the
purpose of warmaking (see Hayden 2007: 20). These criticisms are not without
merit, but fail to address the subtle mechanisms of cooptation inherent in the
doctrine itself. The official endorsement of the doctrine by a director of a human
rights center is itself an instrument of COIN in that it generates the legitimacy
necessary for winning the support of not only the host-nation population, but
also of other so-called strategic audiences, in this case primarily, but not only,
the US public. Indeed, the doctrine not only 'codifies how the institution thinks
about its role in the world and how it accomplishes that role on the battlefield'
(Nagl 2007: xiv), but also seeks to communicate the way the institution presents
itself to a wider, non-military audience. After all, the release of the manual was
well publicized and the document was downloaded more than two million times
within the first two months of its online publication in 2006 (Hayden 2007: 20).

How new is the new doctrine?

When the US announced a 'global war on terror' (GWOT) in response to the
9/11 attacks, many critics pointed to the overall logical inconsistency of the
notion. Francis Fukuyama (cited in Kilcullen 2005: 597) for instance, stated that
'terrorism is only a means to an end; in this regard, a war on terrorism makes no
more sense than a war on submarines'.

Following the continuous failure to address the deteriorating security situation
in post-invasion Afghanistan and Iraq, the term 'global war on terror' was
dropped from the official lexicon and replaced by terms, such as 'the Long War'
and 'Global Contingency Operations' (see Berger and Borer 2007: 198; Wilson
and Kamen 2009). This semantic shift was meant to prepare both the American
public and members of the armed forces for a protracted engagement in both
Afghanistan and Iraq, as well as for a potentially endless fight against global

terrorism. However, many security analysts argued that this semantic shift did not go far enough. They suggested that al-Qaeda's brand of global jihad should rather be seen as a global insurgency that can only be warded off by a counterinsurgency strategy equally global in scope (see Cassidy 2006a: 1–4; Kilcullen 2005: 614–15; Fowler 2005).

In his seminal article 'Countering Global Insurgency', David Kilcullen, a former Australian infantry officer, who also contributed to the field manual, declares that:

> [T]he war [on terror] is best understood as a globalized insurgency initiated by a diffuse confederation of Islamist movements seeking to re-make Islam's role in the world order. They use terrorism as their primary, but not their sole tactic. Therefore counterinsurgency rather than traditional counterterrorism may offer the best approach to defeating global jihad. But classic counterinsurgency, as developed in the 1960s, is designed to defeat insurgency in a single country. It demands measures – coordinated political-military responses, integrated regional and inter-agency measures, protracted commitment to a course of action – that cannot be achieved at the global level in today's international system. Therefore a traditional counterinsurgency paradigm will not work for the present war: instead, a fundamental reappraisal is needed, to develop methods effective against a globalized insurgency.
>
> (Kilcullen 2005: 614–15)

Kilcullen argues that global jihad can only be defeated by a counterinsurgency strategy that operates across global, regional and local levels. This strategy would have 'to interdict global links via a worldwide CORDS[10] program, isolate regional players through a series of regional counterinsurgencies and strengthen local governance through a greatly enhanced security framework at the country level' (Kilcullen 2005: 615). Kilcullen envisages a global strategy of rule that sounds pretty much like Hardt and Negri's (2000: xii) concept of 'Empire': 'a decentered and deterritorializing apparatus of rule that progressively incorporates the entire global realm within its open expanding frontier'. In fact, the global counterinsurgency strategy outlined by Kilcullen is, above all, a global program of rule that seeks to manage and control global interconnectivities in order to interdict global circulations of terror.

But to what extent are general changes in the environment and organization of insurgencies reflected in the new field manual? We should note that the manual is not a document of grand strategy, but centers more on the implementation of the regional and local aspects of Kilcullen's proposal for a three-tiered strategy. Yet, even regional or local battlespaces are shaped by a host of internal and external forces. Every conflict now involves numerous local, regional, transnational, and global stakeholders, ranging from insurgents and counterinsurgents to NGOs and international media outlets. As we have seen above, the new field manual dedicates a whole chapter to the difficulties of achieving unity of effort amongst friendly civilian and military activities (Department of the Army 2007: 53–77). The manual also emphasizes the need for specific contextual cultural knowledge and intelligence-gathering at all levels of command (Department of the Army 2007: 79–135). In 'Appendix B Social Network Analysis and Other Analytical Tools', it also maps out innovative instruments for the production of knowledge not only about insurgent networks, but also about the civilian communities amongst whom they hide (Department of the Army 2007: 305–33). Thus, the new doctrine clearly seeks to address and respond to the globalization of insurgencies and the concomitant complexity of contemporary battlespaces.

However, some critics of the new doctrine argue that it still focuses too much on the Maoist model of insurgency (see Peters 2007: 34; Hoffman 2007b: 71–3). According to Frank Hoffman (2007b: 71), the manual is a 'product of various schools of thought about modern insurgencies, including what can be called the classical school,[11] based on the concepts of Mao and revolutionary warfare'. However, references to Mao's theory of revolutionary warfare and the classical school of counterinsurgency are to a certain extent inevitable, because even highly evolved contemporary forms of insurgency are still wars amongst the people. In the manual's foreword, David Petraeus and James Amos (2007) put it quite succinctly:

> You cannot fight former Saddamists and Islamic extremists the same way you would have fought the Viet Cong, Moros, or Tupamaros; the application of principles and fundamentals to deal with each varies considerably. Nonetheless, all insurgencies, even today's highly adaptable strains, remain wars amongst the people. They use variations of standard themes and adhere to elements of a recognizable revolutionary campaign plan. This manual therefore addresses the common characteristics of insurgencies. It strives to provide those conducting counterinsurgency campaigns with a solid foundation for understanding and addressing specific insurgencies.
>
> (Petraeus and Amos 2007: xlv)

There are, therefore, both continuities and discontinuities between 1960s and contemporary doctrine. Current doctrine is based on the assumption that insurgencies are marked by a tension between broad historical trends and constant change through adaptation. On the one hand, every insurgency is regarded as a struggle for the support of the population; on the other, the context within which this struggle occurs and the tactics and forms of organization employed in this struggle, are seen as singular. This is why the manual stresses the need for cultural knowledge, bottom-up intelligence-gathering and a number of new analytical tools such as social network analysis. Indeed, the emphasis on specific contextual socio-cultural analysis seems to mark a departure from older doctrine, which tended to lump all insurgencies together by treating them as a result of blocked modernization (see Department of the Army 2007: 79–135; Clemis 2009; Heuser 2007: 167; Kienscherf 2010; Shafer 1988: 110–32; United States Government 1962b: 4–5).

But in line with its predecessor, the new doctrine still prescribes a combination of security and development, in order to pacify the host-nation and rebuild its governmental capacities so that it may eventually be able to secure itself from both internal and external threats (Department of the Army 2007: 34–51, 151–97; see also United States Government 1962b: 7, 10–11, 12–15). This focus on what is essentially nation-building seems like a far cry from former Secretary of Defense Donald Rumsfeld's declaration (cited in Berger and Borer 2007: 197), made just before the overthrow of Saddam Hussein, that the US should move 'beyond nation building'.

This brings us to one of the most fundamental differences between 1960s counterinsurgency doctrine and its contemporary counterpart. We have already seen that in the 1960s, counterinsurgency was a presidential priority; that is to say, the promulgation of the doctrine was prompted by President Kennedy himself, as well as by other leading members of his administration. Counterinsurgency was thus imposed on both military and civilian agencies. And Kennedy faced strong resistance, especially from members of the armed forces, some of who were less than enthusiastic about the president's concern with counterinsurgency. What is more, Kennedy himself did not trust the military: 'I know the Army is not going to develop this counterinsurgency field and do the things that I think must be done unless the Army itself wants to do it' (cited in Krepinevich 1986: 31). In stark contrast, the recent push for an up-dated doctrine came out of the military itself. This push was prompted by the stiff resistance encountered by US forces after the ousting of Saddam Hussein, caused by the Bush administration neglecting to prepare plans for the post-war reconstruction of Iraq (or Afghanistan for that matter). Indeed, President Bush, and his former Secretary of Defense Rumsfeld, repeatedly stated that 'we don't do nation building', while Secretary of State, Colin Powell, whose department was charged with developing post-war reconstruction plans, was frequently sidelined. However, at the same time, many Army and Marine Corps mid-career officers posted in Iraq faced a constantly deteriorating security situation as well as steadily mounting numbers of US casualties. As we have seen above, the ideas and experiences of mid-level commanders played a significant role in shaping the new doctrine. This clearly reverberates with one of the central tenets of the manual, namely that in order to be able to defeat insurgents, the army must become a more flexible, more adaptive and less bureaucratic learning organization.

Here again, the need for socio-cultural knowledge and bottom-up intelligence-gathering enters the equation. Knowledge about insurgents and their socio-cultural environment is also produced in and through operations on the ground, which in turn are to be constantly (re)adjusted in response to the knowledge they are expected to yield. Hence, tactical operations are supposed to become both the product and producer of knowledge. Current doctrine, therefore, seeks to integrate the interaction between tactics, operations and knowledge into the very organization of the armed forces. In short, the military is expected to become a learning organization – a highly flexible and adaptive machine for the production of knowledge through the exercise of power/violence and the effective exercise of power/violence through the production of knowledge.

However, it remains highly questionable whether the US military can institute the necessary reforms to become such an organization. Turning an enormously bureaucratic and path-dependent institution into a flexible, decentralized learning organization would require a reform program of gigantic dimensions. Moreover, there is a lot of opposition to such reform from within the military and the Pentagon. Many high-ranking officers and Pentagon officials still cling to the tradition of conventional high-tech warfare (see Bacevich 2008). In fact, two particular features of counterinsurgency operations go a long way in explaining why some members of the US armed forces would rather avoid such types of conflict. First, counterinsurgency operations are inevitably part of wider attempts at establishing legitimate governmental structures. This requires a vast array of non-military expertise, which is not necessarily present within the existing force structure. What is more, development and reconstruction efforts tend to take place in an insecure or even hostile environment and thus have to be tightly coupled with the provision of security (see Choharis and Gavrilis 2010). Therefore, these tasks cannot be easily farmed out to civilian agencies either. Second, counterinsurgents face unconventional, elusive, 'asymmetric' or 'irregular', enemies who hide amongst the civilian population. This makes US conventional, firepower-centered military superiority largely irrelevant. As Ucko puts it:

> Effective operations require identifying, locating, and closing in on an elusive adversary – a demanding challenge, even more so in a foreign land where the language barrier is high, the local police structures are weak, and the loyalties of the population are split.
>
> (Ucko 2009: 2)

Conclusion

Generally speaking, counterinsurgency doctrine seeks to articulate security and development into a governmental program for pacifying spaces and populations that are viewed as threats to the international system of (liberal) states, in order to eventually (re)integrate them into a liberal global order (see Kienscherf 2011).

The (at least partial) reorientation of US military strategy towards counterinsurgency was the outcome of discursive and material struggles amongst soldiers, civilian policymakers and private security consultants. Counterinsurgency has been rehabilitated by a group of experts comprising members of the armed forces as well as civilian academics, journalists and private consultants. These counterinsurgency professionals have managed to reshape discourses on security and military strategy, both within the US armed forces and beyond. They have, moreover, successfully convinced both a Republican and a Democratic administration to adopt at least some of their prescriptions (Bacevich 2010: 182–221). The Bush administration sanctioned a counterinsurgency approach for Iraq in 2005–2006, and the Obama administration came out in support of General

McChrystal's counterinsurgency strategy for Afghanistan in 2009. However, due to the at best qualified success in pacifying Iraq and Afghanistan, and steadily mounting budgetary constraints, we are unlikely to see any large-scale US expeditionary counterinsurgency efforts in the near future. But as long as there is no resurgence of major interstate tensions, rationalities and practices geared towards pacifying dangerous spaces and populations through a combination of security and development, albeit on a much smaller scale than in Iraq and Afghanistan, will likely remain on the top of the US security agenda.

3 Domestic pacification

Introduction

According to a report by the US-based Center for Investigative Reporting (Becker and Schulz 2011): since 9/11, US local police agencies have spent $34 billion in federal grants on military-type equipment, such as body armor, bomb-detection robots, high-powered assault rifles, communication equipment, etc. (see also Democracy Now 2011b). Most of the funds were provided by the Department of Homeland Security. The money was awarded in the form of block grants and was primarily intended for counterterrorism purposes. But, as there was little governmental oversight, most police departments just went on a spending spree and stocked up on expensive military equipment. Between 1968 and 1982, the Law Enforcement Assistance Administration (LEAA) also handed billions of dollars in block grants to local police departments. As with the homeland security grants today, most of the money was spent on military gear. However, militarized police arsenals are not the only evidence of the creeping militarization of the police. From the late 1960s, rationalities and practices of policing have increasingly turned into the domestic equivalent of counterinsurgency-style pacification campaigns that tend to target particular populations and spaces:

> The drugs war is a means by which the 'low intensity conflict' of pacification is brought back into the domestic frame, via a replication of one of the fundamental tropes of security discourse: the articulation of an 'emergency situation' with a 'clear and present danger' threatening the fundamental fabric of society.
> (Neocleous 2011: 202; see also Campbell 1998; Dunn 1996; Klare 1988; Kuzmarov 2009; McCoy 2003)

At the same time, the federal government has become increasingly involved in the hitherto mainly local domain of policing. Growing federal involvement, in and the increasing militarization of, US policing were, above all, spurred by mounting concerns over domestic dissent and illegal drugs.

During the 1960s, American social order seemed to be crumbling. In the face of soaring crime rates, protests, violent riots and a protracted and increasingly bloody war in the jungles of Southeast Asia, domestic dissent was framed as a threat to national security and illegal drugs came to be problematized as a clear and present danger to 'the fundamental values and vitality of the state' (Morales 1989: 149).

The late 1960s and early 1970s saw both a massive police buildup and increasing federal involvement in the hitherto predominantly local domain of policing. These developments were, above all, driven by overlapping efforts to suppress internal dissent and combat the sales and consumption of illicit drugs and narcotics. Indeed, sweeping government efforts to crack down on domestic dissent were folded into the war on drugs, which provided a convenient cover for the repression of militancy. Christian Parenti (1999) even goes as far as to argue that Nixon's war on drugs was primarily geared towards suppressing domestic dissent. In a similar vein, some authors contend that, when the war on drugs was increasingly internationalized from the late 1980s onwards, it 'serve[d] to mask the U.S. counter-intelligence and paramilitary presence abroad' (Bullington and Block 1990: 39; see also Marshall 1987; Morales 1989; Stokes 2005).

Nixon and the war on drugs

Confronted with a mounting domestic crisis and an unwinnable war abroad, President Johnson decided to also wage a domestic war on crime:

> Today, I ask every Governor, every mayor, and every county and city commissioner and councilman to examine the adequacy of their state and local law enforcement systems and to move promptly to support the policemen, the law enforcement officers and the men who wage the war on crime day after day in all the streets and roads and alleys in America.
>
> (Johnson 1968: 728; cited in Simon 2007: 99)

Johnson's statement cast the streets of America as battlefields where brave men, who do not get all the support they need from their political leaders, bravely fight the sinister enemy of crime.[1] He saw crime as a national issue that called for more federal involvement in state and local government – nothing short of a complete reform of governance (Simon 2007: 99).

In 1968, the Johnson administration combined the Bureau of Narcotics, in the Treasury Department, and the Bureau of Drug Abuse Control (BDAC), in the Department of Health, Education and Welfare, into the Bureau of Narcotics and Dangerous Drugs (BNDD), which came to be overseen by the Department of Justice (Drug Enforcement Administration 2009: 5). He also appealed to Congress to set up 'a new "super agency" to strengthen ties between the federal government and local police' (Parenti 1999: 6). The Law Enforcement Assistance Administration (LEAA) was created in 1968 as part of the Omnibus Crime Control and Safe Streets Act. Until its abolishment in 1982, the LEAA would spend billions of dollars in a scramble 'to reshape, retool, and rationalize

American policing' (Parenti 1999: 6; see also Epstein 1977). The LEAA came to play a major part in providing military hardware and training to local law enforcement agencies.

By and large, 'Johnson laid the groundwork for the tremendous combination of police power, surveillance, and incarceration that today so dominates domestic politics' (Parenti 1999: 6). What is more, according to legal scholar Jonathan Simon, the Safe Streets Act marked a fundamental realignment of US politics – the advent of crime as a rationality of government:

> When we govern through crime, we make crime and the forms of knowledge historically associated with it [...] available outside their limited subject domains as powerful tools with which to interpret and frame all forms of social action as a problem for governance.
>
> (Simon 2007: 17)

But Nixon (1973), who declared an 'all-out global war on the drug menace' and thus 'helped turn the Kennedy-Johnson war on crime into a Vietnam-like conflict with federal funding and training of state and local police to fight the war' (Simon 2007: 54), would take what Simon (2007) calls 'governance through crime' several steps further. A few months after he took office, Nixon informed Congress about what he viewed as a new threat to national security:

> Within the last decade, the abuse of drugs has grown from essentially a local police problem into a serious national threat to the personal health and safety of millions of Americans. [...] A national awareness of the gravity of the situation is needed: a new urgency and concerted national policy are needed at the federal level to begin to cope with this growing menace to the general welfare of the United States.
>
> (Nixon 1969: 57A)

The Nixon administration went to work straight away and drew up a pugnacious anti-crime bill. This bill contained a number of highly controversial measures, such as 'preventive detention' and so-called 'no-knock' warrants, which gave police officers the power to kick in doors without prior warning.

While Nixon's proposals were debated in the House and Senate between 1969 and 1970, a number of hardliners lectured the public about the dangers of drugs. Christian Parenti (1999) shows that even American woes in Vietnam were suddenly linked to drugs:

> According to one eyewitness testifying before Congress, 'At least 60 percent of the soldiers in Charlie Company, the unit involved in the My Lai incident, had smoked marijuana at least once. Some soldiers smoked marijuana the night before they went to My Lai on the day of the alleged massacre.' Senator Thomas Dodd, a Democrat from Connecticut, concluded that 'in Vietnam dangerous drugs and even heroin are almost as available as candy

bars.' Ronald Ridenhour, the helicopter door-gunner who witnessed, researched, and then exposed the barbarism of My Lai, concurred; most troops in Vietnam smoked pot. But he denied that had anything to do with *why* Charlie Company massacred a village during Operation Song My: 'Many Americans are looking for any reason other than a command decision.' The real crimes were assiduously avoided. 'Did the Viet Cong smoke marijuana?' asked a concerned Senator Dodd. The parade of witnesses seemed to think not – yet another unfair advantage. The message was simple: America was under attack, and even its war crimes were just aberrations, animated by heroin and weed.

> (Parenti 1999: 10–11; see also Congressional Quarterly Incorporated 1971: 539–41)

Ironically, besides hampering the war effort by sapping US soldiers' will and ability to fight, drugs were also said to incite troops to commit atrocities. Drugs were, moreover, thought to undermine domestic support for the war. Indeed, many commentators believed that the increasingly violent protests of students and minorities were fuelled by illegal drugs. In the early 1970s, drugs came to be problematized as a biopolitical threat to the health of both individual bodies and the overall social body. This led to a flurry of activities at the level of both legislation and policing.

Alongside the enactment of criminal law and the deployment of police tactics targeting particular populations, the construal of narcotics as a biopolitical threat to the vitality of the nation produced the category of narco-delinquency, which fed back into the discursive production of particular spaces, populations and activities as risks:

> The production of narco-delinquency, for example, is a dynamic *transnational* process that targets specific populations, dispersed by local criminal justice practices that shape where, when, and against whom to apply the force of the law. This process is fed by biopolitical practices which continuously script and rescript illegal drugs as a dangerous threat to individual and social bodies, rather than as embedded in relations of domination and resistance. The state consolidates and disperses discourses of narco-danger that emanate from elite insecurity and hysteria about the 'scourge of drug addiction,' creating the category of narco-delinquency that justifies the application of the criminal justice function, especially against marginalized populations.
>
> (Corva 2008: 181, original emphasis)

Consequently, the problematization of narcotics as a threat to security has given rise to the category of narco-delinquency. This, in turn, has reinforced biopolitical discourses of threat while sanctioning the targeting of populations that are construed either as posing a narcotics-related risk or as being at-risk of narco-delinquency.

The Nixon administration's goal to 'contain the growing threat of organized political rebellion and the culture of disobedience and disrespect that fed it' (Parenti 1999: 9) has been greatly facilitated by 'discourses of narco-danger' (Corva 2008: 181). Nixon's Chief of Staff, H. R. Haldeman (1994: 54; cited in Parenti 1999: 12) confided to his diary that '[President Nixon] emphasized that you have to face the fact that the whole problem is really the blacks. The key is to devise a system that recognizes this while not appearing to.' The system devised was a counter-narcotics program primarily targeted at street level dealers and consumers in African-American neighborhoods.

But when Nixon ordered the Bureau of Narcotics and Dangerous Drugs (BNDD) to focus on street level dealing instead of going after the higher echelons of the narcotics business, the BNDD resisted. Consequently, in 1972, the Nixon administration issued an executive order calling for the establishment of a new counter-narcotics agency, the Office of Drug Abuse Law Enforcement (ODALE), which reported directly to the White House and whose primary objective was 'to bring federal resources to bear on the street-level heroin pusher' (Drug Enforcement Administration 2009: 6; Epstein 1977: 212). Equipped with military-spec gear, ODALE's 300 or so agents were deployed in inner-city ghettos to track down street level dealers. ODALE field agents played the role of 'drug war irregulars', equivalent to the use of special operations forces in expeditionary counterinsurgency operations:

> From 1972 through 1973 these ODALE squads – usually augmented with cross-deputized officers from local forces – roamed their areas of operation at will, using 'no-knock warrants,' preventive detention, and the special grand juries to raise hell and make headlines on the streets of a few big cities.
>
> (Parenti 1999: 13)

But the headlines were not always positive. Throughout early 1973, ODALE was regularly accused of raiding the homes of innocents who were allegedly held at gunpoint, insulted and threatened, while officers searched the premises. This prompted Nixon to fold both ODALE and the BNDD into the new Drug Enforcement Administration (DEA).

With a current budget of $2.02 billion and 226 offices across the United States, the DEA is now the lead agency in the war on drugs (Drug Enforcement Administration 2011). What is more, since the war on drugs has been progressively globalized, the DEA also has a sizable global presence (see Nadelmann 1993). As of 2011, there are 83 DEA offices in 63 countries around the globe (Drug Enforcement Administration 2011). Vying for a greater slice of the homeland security budget, the DEA has also sought to link the fight against drugs with the war on terror. In the current Administrator Michele M. Leonhart's 'Vision for the DEA', priority number one is to '[d]isrupt and dismantle the major drug trafficking supply organizations and their networks, *including organizations that use drug trafficking proceeds to fund terror*' (Drug Enforcement Administration

2011: emphasis added) Whereas the DEA now aims to articulate the war on drugs as part of the war on terror, in the sixties and seventies, the DEA and its predecessors sought to incorporate it into the fight against domestic militancy.

COINTELPRO

From the mid-1950s to the early 1970s, there was also a whole series of much more direct, albeit highly secretive, attacks on oppositional groups within the United States. In 1956, the FBI launched its infamous Counterintelligence Program (COINTELPRO) to disrupt the US Communist Party. During the 1960s, COINTELPRO was massively extended to target a spate of domestic political organizations: the Ku Klux Klan, the Nation of Islam and the Black Panther Party, as well as organizations of the Old and New Left, including Civil Rights and antiwar organizations (Blackstock 1988; Churchill and Wall 2002; Cunningham 2003a, 2003b; Drabble 2004; United States Senate 1976). According to the Select Committee to Study Governmental Operations with Respect to Intelligence Activities of the United States Senate (United States Senate 1976), better known as the Church Committee after its chairman Frank Church, the FBI used World War II counterintelligence tactics, 'defined as those actions by an intelligence agency intended to protect its own security and to undermine hostile intelligence operations', against 'perceived domestic threats to the established political and social order' (United States Senate 1976: 4). The FBI's arsenal of tactics comprised discrediting individuals through false accusations, sowing dissent within and between groups by forging documents and planting inaccurate reports in the news media, wrongful imprisonment and the use of violence. COINTELPRO actions thus ranged from infiltration and harassment to psychological warfare and even direct action, including targeted assassinations (Chomsky 1997; Glick 1989). What is more, the program was highly secretive and information about it was only shared on a 'need-to-know' basis.

In 1971, the Citizens' Commission to Investigate the FBI broke into an FBI field office, stole several COINTELPRO-related files, and leaked them to the news media. This led to a flurry of lawsuits against the FBI, which resulted in the release of even more documents. In 1976, the Church Committee launched an official inquiry into COINTELPRO activities. Its final report concludes that many of the FBI's actions were clearly unconstitutional:

> In these programs, the Bureau went beyond the collection of intelligence to secret action defined to 'disrupt' and 'neutralize' target groups and individuals. [...] [T]he Bureau conducted a sophisticated vigilante operation aimed squarely at preventing the exercise of First Amendment rights of speech and association, on the theory that preventing the growth of dangerous groups and the propagation of dangerous ideas would protect the national security and deter violence. Many of the techniques used would be intolerable in a democratic society even if all of the targets had been involved in violent activity, but COINTELPRO went far beyond that. The

unexpressed major premise of the programs was that a law enforcement agency has the duty to do whatever is necessary to combat perceived threats to the existing social and political order.

(United States Senate 1976: 3)

COINTELPRO was designed as a domestic program of pacification, employing primarily covert and often highly illegal means to target individuals and groups that were construed as threats to the liberal order. What is more, the history of COINTELPRO clearly shows up security professionals' routine deployment of emergency powers against expressions of domestic dissent.

In 1971, the FBI officially terminated COINTELPRO. However, since then, similar techniques have been used and are still employed, albeit it in a much more decentralized, case-by-case manner, which makes democratic oversight even more difficult (Glick 1999: xii). According to the Church Committee (United States Senate 1976: 14), 'Attitudes within and without the Bureau demonstrate a continued belief by some that covert action against American citizens is permissible if the need for it is strong enough.' The war on drugs, moreover, served as a convenient vehicle for continuing many COINTELPRO-style activities under a much more legitimate mantle. As Brian Glick (1999: xiii) put it, 'Anti-communism – the time-honored rationale for political police work – has been augmented by "counter-terrorism" and "the war on drugs," pretexts that better resonate with current popular fears.' This has turned 'domestic covert operations' into 'a permanent feature of U.S. politics' (Glick 1999: xv). More generally, what is at stake here is not just the protection of a given socio-political order against perceived threats, but the constant (re)production of liberal order through the identification, tracking and both covert and overt targeting of illiberal others.

The war on drugs under Reagan

After a brief lull under the Ford and Carter administrations, the war on drugs was ratcheted up again under the Reagan administration. President Reagan quietly stepped up federal crime control efforts by increasing the budget of the FBI, the Bureau of Prisons, and the DEA. The Reagan administration also launched numerous anti-narcotics programs and task forces, such as the massive multi-agency Organized Crime Drug Enforcement Task Force Program (OCDETF), which mobilized 200 US attorneys and 1,200 agents from the DEA, Customs, the FBI, the Bureau of Alcohol, Tobacco, Firearms and Explosives (BATF), the Internal Revenue Service and the US Marshals Service (Parenti 1999: 47).

In 1984, another sweeping new anti-crime act was passed. The so-called Comprehensive Crime Control Act (CCCA), which was described as 'one of the most far reaching anti-crime measures enacted since the 1968 Omnibus Crime Control and Safe Streets Act' (Congressional Quarterly Incorporated 1984: 215; cited in Parenti 1999: 50), contained a host of tough new measures, such as mandatory minimum sentences, the establishment of a Sentencing Commission to set strict sentencing guidelines and the elimination of federal parole. One of the most striking provisions of the CCCA was an expansion of asset forfeiture statutes, which stipulated that the government could now seize not only 'all profits from drug trafficking and all assets purchased with these profits', but also 'all real property that was used in or intended to be used in a drug trafficking offense' (Jensen and Gerber 1996: 423).

Asset forfeiture statutes were first enacted in the 1970s as part of the Comprehensive Drug Abuse and Control Act, but were limited in scope and rarely used. They were expanded in 1978 to allow the seizure of assets not directly linked to drug crimes (Jensen and Gerber 1996: 422–3; Parenti 1999: 50). But with the 1984 crime bill, the seizure of assets really took off. Many local police forces now 'formed special assets-seeking narcotics squads and mounted full-scale operations of pillaging and plunder' (Parenti 1999: 51).

Reagan's war on drugs gathered even more pace when a dangerous new substance – 'crack', a cheap smokeable form of cocaine – began to hit the streets of deprived inner-city neighborhoods by the mid-1980s. Congress promptly responded by passing the Anti-Drug Abuse Act in 1986, which set stiff new mandatory sentences for drug possession.[2] When Reagan (1986) signed the Act into law, he described his and his wife's efforts to combat narcotics in starkly militaristic terms:

> Let me take a moment here and salute a special person who has turned the fight against drug abuse into a national crusade. She started long before the polls began to register our citizens' concern about drugs. She mobilized the American people, and I'm mighty proud of her. [...] [T]oday marks a major victory in our crusade against drugs – a victory for safer neighborhoods, a victory for the protection of the American family. The American people want their government to get tough and to go on the offensive. And that's exactly what we intend, with more ferocity than ever before.
>
> (Reagan 1986: 1447)

While Nancy Reagan marshaled public opinion and law-makers scrambled to draw up ever tougher legislation, the police conducted their own 'crusade against drugs' on the streets of major cities.

The 1980s saw a spate of raids and ghetto sweeps in which heavily armed paramilitary police arrested thousands of mostly black young men. In April 1984, the Los Angeles Police Department (LAPD) launched Operation HAMMER, 'arresting more black youth than at any other time since the Watts Rebellion of 1965' (Davis 1992: 267–8). According to Mike Davis (1992), Los Angeles was then gripped by a massive anti-gang frenzy, because gangs were seen as the chief distribution networks for crack:

> In the official version, which Hollywood is incessantly reheating and further sensationalizing these gangs comprise veritable urban guerrilla armies

organized for the sale of crack and outgunning the police with huge arsenals of UZI and Mac-10 automatics. Although gang cohorts are typically hardly more than high-school sophomores, local politicians frequently compare them to the 'murderous militias of Beirut'.

(Davis 1992: 268)

A local mayor even went as far as to refer to gang members as 'the Viet Cong abroad in our society' (Mayor James Van Horn of Artesia cited in Meisler 1989: 268).

But Los Angeles was not the only major American city waging a 'crusade against drugs'. During Operation Pressure Point, the New York Police Department (NYPD) conducted a whole series of sweeps, stings and 'buy-busts', targeting low-level dealers as well as users, in neighborhoods that also happened to be in the sights of real estate developers (Parenti 1999: 59). Washington D.C., Miami, Philadelphia, and Orange County, California, launched their own massive anti-drug operations. What all these operations had in common was that they targeted particular groups of people (mainly street-level dealers and users) in particular areas (notably non-white, inner-city neighborhoods). These areas were swept by paramilitary police units in an effort to pacify them. This clearly shows that the 'war' in war on drugs has been more than just a metaphor. Indeed, from the 1980s onwards, many police departments have waged a veritable low-intensity war against drug-dealers and users. To put it bluntly, the war on drugs fought on the streets of America marked a transposition of Third World-style low-intensity conflicts into the cities of the first world, or rather into what came to be construed as pockets of the Third World within major US cities.

Another sweeping Anti-Drug Abuse Act cleared Congress in 1988. According to Christian Parenti (1999), the Act contained numerous 'brutal and authoritarian provisions' (Parenti 1999: 61), the most important of which was the establishment of 'the federal death penalty for persons guilty of participation in a federally defined "criminal enterprise" or any drug-related felony, who intentionally or unintentionally kills another person' (Parenti 1999: 61). The Act also set up the Office of National Drug Control Policy headed by a cabinet level 'drug czar', charged with coordinating anti-narcotics activities between law enforcement agencies, the military and the intelligence agencies. Moreover, besides handing millions to the DEA, FBI, US Marshals and Customs and federal prosecutors, the Act also awarded $2 million to the Department of Defense for training law enforcement agencies, and another $3.5 million for furnishing police with military hardware (Parenti 1999: 61).

However, the Act's most problematic provisions were the ones under the innocuous heading of 'user accountability' that, in Parenti's terms (1999: 61), 'furthered subordination of the state's social service function to its policing functions'. For example, under the so-called 'one strike law' public housing residents committing a crime on or near public housing premises could now be evicted. Jonathan Simon (2007: 194) describes the case of Pearl Rucker, a grandmother and public housing tenant, who was evicted because 'her daughter was arrested for possession of cocaine three blocks from the public housing project where she lived'. Under the Clinton administration, this statute was extended to also include applicants for public housing:

> The new policies authorize and encourage – but do not require – public housing authorities to do more initial screening of potential residents for criminal behavior, and to evict any current tenant deemed threatening to the safety or security of other residents regardless of whether there was an arrest, a conviction, or whether the incident actually took place in public housing.
>
> (Simon 2007: 195)

First, the 'one strike and you're out' provisions are clearly indicative of the inherently liberal distinction between those that can be governed liberally and those that need to be governed through authoritarian means. The law grants public housing authorities the autonomy to decide whether and how to enforce these draconian provisions whereas applicants to, and residents of, public housing are mere targets of authoritarian techniques of social control, no matter whether they have actually committed any crime. Second, these provisions are part of a more general shift from the ideal of rehabilitation to a preoccupation with risk management. Obviously, the goal of this law is not to reintegrate offenders into society, but rather to permanently exclude illiberal subjects from the community, even if they have not been convicted of any crime – all in the name of security. Ultimately this statute thus directly feeds a waste management prison complex. Last but not least, the fact that this law was extended under the Clinton administration shows that being tough on crime has become a bipartisan position and is no longer the prerogative of the Republican Party.

The war on drugs under Bush and Clinton

George H. W. Bush's 1988 presidential campaign was to a large extent driven by crime. Bush fashioned himself as a first-rate crime warrior by portraying Democratic nominee Michael Dukakis as soft on crime, because the latter opposed the death penalty. According to Jonathan Simon (2007: 57), Bush saw crime not only as 'just another social problem, but rather as a metaphor around which a whole range of popular needs might be expressed, a metaphor whose crucial entailment was punishment and a punitive state'. During his election campaign, Bush (1988) even went as far as to frame the conservative cause célèbre of inflation as a crime against elderly Americans:

> There are millions of older Americans who were brutalized by inflation. We arrested it – and we're not going to let it out on furlough. We're going to keep the Social Security trust fund sound and out of reach of the big spenders. To America's elderly I say: 'Once again you have the security that is your right – and I'm not going to let them take it away from you.'
>
> (A 14; cited in Simon 2007: 59)

By casting inflation as a violent criminal stalking defenseless elderly folks, and by promising to lock it up and throw away the key, Bush managed simultaneously to stoke and allay the fears of a group that in recent decades had predominantly supported the Democratic Party (Simon 2007: 59). Bush's speech is another glaring instance of a general tendency in American politics to turn crime into a mode of government. That is to say, crime is deployed as a metaphor to make other fields of government intervention (such as the economy) intelligible, and to legitimize intervention in these fields. In fact, crime and conflict have become the only domains where federal intervention is still seen as both legitimate and desirable.

The 1989 National Defense Authorization Act, which labeled illegal narcotics as a clear and present threat to US National security, shows up the growing militarization of the Bush administration's counter-narcotics efforts. The Act turned the Department of Defense into:

> the lead agency to detect and monitor illegal drug shipments into the country; to integrate certain command, control, and technical intelligence assets to ensure they are dedicated to drug interdiction; and to approve and fund state plans for using ARNG [US Army National Guard] soldiers and Air National Guard (ANG) airmen to support law enforcement agencies (LEAs) and community-based organizations (CBOs).
>
> (Cole 2005: 70)

Bush also escalated the war on drugs by launching the so-called kingpin strategy, which was directed at the leaders of major transnational cartels. From its creation in 1973, the DEA had been constantly criticized for its failure to go after major drug bosses. During the 1980s and 1990s, the DEA, therefore, developed a number of innovations in its undercover operations (including controlled deliveries and reverse stings), expanded its intelligence collection and analysis capabilities and increased the use of electronic surveillance technology, in an attempt to target the higher echelons of the transnational drug trade (Kenney 2007: 80). Interestingly, Michael Kenney maintains that the moniker 'cartel' is both misleading and politically self-serving:

> Beginning in the early 1980s, as numerous trafficking enterprises extended their reach into American drug markets, a misconception developed that the Colombian cocaine trade was run by a handful of massive, vertically integrated 'cartels' that restricted production and set international prices.
>
> (Kenney 2007: 25)

Yet, Colombian cocaine production and distribution have always been part of a highly competitive business environment, where 'flexible exchange networks expand and contract according to market opportunities and regulatory constraint' (Kenney 2007: 26). But the term 'cartel' serves a political purpose in that it helps mobilize the resources deemed necessary to fight such a formidable foe. Thus, the very problematization of drug trafficking organizations in terms of 'cartels' has played a pivotal role both in mobilizing people and resources around a costly war on drugs and in justifying these mobilizations.

Addressing the International Drug Enforcement Conference in Miami on 27 April 1989, President Bush (1989) equated the fight against drugs with a world war of epic proportions:

> I'm here today to talk about war: first, to see cocaine trafficking for what it is – an attack aimed at enslaving and exploiting the weak; second, to confront what's become a world war. [...] And I've said it before: The war on drugs is no metaphor. We've been slower to recognize that it is also a world war, leaving no nation unscathed, one in which Hong Kong bankers and Bolivian growers and Middle Eastern couriers and west coast wholesalers all play insidious roles. And it is especially acute in this hemisphere, where an explosive cycle of drugs, dependency, and dollars has escalated clear out of control.
>
> (Bush 1989)

Bush portrayed himself as spearheading an actual war effort. What is more, he described the war on drugs as both spatially and temporally indeterminate: it spans the whole globe and since it does not target one specific state, group or individual it is also potentially open-ended.

How open-ended this 'world war' would be, became obvious when a Democrat entered the White House. According to Jonathan Simon (2007: 59), Clinton's victory over the incumbent Bush was partly due to the fact that during the 1992 campaign, Clinton 'was prepared to match Bush on punitiveness toward crime and drugs'. Indeed, when he was in office, Clinton proved to be a diligent crime fighter. Although he did not push for any new crime legislation during his first year in office, in 1993 (shortly after the L.A. Riots) Clinton promoted a new 'get-tough-on-crime' piece of legislation, containing provisions for the hiring of 100,000 new police officers, the introduction of new federal death penalty crimes and restrictions on federal appeals in capital cases. The Violent Crime Control and Law Enforcement Act cleared Congress in 1994, and was greeted with the usual fanfare as 'an unprecedented federal venture into crime-fighting' (Congressional Quarterly Incorporated 1994: 273; cited in Parenti 1999: 65).

In 1999, Clinton also escalated the war on drugs internationally by launching the now infamous Plan Colombia, which has folded counter-narcotics operations into counterinsurgency and vice versa. In response to a general increase in guerrilla attacks and kidnappings in the wake of stalled peace talks between the FARC (Fuerzas Armadas Revolucionarias de Colombia – Revolutionary Armed Forces of Colombia, a Colombian insurgent organization) and the Colombian government, and the recognition that the seemingly successful kingpin strategy had failed to stem the flow of drugs into the US, the Clinton administration decided to frame Colombian instability as a threat to US national security (Crandall 2002: 162; see also Stokes 2005). Above all, Plan Colombia centered on the provision of both military assistance and humanitarian aid to the Colombian government. Thus, in many respects the plan was a counterinsurgency-style combination of security and development. But the plan was presented to Congress as a new chapter in the war on drugs, for 'the White House knew that few members of Congress would oppose assistance to help fight the drug war, and therefore took painstaking efforts to distinguish "counter-insurgency" from "counter-narcotics" initiatives' (Crandall 2002: 163).

Plan Colombia continues to shape US–Colombian relations. In October 2009, the government of Colombia granted the Pentagon the use of seven military bases and a number of other smaller facilities. And Colombia still receives billions in military aid. According to Greg Grandin (2010), Plan Colombia ought to be seen as 'the Latin American edition of GCOIN, or Global Counterinsurgency' (Grandin 2010: 9), aimed at establishing a 'unified, supra-national counterinsurgent infrastructure' (Grandin 2010: 11), in order to counter what Pentagon planners describe as a fusion between the drug trade and global terrorism. Indeed, a number of security pundits are demanding that due to the ever more intricate interrelation between drugs and violent conflict, potentially global counter-narcotics efforts should become an integral part of a global US stabilization strategy (see, for example, Kan 2009; Kilcullen 2005, 2009).

Managing risky populations

In *Policing the Risk Society*, R. V. Ericson and K. D. Haggerty (1997) suggest that contemporary policing is best understood in terms of risk management. The significant role of risk management in contemporary liberal governance is now widely accepted across the social sciences. Whereas major societal risks were originally associated with the unintended ecological consequences of industrialization, the concept of risk now covers a whole swath of events, processes and developments that are seen as detrimental to the security of both people and states (Lyon 2005: 73; see also Beck 1992; Amoore and De Goede 2008; Aradau and van Munster 2008; De Goede 2008; Epstein 2008).

According to Ericson and Haggerty (1997: 85), liberal democracies are, above all, risk societies in which 'governance is directed at the provision of security'. In this context, rationalities and practices of policing are aimed at identifying, tracking, managing, containing and/or eliminating risks. And since the 'yearning for security drives the insatiable quest for more and better knowledge of risk' (Ericson and Haggerty 1997: 18), police officers are now above all knowledge-workers, whose primary task is to sort individuals, populations and spaces into risk categories, and act according to these categorizations. Consequently, policing centers on 'identifying, classifying, and managing groups sorted by levels of dangerousness' (Feely and Simon 1994; cited in Lyon 2005: 75). The sorting of individuals, spaces and populations into categories of risk is, moreover, both product and producer of a sliding scale of illiberality that, as we have seen in Chapter 1, always tends to bleed into a binary opposition between friend and enemy.

Ericson and Haggerty (1997) note that a risk management approach to policing manifests itself, above all, in the now predominant paradigm of community policing. Community policing is widely touted as a compliance-based form of law enforcement that rests on consent rather than coercion. Community policing can, moreover, be read as characteristic of a hands-off liberal mode of government that frets over governing too much (Ericson and Haggerty 1997: 70–5). Ericson and Haggerty (1997: 67), moreover, contend that 'community policing rejects previous models of policing, including militarism (order maintenance), legalism (law enforcement), and professionalism (public service)'. Yet, the apparently compliance-based rationality of community policing does entail rather coercive practices (see Herbert 1999). Or, to be more precise, risk management sets the parameters for other more robust practices of policing, because some individuals, populations and spaces are slotted into risk categories that render them impervious to compliance-based approaches. A risk management approach to policing is, moreover, not so much directed at maintaining a pre-existing order, but rather at actively (re)producing order. What is more, in contrast with traditional law-enforcement approaches to policing, which sought to react to crimes, solve them and immobilize the perpetrators, community policing is preemptive in that it aims to reduce the overall risk of crime by working closely with at-risk communities (see Friedmann and Cannon 2008; Green and Mastrofski 1987; Moore and Trojanowicz 1988; Moore 1990; Silverman and Della-Guistina 2001).

'Broken-windows', or 'quality of life', policing is another preemptive approach to providing domestic security, because it seeks to clamp down on minor infractions of the law, in order to prevent the commission of more serious criminal acts. The broken-windows theory was first advanced by criminologists James Q. Wilson and George Kelling (1982). Their argument is strikingly simple:

> [A]t the community level, disorder and crime are usually inextricably linked, in a kind of developmental sequence. Social psychologists and police officers tend to agree that if a window in a building is broken *and is left unrepaired*, all the rest of the windows will soon be broken. This is as true in nice neighborhoods as in run-down ones. Window-breaking does not necessarily occur on a large scale because some areas are inhabited by determined window-breakers whereas others are populated by window-lovers; rather, one unrepaired broken window is a signal that no one cares, and so breaking more windows costs nothing. (It has always been fun.)
>
> (Wilson and Kelling 1982: 2)

Small offenses, such as window smashing, graffiti, loitering, public drinking, etc., may lead to a 'breakdown of community controls' and thereby pave the way for a much more serious *criminal invasion*:

> Though it is not inevitable, it is more likely that here, rather than in places where people are confident they can regulate public behavior by informal

controls, drugs will change hands, prostitutes will solicit, and cars will be stripped. That the drunks will be robbed by boys who do it as a lark and the prostitutes' customers will be robbed by men who do it purposefully and perhaps violently. That muggings will occur.

(Wilson and Kelling 1982: 2)

Police officers are thus supposed to get out of their patrol cars and work closely with other public agencies, so that they can deal with any deteriorations of physical space, such as abandoned buildings and broken windows, and crack down on minor criminality that is said to develop in such spaces (Wilson and Kelling 1982).

In the 1990s, Mayor Rudolph Giuliani sought to implement a 'quality of life' policing strategy in New York City. During his election campaign of 1993, he frequently lambasted incumbent David Dinkins with letting petty crime undermine the overall quality of local community life (Purdham 1993: B1; cited in Silverman and Della-Guistina 2001: 946). In 1994, mayor-elect Giuliani then tasked his newly appointed Police Commissioner, William Bratton (former head of New York Transit Police and widely acclaimed for his crackdown on crime on the subway) with putting what became known as the 'zero tolerance' strategy to work. In his memoirs Bratton wrote, 'If you peed in the street, you were going to jail. We were going to fix the broken windows and prevent anyone from breaking them again' (Bratton and Knobler 1998: 229; cited in Wacquant 2009b: 260). At the same time, the New York Police Department saw broad bureaucratic restructuring, a massive expansion in terms of financial resources and manpower, and the rolling out of new technologies, the most prominent of which was CompStat (short for computer statistic), a system for tracking the geographical distribution of crimes in real time (Wacquant 2009b: 260–1).

Loïc Wacquant (2009b: 261) argues that the transformation of what used to be a 'cowardly, puffing, and passive as well as corrupt' bureaucracy into 'the veritable simile of a zealous "security firm," endowed with colossal human and material resources and an offensive outlook' was probably more of a factor in NYPD's alleged successes in crime fighting than the adoption of a broken-windows strategy. What is more, the broken-windows theory merely served as pseudo scientific smokescreen for 'conventional police wisdom' (Wacquant 2009b: 265). As Bratton's Deputy Police Commissioner, Jack Maple declared in his autobiography, ' "Broken Windows" was merely an extension of what we used to call the "Breaking Balls" theory' (Maple and Mitchell 1999: 152; cited in Wacquant 2009b: 265). But even the most well-funded police department cannot just 'break the balls' of everyone who pees in the street. Due to finite resources and manpower, quality of life policing does not happen everywhere all the time, but tends to be aimed at particular populations and spaces (see Maple and Mitchell 1999; Silverman and Della-Guistina 2001; Wacquant 2009b):

Properly applied assertive policing can, however, mean selective enforcement, as part of overall strategies, targeted to specific problems [...].

Strategies may include a vast array of tactics including car searches, warrant checks and a range of community and social agency involvement. All, however, are directed towards particular problems based on their geographical and temporal crime distribution that we know generally fall into clusters.

(Silverman and Della-Guistina 2001: 954)

In fact, broken-windows policing is just an umbrella term for rationalities and practices of policing that target particular populations and spaces, most notably poor non-white populations in inner city neighborhoods. Risky populations and so-called 'crime hot spots' are identified by means of risk-management technologies, such as geographical crime mapping technologies. Compliance-based modes of policing are, moreover, backed up by an increasingly para-militarized approach, under which the 'big guns' are trained on those illiberal subjects who are risk-profiled as enemies of the liberal order.

Paramilitary policing

Kraska and Kappeler (1997) document the massive proliferation of paramilitary policing in the United States since the 1970s. Police paramilitary units (PPUs), also known as SWAT (Special Weapons and Tactics) teams, are frequently trained by military Special Forces. Many of their members used to serve in commando-type units, such as the Navy Seals, Delta Force, Army Rangers or Marine Force Recon, and their military-spec hardware 'would generate envy among the militaries in many small countries' (Churchill 2002: xxxiv; see also Kraska and Kappeler 1997). What is more, SWAT-type gear has also increasingly spilled over into regular police units. For instance, even beat cops now regularly wear body armor, sport powerful 9 mm automatics instead of the old .38 caliber 'Police Special' revolvers, and have swapped their shotguns for assault rifles (Churchill 2002: xxxiv; Becker and Schulz 2011).

When the first police paramilitary units were set up in the 1960s and 1970s, their mission was limited to exceptional situations such as hostage takings, sniper attacks and terrorism, but as the war on drugs gathered pace during the early 1980s, their brief was greatly expanded (see Balko 2006; Kraska and Kappeler 1997: 4; Churchill 2002: xxxiv–vii). What is more, it seems as if from their inception, paramilitary police units were also supposed to play a major part in the suppression of political militancy. The first SWAT team was fielded by the Los Angeles Police Department (LAPD), with support from the Federal Bureau of Investigation (FBI) in the late 1960s and early 1970s, to target African-American militants, such as the Black Panther Party and the Symbionese Liberation Army (Churchill 2002: xxxv).

Kraska and Kappeler's survey (1997: 5–12) of 548 US police departments found that in the course of the war on drugs, police paramilitary units became involved in an ever wider set of activities, such as servicing search and arrest warrants (especially 'no-knock entries') or conducting saturation patrols in high crime areas. A spokesperson of 'one highly acclaimed community policing department' gave the following description of such patrols:

> We're into saturation patrols in hot spots. We do a lot of our work with the SWAT unit because we have bigger guns. We send two, two-to-four men cars, we look for minor violations and do jump-outs either on people on the street or automobiles. After we jump out the second car provides periphery cover with an ostentatious display of weaponry. We are sending a clear message: if the shootings don't stop, we'll shoot someone.
>
> (Cited in Kraska and Kappeler 1997: 10)

Kraska and Kappeler (1997: 12–13), moreover, show that community policing and paramilitary policing are not mutually exclusive, but complementary, strategies (see also Herbert 1999: 156). Laden with metaphors that bear a striking resemblance to the counterinsurgency literature we encountered in the previous chapter, paramilitary police patrols are often seen as a first step towards enabling communities to regain their neighborhoods. Kraska and Kappeler (1997: 13) quote two police commanders who see community policing and paramilitary policing as inextricably intertwined:

> We conduct a lot of saturation patrol. We do 'terry stops' and 'aggressive' field interviews. These tactics are successful as long as the pressure stays on relentlessly. The key to our success is that we're an elite crime fighting team that's not bogged down in the regular bureaucracy. We focus on 'quality of life' issues like illegal parking, loud music, bums, neighbor troubles. We have the freedom to stay in a hot area and clean it up – particularly gangs. *Our tactical enforcement team works nicely with our department's emphasis on community policing.*
>
> (Kraska and Kappeler 1997: 13, emphasis added)

> It's going to come to the point that the only people that are going to be able to deal with these problems are highly trained tactical teams with proper equipment to go into a neighborhood and *clear the neighborhood and hold it*; allowing community policing and problem oriented policing officers to come in and start turning the neighborhood around.
>
> (Kraska and Kappeler 1997: 13, emphasis added)

The militarized language of the last quote is particularly illustrative in this respect. Indeed, this particular police commander seems to view his task in terms of a counterinsurgency-inspired pacification strategy, that consists of occupying and holding a troubled area so that community policing officers can then start to (re)build trust and use informal community controls, in order to permanently stabilize the area.

Domestic pacification

Both community policing and counterinsurgency emphasize cooperation with the local population, in order to gather intelligence about insurgents or criminals and bolster informal modes of social control that are supposed to prevent community members from turning into insurgents or criminals. Friedmann and Cannon summarize the role of police-community partnerships in community policing as follows:

> Each law enforcement-community partnership is expected to rebuild citizen trust of the police, activate the informal social control processes that contribute to deviance prevention, and allow police access to the various information rooted in their jurisdiction.
>
> (Friedmann and Cannon 2008: 11)

We have already seen that, according to the current *Counterinsurgency Field Manual* (Department of the Army 2007: 51), 'at its core, COIN is a struggle for the population's support', and that in order to achieve the ultimate goal of winning the 'hearts and minds' of the populace, soldiers and marines require a thorough understanding of the host-nation's culture and society.

The compliance-based rationality of community policing is, in fact, informed by experiences of counterinsurgency-style pacification. Christian Parenti (1999: 24–6) suggests that community policing is the soft side of the militarization of the police, a community relations effort aimed at winning the hearts and minds of embattled communities. According to an article in the *FBI Bulletin*, 'community relations efforts were born in the turbulent sixties as police concentrated on rebuilding their image, gaining community support and cooling the brush fires of violence' (Federal Bureau of Investigation 1974: 23; cited in Parenti 1999: 24). Indeed, in the late 1960s, the authorities came to realize that the riots in the predominantly black inner-city ghettos were frequently compounded, if not caused, by police brutality. The Kerner Commission on Civil Disturbances (United States Government 1967: 206) put it as follows: 'Invariably the incident that ignites disorder arises from police action. Harlem, Watts, Newark and Detroit – all major outbursts of recent years – were precipitated by routine arrests of Negroes for minor offenses by white police.' As a result, the police were supposed to become more attuned to minority communities. Community relations thus became a tactical element within a nonetheless heavily militarized policing strategy – a tactic that, according to Parenti, was itself borrowed from the military. Indeed, Parenti (1999) draws very explicit parallels to counterinsurgency efforts in Vietnam:

> The gendarmerie needed to become more thoroughly insinuated into the communities they policed. And law enforcement, traduced by a decade of its own misdeeds, was in need of re-legitimization. But this 'soft' side of the great leap forward borrowed just as heavily from the military, as did helicopter patrols, computer systems, SWAT teams, and regional anti-riot plans.

As in Vietnam, so too in the cities the battle for 'hearts and minds' was as essential as any satellite photo or high-tech firepower. [...] If, in the police view, the much storied "militant Negro" was the domestic equivalent to the Viet Cong, then the soft community police strategies – like block watches and police community alliances – were domestic parallels to the 'strategic hamlets' of South Vietnam.

(Parenti 1999: 24–5)

Many practitioners saw their job in similar terms. In the 1960s and 1970s, many politicians and high-ranking police officers were obsessed by what they saw as a threat to public order posed by, primarily, left-wing militants. In a 1968 report entitled *Guerrilla Warfare Advocates in the United States*, the House Un-American Activities Committee contended that domestic oppositional movements, most notably black liberation groups, increasingly advocated the use of Third World-style guerrilla tactics at home (House Un-American Activities Committee 1968, cited in Neocleous 2011: 205). According to an article in the *FBI Bulletin*, entitled 'Trends in Urban Guerrilla Tactics': 'New tactics and techniques have been developed in the United States by a small number of criminals who style themselves urban guerrillas' (Federal Bureau of Investigation 1973; cited in Parenti 1999: 17). In his article 'Law Enforcement Faces the Revolutionary-Guerrilla Criminal', then FBI director, J. Edgar Hoover, struck a similar note:

[N]ever before in the history of American law enforcement has our profession faced such inflamed bitterness and hostility and such purposive intentions to wreak havoc against police officers through injury, maiming and outright murder. [...] Ideological and revolutionary violence in the nation is on the increase.

(Hoover 1970; cited in Parenti 1999)

Indeed, while members of the New Left proclaimed their solidarity with wars of national liberation in the Third World, and drew on the tactics of Mao, Che Guevara, Marighella and Ho Chi Minh (Berger 2006, 2010), the authorities charged with responding to, and ultimately repressing, militancy took their cue from counterinsurgency doctrine. A 1966 article with the ominous title: 'Police-Military Relations in a Revolutionary Environment' published in *The Police Chief*, explicitly discussed the domestic applicability of counterinsurgency lessons and praised the 'value of an effective police organization – both civil and military – in maintaining law and order, whether in California, Pennsylvania, Mississippi, or the rice paddies and jungles of Vietnam' (Rudziak 1966; cited in Parenti 1999: 18).

Domestic policing has, in fact, morphed into 'a variation of counterinsurgency as crime is increasingly administered and contoured as a mode of clandestine economic circulation' (Feldman 2004: 334). It is increasingly concerned with the preemptive identification, tracking and targeting of illicit flows of people and goods that are hidden amongst licit everyday circulations (see Amoore and De Goede 2008; Aradau and van Munster 2008; Graham 2010; De Goede

2008). Domestic policing thus faces the same challenge as counterinsurgency: whereas counterinsurgents have to identify insurgents who hide amongst a civilian population, police forces have to identify potential and actual criminals as well as illicit flows of contraband amongst the everyday activities of ordinary people.

Practices derived from expeditionary counterinsurgency operations have been, and continue to be, adapted to the pacification of risky neighborhoods in the homeland. Areas are first risk-profiled by means of geographical crime mapping technologies. High-risk areas then become the target of paramilitary units that conduct saturation patrols, no-knock entries, serve warrants, and engage in 'quality of life' policing. Once an area is pacified, community policing proper begins and the police seek to establish a rapport with the local community, in order to prevent the neighborhood from reverting back to its former high-risk status. This phase also coincides with a crackdown on small-scale crime, and the implementation of situational crime prevention methods that seek to design the overall physical environment in such a way as to prevent criminal behavior from occurring in the first place. This may include target-hardening of public places through CCTV cameras, fences, walls and spotlights as well as 'bum-proof' benches and classical music, which is supposed to keep youths and drug-addicts at bay (see Parenti 1999; Davis 1992). In fact, this is what the US Justice Department called the 'Weed and Seed Program': weeding out undesirable elements in the community, while planting the seed for sustainable revitalization to keep these elements out (see Lyons 1999: 1). In brief, contemporary policing seeks to identify risky communities and spaces and aims to violently exclude the risk factors in order to provide long-term stability and security.

Rationalities and practices of policing thus present us with a complex alignment of technologies (information, communication and surveillance technologies, but also more low-tech tools such as fences, walls, etc.), modes of knowledge production (crime rates, geography, knowledge about particular communities, etc.), organizations (different police units, community organizations, businesses, etc.) and tactics (raids, saturation patrols, no-knock entries, enlisting the help and support of community organizations, etc.). All these elements converge into a pacification strategy targeting populations and spaces that are considered to be inimical to the liberal order. Indeed, US policing forms a complex governmental machine that connects up various forms of expertise, modes of knowledge production, technologies, organizations and institutions and techniques and tactics. And this governmental machine is, above all, geared towards pacifying the racialized poor.

Ever since the race riots erupted in inner city ghettos across the United States in the late 1960s, the '(semi-)welfare state' has been steadily dismantled, only to be replaced by 'a police and penal state for which the criminalization of marginality and the punitive containment of dispossessed categories serve as social policy at the lower end of the class and ethnic order' (Wacquant 2009b: 41). Rationalities and practices of domestic policing seek to permanently exclude elements that are construed as threats to the liberal order through warehousing them in prisons, while trying to re-integrate less risky illiberal elements into the liberal order through highly disciplinary workfare programs. Not only does policing combine care with control, but it also merges government in the sense of attempting 'to structure the possible field of action of others' (Foucault 2000c: 341) with violence in the sense of violently excluding bodies from society through the deployment of military-type tactics, doctrines and equipment. The fight against domestic militancy, and the war on drugs, functioned as major vehicles for inserting rationalities and practices of expeditionary pacification into the US homeland. What is more, these rationalities and practices have been assembled into a biopolitical strategy for the pacification of dangerous life.

Conclusion

Policing in the United States forms a highly heterogeneous field: law enforcement practices differ from state to state and even from municipality to municipality. In fact, in the United States, policing is primarily a municipal affair. Yet, from the 1960s onwards, the federal government became increasingly involved in law enforcement. Federal involvement in policing has been shaped by three interrelated trends: First, federal concerns over policing have become more and more dominated by rationalities and practices of pacification directed at particular populations and spaces. Second, the development and deployment of these rationalities and practices have, moreover, been contoured by two overlapping problematizations of insecurity, namely, the alleged threat of domestic militancy (especially amongst dispossessed minority groups) and the supposed danger of a narcotics and drugs epidemic. Third, and in a more general sense, rationalities and practices of policing have been shaped by a tension between government through freedom, and government through more authoritarian means.

The war on drugs to a large extent anticipated the war on terror. Like the war on terror, America's drug war has been both spatially and temporally indeterminate (which is also borne out by the fact that it is still ongoing, albeit somewhat on the backburner); it erodes the distinction between warfighting and policing and hence also results in a complete intermingling of domestic public safety and foreign defense. Michael Hardt and Antonio Negri put it quite succinctly:

> In the context of this cross between military and police activity there is ever less difference between inside and outside the nation-state: low-intensity warfare meets high-intensity policing. The "enemy", which has traditionally been conceived outside, and the "dangerous classes," which have traditionally been inside, are thus increasingly indistinguishable from one another and serve together as the object of the war effort.
>
> (Hardt and Negri 2004: 14–15)

What Hardt and Negri call the 'enemy' and the 'dangerous classes' are those who cannot be governed liberally, who are seen as threats to liberalism and

4 Geographies of security

Introduction

Governmentalities of security materialize in space. As Eyal Weizman puts it (2007: 106–7), '[security] erects barriers and channels and rechannels the flow of people and resources through space. According to the logic of security, only a constantly configured and reconfigured environment is a safe environment'. At the same time, problematizations of insecurity tend to cluster around the increasing mobility of dangerous circulations as well as concerns over 'activities that threaten ' "our" values, "our" way of life' (Walters 2004: 247).

The mobility of people, goods, and information is now widely seen as a defining characteristic of late modernity in general and of globalization in particular. Since the end of the Cold War, over-hyped accounts of a borderless world to be brought about by advances in communication technology, transportation and economic globalization have been all the rage. The pivotal role of borders in the late modern mobility regime, however, was generally ignored. As Zureik and Salter point out:

> Inter-state borders – of various significance – are central to the global mobility regime, the international system in both political and economic spheres, and to national identity. Inter-state frontiers always reflect the over-determination of economic, military, and cultural boundaries.
>
> (Zureik and Salter 2005: 3)

Above all, borders serve to demarcate the territory over which a state exerts control not only from the territory of other states, but also from the general sphere of international relations. Interstate borders thus provide the material basis for the mythical distinction between the domesticated territory of states and the anarchic sphere of international relations, and hence also for the academic divisions that flow from it.

But borders are more than just physical barriers between states. More generally, they are also geared towards tracking, targeting and managing flows of people, goods and information in space. They are sorting mechanisms that (re)produce divisions between risky and risk-free circulations, and inscribe them in space.

Moreover, borders should not only be thought of in terms of traditional points of entry that allow movement into and out of a clearly demarcated territory. As Mark Salter argues:

> From the macro-politics of inside/outside, we see the emergence of a micro-politics of surveillance nets and vulnerable nodes. Thus, we have seen a sea change in our notion of territoriality, wherein the anxiety which was previously centred on the border has been projected onto a set of internal security measures (such as airport security and mall surveillance).
>
> (Salter 2005: 41–2)

In fact, territorial borders between states at the national level, and between communities at the local level, have merged into 'a "multiplicity of control points" that become distributed along key lines of circulation and key geographies of wealth and power, crossing territorial lines between states as well as those within and beyond those boundaries' (Graham 2010: 89; see also Côté-Boucher 2008).

Bordering is thus a pivotal security practice. Bordering materializes in what will be called *geographies of security*. Geographies of security can take a variety of concrete forms, from traditional territorial borders to the target-hardening of public and commercial spaces. What they all share is a concern with performing a distinction between safe and dangerous circulations. Indeed, geographies of security seek to inscribe the biopolitical distinction between risky and risk-free individuals, populations and spaces into the built environment through a multiplicity of visible and invisible checkpoints that now dot both the American homeland and the entire globe (see Dudley 2007: 3; Shapiro 2009).

Armed with high-tech surveillance equipment and sophisticated risk management techniques, increasingly militarized territorial borders (and also 'target-hardened' (semi-)public spaces, such as shopping malls) now serve to identify, locate and ultimately interdict risky circulations (Salter 2005, 2008a, 2008b; Lyon 2008; Lahav 2008). But since practices of sifting risky from risk-free circulations also frequently end up confining particular individuals and populations to jails, prisons, penitentiaries and other detention facilities, we will also examine those authoritarian geographies of security that increasingly serve to permanently exclude undesirable populations.

Command, control, surveillance and reconnaissance

Geographies of security assemble tactics, technologies and forms of knowledge (production) into complex machines geared towards distinguishing between risky and risk-free flows. Since sifting risky flows from risk-free everyday circulations presents enormous challenges, geographies of security rely on increasingly sophisticated technological fixes to the perennial problem of rendering circulations visible and, ultimately, knowable.

In the early 1960s, defense contractors, such as the aerospace company Lockheed, and defense research institutions, such as the RAND Corporation, scrambled to find profitable new markets beyond the purely military domain (Light 2002: 607–8). For a decade or so, city planning and management became a profitable sphere of activity for defense experts as well as major aerospace companies. After all, the technocrats of the Military–Industrial Complex were at the cutting edge of information and communication technology and had ample expertise in the practical use of information systems, simulations and systems analysis. It was widely believed that the advanced knowledge and technologies of the defense and aerospace community could help manage and control the complexities of contemporary urban life. Many American city governments thus partnered up with military think tanks and/or defense contractors (Light 2004).

The deployment of military expertise and technologies in the context of urban planning and management was greatly boosted by the overall 'urban crisis' of the 1960s. During the 'long, hot summers' from 1965 to 1968, civil disorders, demonstrations, and full-fledged urban riots were the order of the day. On top of these urban upheavals, there were regular threats of bomb attacks and sabotage as well as a general increase in violent and supposedly drug-related crime. While the National Guard and even regular Army units were deployed in the streets of American cities to quell urban rioting, '[d]efense intellectuals from institutions such as RAND and Lockheed, already seeking urban markets, found further opportunities for work in the violence that had engulfed American cities' (Light 2002: 609):

> A shared vision of the escalating "urban crisis" as a national security crisis transformed urban problems into strategic challenges to be met through techniques and technologies of command, control, communication, intelligence, surveillance and reconnaissance.
>
> (Light 2002: 609)

Military systems of command, control, communication, surveillance and reconnaissance seemed to allow for the identification, real-time monitoring and preemption of urban decay in general and criminal activity in particular. According to historian Jennifer S. Light (2004: 404), 'With these tools, urban planners could analyze urban data and propose new physical plans and social programs to thwart any immediate threats.' The application of sophisticated military technologies to problems of urban planning and management amounted to the deployment of a veritable logistics of perception as a basis for more targeted forms of urban governance. Contemporary urban governance is, above all, an attempt to manage risks. But risky spaces, populations and activities need to be identified, located and tracked before they can be targeted by the full range of governmental programs: from assistance to militarized coercion. And this is precisely what military technologies of command, control, communication, surveillance and reconnaissance seemed to offer.

However, in spite of successes in some areas (notably increases in the efficiency of traffic flow as well as firefighter and police dispatch) by the beginning of the 1970s, there was mounting evidence that the adoption of military technologies did not provide an easy fix to the nation's multiple urban problems. Indeed, the implementation of this high-tech fix was beset by a fundamental problem: 'goals such as improving the quality of community life and neighborhood revitalization were not as easily reduced to mathematical form as military objectives; decisions could not always be implemented' (Light 2004: 405). Furthermore, city planners and defense analysts alike came to realize that 'the nation's cities faced challenges that were more difficult than those confronting defense planners organizing a military campaign or a satellite launch' (Light 2004: 405). Light also notes that '[m]en with experience in both defense and urban analysis, such as former Deputy Assistant Secretary of Defense and later Urban Planning Institute President William Gorham, publicly admitted that cities were more challenging' (Light 2004: 405).

But were they really? While military technology and expertise was touted as an easy fix to America's urban problems, the US military had already become bogged down in a bloody conflict that proved as impervious to technological fixes as America's cities. The Vietnam War was about more than just a series of targets to be identified, tracked and serviced. In fact, this war brought the fundamental dilemma between universally applicable algorithms and messy local situations into as sharp a relief as the apparent ungovernability of America's cities. Today, the search for technological fixes to the perennial problem of interdicting risky circulations continues unabated.

Interdicting 'risky' circulations

Interdiction forms the key technique for filtering out risky circulations. In the Pentagon lexicon, interdiction includes several (often overlapping) phases, 'including detection, identification [...], interception, tracking and monitoring, apprehension, search, seizure, and arrest' (Dunn 1996: 108). Interdicting risky circulations, moreover, hinges on the preemptive tracking and targeting of mobile bodies and objects. In her discussion of 'algorithmic war' – defined as 'a stitching together of the mundane and prosaic calculations of business, the security decisions authorized by the state, and the mobilized vigilance of a fearful public' (Amoore 2009: 50) – political geographer Louise Amoore, argues that practices of security aim to identify, localize, name and depict risky populations, bodies and goods 'in advance of any possible future strike or intervention' (Amoore 2009: 56). Practices of security thus seek to preempt danger by interdicting, sometimes through the use of lethal force, threats before they become manifest. Interdiction thereby relies both on surveillance technologies, such as motion sensors, CCTV cameras, night vision equipment, biometrics, etc. and on risk management techniques, such as the use of algorithms, 'to connect the dots' by mapping probabilistic relations between data entries stored in vast and increasingly interconnected databases (see for example, Amoore 2008, 2009; Aradau and van Munster 2008; Muller 2005). For instance, social network analysis is now widely used to identify and target both insurgent and criminal networks. Social network analysis seeks to locate and map the distribution of nodes within a network so that they can be targeted in a more discriminate fashion. According to Marieke de Goede (2008: 105–6), 'Social Network Analysis is perceived to be an imaginative and innovative risk technique in the war on terror that enables the preemptive identification and disruption of potential suspects.' The current *Counterinsurgency Field Manual* (Department of the Army 2007: 305–33), for instance, contains an appendix outlining the benefits of social network analysis for counterinsurgency operations. In their counterinsurgency efforts in Iraq and Afghanistan, the US armed forces have used a variety of instruments for rendering the so-called human terrain intelligible. Besides the use of the usual high-tech surveillance equipment, the US military has also resorted to the expertise of civilian social scientists, above all anthropologists. Social scientists have been deployed as so-called Human Terrain Teams alongside combat forces in both Iraq and Afghanistan. Through these teams, counterinsurgents have sought to combine the analysis of local social networks with the spatial analysis of human and physical geography, in order to map and risk-categorize individuals and communities so that practices of targeting could be adapted to their level of risk (see Kienscherf 2010: 131–35). The Human Terrain System will be discussed in more detail in Chapter 5.

Global borderlands

Historically, the distinction between safe and dangerous individuals (and populations and spaces) manifested itself in the relation between European metropolises and the colonial periphery but also, within the metropolis, in the relation between the bourgeoisie and the so-called dangerous classes. Today, this distinction structures the global relations between the developed and a so-called developing world that is regularly subjected to measures ranging from the seemingly benign, such as humanitarian and developmental assistance, to a whole arsenal of coercive means, including full-fledged military intervention. Domestically, this distinction presents itself in the divisions between ordinary, mostly white middle-class citizens and an overdetermined subaltern population of so-called undeserving poor, illegal aliens and criminals who are also subjected to instruments ranging from (often paternalistic) therapeutic assistance, to all-out coercion. As previously noted, these divisions are based both on a binary opposition between safe and dangerous subjects and a scale of dangerousness based on a rationality of risk management.

Counterinsurgency-style pacification helps us conceptualize rationalities and practices of liberal security both domestically and globally because it encompasses the full range of measures for dealing with risky populations, from developmental assistance to the full-scale deployment of combat troops and/or paramilitary police forces.

Expeditionary counterinsurgency efforts mostly target ungoverned spaces, dark spots on the world map that are disconnected from the globalized networks of licit circulations, and are seen as breeding grounds for dangerous circulations (Kilcullen 2005, 2009). Counterinsurgency aims to pacify these illiberal spaces by (re)establishing control over the population in order to weed out dangerous elements. These pacification efforts are centered on a distinction between an active minority supporting the insurgency, an active minority opposing it and a neutral or passive majority that can swing either way (Department of the Army 2007: 36). In targeting what are, in fact, construed as dangerous spaces and populations, counterinsurgency relies both on a scale of dangerousness and a distinction within the targeted population between those that can be won over through non-lethal ways and those hardliners that need to be taken out by force. These divisions are then inscribed into space through practices of bordering and materialize in geographies of security.

In expeditionary counterinsurgency, geographies of security first of all serve the traditional purpose of protecting the territorial integrity of the host- nation. Above all, border control is supposed to deny cross-border support and sanctuary to insurgents (Celeski 2006: 51). But counterinsurgents also seek to configure host-nation space in such a way as to be able to separate the civilian population from the insurgents. Such practices have a profoundly imperialist genealogy (see Galula 1964; Hunt 1995; Marshall 2010; McClintock 1992; Townshend 1986; Tyner 2009: 97–104).

The practices of British imperial policing and French counter-revolutionary warfare had a huge influence on the formation of contemporary counterinsurgency doctrine (see Marshall 2010). Many counterinsurgency enthusiasts today tout the British practice of imperial policing as a viable model for current campaigns (see Crawshaw 2007; Nagl 2005). As Michael Crawshaw puts it in a paper published by the UK Defence Academy:

> The 'British Model', tied as it is to the era of colonial counter-revolutionary war and earlier, is dated. Nevertheless, much of its methodology can be applied to modern insurgencies *provided that there is a legitimate indigenous government capable of taking ownership of the campaign.*
>
> (Crawshaw 2007: 31 original emphasis)

In particular, the so-called 'hearts and minds' approach to counterinsurgency, which the British are widely held to have pioneered, is frequently heaped with praise in the counterinsurgency literature[1] (see Long 2006: 21–23).

The French model of counter-revolutionary warfare differed from British imperial policing only in the extent 'to which it sought not to maintain or manage the existing status quo, but rather to actively physically and mentally *transform* the societies concerned, in order to produce more loyal clients' (Marshall 2010: 242 original emphasis). In the words of French veteran and counterinsurgency expert, David Galula (1964: 95), whose work also heavily informed the current US *Counterinsurgency Field Manual* (Department of the Army 2007), 'the basic mechanism of counterinsurgency warfare [...] can be summed up in a single sentence: Build (or rebuild) a political machine from the population upwards'.

French policy centered on isolating the insurgents from the population. To this end, French counterinsurgent forces sought to divide operational space into color-coded zones, physically marked off by fences and watchtowers: white for government-controlled areas; pink for contested zones; and red for insurgent-controlled areas. Accordingly, the task of the counterinsurgents was to turn pink areas white and red areas first pink and then white (Galula 1964: 49; Marshall 2010: 243).

A strikingly similar approach was adopted during the 'surge' in Iraq: the cities of Baghdad and Ramadi were divided into sectors that 'were subjected to intense yet discriminate infantry operations and were cordoned off with checkpoints and barriers; the population was issued identity cards, and any travel to and from the area was strictly controlled' (Ucko 2009: 128). Officers frequently referred to these fenced-in neighborhoods as 'gated communities' (see Brulliard 2007; Kilcullen 2007b). David Kilcullen (2007b) contends that, 'Gated Communities in counterinsurgency are like tourniquets in surgery' – an effective, albeit somewhat painful, instrument for breaking the cycle of violence. He suggests that 'gated communities' can achieve this in three ways:

> First, it makes it much harder for terrorists to infiltrate a community. We only establish perimeter security (checkpoints, T-walls, etc.) once the area has been cleared and secured, close relations are established with the population, and we have troops on the ground securing the district in conjunction with the people. Once the gated community goes in, this makes it much harder for extremists to re-enter.
>
> Second, the perimeter controls make it much harder for terrorists to launch attacks from within that district, because they have to smuggle a car bomb or suicide vest out, through a limited number of controlled access points. This reduces extremists' ability to use gated districts as a base to attack neighboring areas.
>
> Third, if the terrorists do manage to mount an attack, the security controls protect the gated community against retaliation by "death squads". This reduces fear within the community, alienates extremists from the population (since they can no longer pose as defenders) and emboldens people, who would otherwise be too intimidated, to tip off the security forces to enemy presence.
>
> (Kilcullen 2007b)

Kilcullen's account shows that once an area is cleared of insurgents, geographies of security are put in place so that the insurgents can be kept out. This takes the form of a complex assemblage of *technologies* (technologies of command, control, communication, surveillance and reconnaissance, biometrics and also fences, walls, checkpoints, etc.), *modes of knowledge-production* (gathering of census data, mapping the physical and human terrain and so forth), *organizations* (US and allied military units, host nation security forces, international aid organizations etc.) and *tactics* (saturation patrols, raids, searches and seizures, enlisting the help of the local community etc.).

This clearly shows how counterinsurgency-style pacification seeks to be implemented through the management and control of movement and how geographies of security are imposed upon 'ungoverned spaces', in order to locate, track and target dangerous elements hiding amongst civilian populations.

Domestic borderlands

In *The Militarization of the U.S.–Mexico Border*, Timothy Dunn asserts that:

> since the mid-1970s, 'border control' has emerged as a salient topic in U.S. politics, with concern for it often spurred on by sensationalist portrayals of undocumented immigration, drug trafficking, and occasionally even the threat of terrorism as critical issues for the U.S.–Mexico border region.
>
> (Dunn 1996: 1)

This has led to gradual militarization of the US–Mexico border through the application of Low-Intensity Conflict (LIC) doctrine (Dunn 1996).

Both Low-Intensity Conflict and counterinsurgency doctrine are characterized by a blurring of internal and external security, a 'policization' of the military and a militarization of the police, as well as an emphasis on so-called pacification or population control:

> The larger objective of LIC doctrine is to effect social control over targeted civilian populations by drawing selectively from this vast continuum of tactics to address any threat to stability (from a broad range of security concerns) in a manner that theoretically is more judicious and appropriate than are heavy-handed, less discriminate, conventional military approaches.
>
> (Dunn 1996: 148)

This is also an apt characterization of counterinsurgency and stability operations. David Ucko (2009: 9–11) suggests that counterinsurgency and stability operations share three significant features: (1) they occur in a context of hostile activity, (2) the stabilization effort forms part of a wider state-building initiative and (3) the stabilizing force is deployed in the midst of a civilian population. The deployment of military tactics, technologies and troops along the US–Mexico border exhibits all these features.

First, as the Reagan, Bush and Clinton administrations massively escalated the war on drugs, it was transformed from a rhetorical device into an actual low intensity conflict that was (and still is) fought not only along the US–Mexico border, but also in the streets of deprived urban neighborhoods. Dunn quotes a leading federal counter-narcotics official,[2] who at the beginning of the 1990s baldly stated, 'We are engaged in something akin to a guerrilla war along the border against well-entrenched and well-organized trafficking groups' (quoted in Dunn 1996: 3). Ever since drugs were declared a threat to national security, drug trafficking has been habitually scripted as a hostile activity that mandates the deployment of a wide range of security assets. Swaths of the border region (as well as certain inner-city neighborhoods) have thus regularly been designated as quasi-hostile environments that can only be pacified through paramilitary operations (Dunn 1996: 112).

Second, considering the deployment of military tactics, technologies and personnel along the border as part of a wider attempt at state-building may, at first glance, seem like a bit of a stretch. However, bordering has always played a major part in state-making, for the simple reason that borders demarcate state-controlled territory both from the territory of other states and from the international sphere. And borders are also a central factor in the construction of national identity, because they materialize the distinction between who (and what) is to be included and who (and what) is to be excluded from the imagined community of the nation(-state). More generally, borders are always geared towards establishing and/or protecting a social, political, economic and cultural order, which is more likely than not state-centric.

Third, it goes without saying that the militarization of the border occurs in the midst of a civilian population (on both sides of the border) as well as amongst regular day-to-day, cross-border traffic.

The militarization of the US–Mexico border has many facets, but is most glaringly exemplified by the use of military weapons and tactics, the provision of military training to border guards and the actual deployment of troops in the border region. For example, in 1984, the Border Patrol Tactical Team (BORTAC) was set up. This small elite unit 'received special training in riot control, counterterrorism, and other paramilitary activities similar to the training provided to US marshals and the FBI Special Weapons and Training (SWAT) teams' (Dunn 1996: 52). Like SWAT teams and other paramilitary police units, BORTAC is modeled on military special operations forces (Kraska and Kappeler 1997). In fact, over the last three decades, the Department of Defense (DoD) has routinely provided training, support (e.g., aerial surveillance) and equipment, such as night vision gear and portable ground radar, to civilian border control and law enforcement agencies. Yet the military has not just doled out training and equipment – US armed forces have also been deployed along the US–Mexico border to actively support drug interdiction efforts. One of the first full-fledged joint operations conducted by the military and civilian law enforcement agencies was Operation Alliance, which was launched in 1986 (Dunn 1996: 113). As Dunn writes:

> Regardless of its actual effectiveness, Operation Alliance certainly increased the scope and range of collaboration between a wide variety of governmental entities (ranging from the Department of Defense to local police), and greatly expanded the amount of resources and equipment deployed (however misguidedly) along the U.S.–Mexico border. [...] On the whole, it appears that this particular law enforcement project provided much of the organizational infrastructure for border-area law enforcement between 1986 and 1992, as it presided over the coordination and implementation of a growing drug enforcement effort there.
>
> (Dunn 1996: 116-7)

Moreover, 'Operation Alliance's scope extended well beyond drug enforcement' (Dunn 1996: 113). Dunn quotes the operation's senior tactical coordinator, James Bowen, who stated that 'Operation Alliance was established to interdict the flow of drugs, weapons, *aliens*, currency, and other contraband across the southwest border' (Dunn1996: 113 original emphasis).

The militarization of border control has received a further boost after the 9/11 attacks (Graham 2010; Sparke 2006). But, as of 2011, Mexican political instability is frequently construed as a cross-border threat of similar, or even greater, proportions than international terrorism. Mexico's own domestic war on drugs has escalated dramatically, with 7,200 victims of drug-related violence in 2008 alone. A Pentagon report, published in November 2008, concluded that due to the 'sustained assault and pressure by criminal gangs' (United States Joint Forces Command 2008: 40) Mexico's government, police and judicial structures might collapse; and that this could ultimately turn Mexico into a failed state, which might pose a severe threat to US homeland security. While a number of senior intelligence officials disputed the report's claims, the Obama administration responded to the study's warnings by drawing up a 'multi-agency security plan for the border' (Hsu and Sheridan 2009). Indeed, a number of security experts now warn that Mexico's drug wars pose an even greater threat to US stability than al-Qaeda (see Bunker 2010, 2011a, 2011b; Sullivan and Bunker 2011; Bunker and Sullivan 2011).

The attacks on 9/11 seem to have quashed hopes for a borderless world. However, in the United States there has been a long-standing tension between economic demands for smooth cross-border movement, and geopolitical demands for a secure homeland. On the one hand, business leaders and pro-business politicians have extolled the virtues of borderless regionalism and transnational trade agreements, such as the North American Free Trade Agreement (NAFTA); on the other, anti-immigration groups and drug warriors have lobbied for more and better border-hardening measures. US border control has thus long faced the daunting task of negotiating between demands for the unfettered movement of capital, goods and, to a far lesser extent, people; and demands for the often violent exclusion of goods and people held to pose a threat to the homeland.

In order to resolve the tension between economic and homeland security, the governments of Canada and the United States signed the 'Smart Border Declaration and Associated 30-Point Action Plan to Enhance the Security of Our Shared Border While Facilitating the Legitimate Flow of People and Goods' in December 2001 (Sparke 2006, 2008; United States Customs and Border Protection 2009). This has given rise to a joint Canadian–US program called NEXUS that allows pre-approved low-risk travelers to avoid long waiting times at border crossings through the use of RFID-enabled smartcards and self-serve kiosks. As the official US Customs and Border Protection Website describes it:

> The NEXUS program allows pre-screened travelers expedited processing by United States and Canadian officials at dedicated processing lanes at designated northern border ports of entry, at NEXUS kiosks at Canadian

preclearance airports, and at marine reporting locations. Approved applicants are issued a photo-identification, proximity Radio Frequency Identification (RFID) card. Participants use the three modes of passage where they will either present their NEXUS card or have their iris scanned and make a declaration.

(United States Customs and Border Protection 2009)

The US–Mexico equivalent is called SENTRI. There is also a pre-clearance program for goods called Free and Secure Trade (FAST). All these programs are combined with an increasing militarization of the border through sensors, aerial surveillance, and other border-hardening measures, such as bollards, tire-shredders, electric gates, etc. (Sparke 2006: 168). Smart Borders are thus set to provide a technological fix to the problem of performing the biopolitical distinction between flows whose movement has to be facilitated, and flows that need to be interdicted.

According to political geographer Matthew Sparke, smart border technology has profound consequences for conceptions of citizenship. A kinetic elite (mostly business travelers) enrolled in so-called Smart Border Programs and/or traveling first class or even in private jets, now exists alongside a kinetic underclass (doomed to move much more slowly and uncomfortably) and a subaltern population that is subject to detention, expedited removal, and extraordinary rendition (often in the same type of jets used by the global elite) (Sparke 2006). Indeed, 'the so-called "land of the free" [...] has managed now to combine expedited exceptions to human rights for asylum seekers with the expedited border-crossing rights for business elites' (Sparke 2006: 173). Sparke, moreover, seeks to address the question of whether 'this authoritarian underside' of, or rather permanent exception to, the option of circulation is in fact 'a necessary corollary, a wholly contingent corollary, or some more complex interrelated counterpart to the emergence of elite transnational citizenship under neoliberalism?' (Sparke 2006: 174). He comes to the conclusion that the authoritarian practices of expedited removal and extraordinary rendition are not the inevitable results of a neoliberal rationality obsessed with free circulation. But nor are they 'just a contingent outcome of the exceptional American context with its history of free market capitalism rooted in that most profitable as well as paradigmatic space of exception: the slave plantation' (Sparke 2006: 175). Sparke maintains that there is a more complex entwinement 'between the neoliberal dynamic and the violence of expedited removal and rendition' (Sparke 2006: 175). In fact, these authoritarian practices 'would seem to be structured by a neoliberal double standard: a standard that is like liberalism's own inaugural double standards – with rights for whites in Europe and often utter inhumanity in the colonies' (Sparke 2006: 175). Indeed, the tension between the facilitation of free movement for liberal subjects and objects and the authoritarian practices targeting illiberal subjects and objects, hinges on the fundamental liberal distinction between those that can be governed through the promotion of freedom and those that need to be targeted through authoritarian means or even violence.

The securitization of urban design

This division is also increasingly inscribed at the community level. Crime Prevention through Environmental Design (CPTED, pronounced *sept-ted*), for instance, constitutes an attempt to build the divisions of liberal security into the urban syntax. CPTED hinges on the assumption that 'through the proper design and use of the built environment, it is possible both to reduce the actual incidence of criminal activity and to mitigate the fear of crime' (Parnaby 2006: 2; see also Crowe 2000; Cozens *et al.* 2001; Newman 1972, 1996). This is, above all, based on 'the ability of CPTED experts to effectively identify crime-related risks and render them seemingly concrete and calculable' (Parnaby 2006: 4). In short, CPTED is a rationality and practice of risk management.

CPTED can be traced back to the early 1960s. In her highly influential critique of 1950s urban renewal policies, *The Death and Life of Great American Cities*, first published in 1961, Jane Jacobs (1992) argued that poor design and planning were partly to blame for rising urban disorder and decay. Jacobs held that a complete overhaul of urban planning and design could re-create close community ties that in turn would strengthen informal social control. In *Defensible Space*, Oscar Newman (1972) followed Jacob's lead in blaming the rise of crime on a breakdown of mechanisms of informal social control brought about by the density, heterogeneity, and anonymity of contemporary urban life.[3] Newman sought to provide the building blocks, the design principles: 'for restructuring the residential environments of our cities so they can again become livable and controlled, controlled not by police but by a community of people sharing a common terrain' (Newman 1972: 2). Newman's rather militaristically termed program, 'defensible space', aimed to boost the security, and thereby also the general welfare, of city dwellers:

> Defensible space is a model for residential environments which inhibits crime by creating the physical expression of a social fabric that defends itself. All the different elements which combine to make a defensible space have a common goal – an environment in which latent territoriality and sense of community in the inhabitants can be translated into responsibility for ensuring a safe, productive, and well-maintained living space.
>
> (Newman 1972: 3)

The primary targets of Newman's design intervention were supposed to be residents of public housing – communities living in the most deprived and crime-ridden neighborhoods of the American cityscape. The program of defensible space was devised to pacify deprived inner-city neighborhoods by re-configuring the built environment in such a way as to decrease the opportunities for crime and disorder. At the same time, it sought to empower the residents of public housing projects by providing them with an environment conducive to the re-creation of a sense of community and the (re)construction of informal social control.

But what are the design principles Newman envisaged? Newman's program of defensible space comprises four design principles: *territoriality, natural surveillance, image,* and *milieu* (Newman 1972: 49–50; see also Katyal 2002: 1048–9; Parnaby 2006: 4).

1   *Territoriality*: Refers to 'mechanisms for the subdivision and articulation of areas of the residential environment intended to reinforce inhabitants in their ability to assume territorial attitudes and prerogatives' (Newman 1972: 50). This includes both physical barriers and symbolic markers of territory, such as 'open gateways, light standards, a short run of steps, planting, and changes in the texture of the walking surface', that 'serve to create perceptible zones of transition from public to private spaces' (Newman 1972: 63).

2   *Natural surveillance*: Encompasses 'mechanisms for improving the capacity of residents to casually and continually survey the nonprivate areas of their living environment, indoor and out' (Newman 1972: 50). This includes design features such as glazing and lighting, but also the creation of clear lines of sight. Newman, moreover, stresses that 'the effectiveness of increased surveillance depends on whether the area under surveillance is identified by the observer as falling under his sphere of influence' (Newman 1972: 79).

3   *Image*: Signifies 'mechanisms which neutralize the symbolic stigma of the form of housing projects, reducing the image of isolation, and the apparent vulnerability of inhabitants' (Newman 1972: 50). This includes a whole series of techniques that seek to counteract the fact that '[t]he idiosyncratic image of publicly-assisted housing, coupled with other design-features and the social-characteristics of the resident population, makes such housing a peculiarly vulnerable target of criminal activity'[4] (Newman 1972: 102).

4   *Milieu*: Denotes 'mechanisms of juxtaposition – the effect of location of a residential environment within a particular urban setting or adjacent to a "safe" or "unsafe" activity area' (Newman 1972: 50).

Newman's concept of defensible space had a profound influence on the development of CPTED (see Crowe 2000; Hopper and Droge 2005; Parnaby 2006: 4; Schneider and Kitchen 2002). But over the years, Newman's ideas also underwent some major changes. For instance, in an article on the role of architecture in crime control, legal scholar and former Acting Solicitor General, Neal Kumar Katyal (2002), outlined a different and somewhat more robust list of design features:

Design should: (1) create opportunities for natural surveillance by residents, neighbors, and bystanders; (2) instill a sense of territoriality so that residents develop proprietary attitudes and outsiders feel deterred from entering a private space; (3) build communities and avoid isolation; and (4) protect targets of crime.

(Katyal 2002: 1048–9)

So natural surveillance and territoriality remain in place, but image and milieu are collapsed into the category of community-building, while target-hardening is introduced as a separate principle. Target-hardening is the most robust, coercive, immediate, and hence also most widely adopted, principle of CPTED. Whereas the first three mechanisms seek to somehow empower ordinary people to defend themselves against crime, target-hardening reveals the 'neo-military syntax of contemporary architecture' (Davis 1992: 226). Stripped of its original focus on empowerment and reform, CPTED is often used to exclude the racial and social 'Other' from public spaces. In his discussion of 'fortress L.A.', Mike Davis offers an acerbic account of defensible spaces:

> In many instances the semiotics of so-called 'defensible space' are just as subtle as a swaggering white cop. Today's upscale, pseudo-public spaces – sumptuary malls, office centers, culture acropolises, and so on – are full of invisible signs warning off the underclass 'Other'. Although architectural critics are usually oblivious to how the built environment contributes to seg-regation, pariah groups – whether poor Latino families, young Black men, or elderly homeless white females – read the meaning immediately.
>
> (Davis 1992: 226)

Whereas Newman's concept of defensible space centered around a combination of development and security geared towards inhabitants of public housing projects, current uses of CPTED often tend to focus solely on the security of public and commercial spaces.

Today, CPTED is widely touted as an effective means for both preventing crime and reducing the fear of crime. By all accounts, it has become a burgeon-ing global industry. The International CPTED Association (ICA), which was founded in 1996, has chapters in the United States, Canada, the United Kingdom, the Netherlands and Chile. In 2004, it also launched an international certification program for practitioners of CPTED (International CPTED Association 2009; Parnaby 2006: 20nn).

Patrick Parnaby (2006) discusses the discursive frames used by practitioners and supporters of CPTED in their efforts to demarcate and legitimate their field of expertise. CPTED experts draw on three interrelated frames (Parnaby 2006: 2): First, they tend to posit the criminal event as flowing directly from the pres-ence of a spatially determined criminal opportunity, 'as opposed to the unpre-dictable convergence of myriad factors in both time and space' (Parnaby 2006: 8). Second, they seek to depoliticize the difference between 'legitimate' and 'illegitimate' users of space, and to gloss over the value-laden and politically problematic aspects of spatial design (Parnaby 2006: 9). Mike Davis's quote above shows that securitized spatial design often has the express purpose of excluding racial and social 'Others', and thus ends up reinforcing existing dis-criminatory attitudes and practices. Finally, CPTED experts aim to mobilize their clients 'to become *willing* participants in their own subjugation to the prac-titioner's expertise' (Parnaby 2006: 14). This is achieved through a strategy of responsibilization, geared towards instilling a sense of responsibility for crime prevention in their potential clients.

CPTED seeks to manage the risk of crime through a re-configuration of the built environment based on the logic of security. It is underpinned by a rationality that clusters around precepts of imminent danger, depoliticized differentiation, and responsibilization of people to take charge of their own security needs. Most importantly, the practice and rationality of CPTED illustrates the pervasiveness of the logic of security, which has been progressively absorbed into urban planning and architecture (see, for example, Hopper and Droge 2005).

Driven by rationalities of preemptive policing and problematizations of the unchecked circulation of urban risk, exclusionary spatial practices that inscribe security into everyday geographies – such as trespass laws, parks exclusion laws, off-limit orders, etc. – have proliferated over the last three decades (Herbert and Brown 2006; Beckett and Herbert 2008). As discussed in the previous chapter, broken-windows policing, for example, hinges on the assumption that if minor infractions of the law go unchecked, they may give rise to a much more serious criminal invasion (Wilson and Kelling 1982; Kelling and Coles 1996). Wilson and Kelling slip easily from run-down urban space to undesirable people, such as 'panhandlers, drunks, addicts, rowdy teenagers, prostitutes, loiterers, the mentally disturbed' (Wilson and Kelling 1982: 1). Indeed, their concern with undesirable people and anti-social behavior can easily be used as a call for more muscular policing, so that, in practice, the broken-windows theory is ultimately nothing but a pseudo-scientific confirmation of traditional police folklore (see Wacquant 2009b: 265).

Although broken-windows policing is obviously more concerned with behavior than with space, it is nonetheless underpinned by a spatial logic which happens to be more or less the same as in CPTED (Herbert and Brown 2006: 757–58). According to Steve Herbert and Elizabeth Brown (2006), both broken-windows policing and CPTED are based on four spatial assumptions.

1   The built environment signifies meaning; that is to say, broken-windows and derelict buildings send a message to potential criminals 'that it is a neighborhood ripe for the picking' (Herbert and Brown 2006: 760).
2   Strong territorial attitudes on the part of a built environment's inhabitants are said to signify a sense of community health and the presence of informal social control (Herbert and Brown 2006: 760).
3   There is a clear-cut division between 'known, controllable insiders and unknown, dangerous outsiders', against whom communities have to defend themselves (Herbert and Brown 2006: 760).
4   Last, but not least, both theories are focused on the local neighborhood level and completely disregard more macro-scale processes (Herbert and Brown 2006: 761).

The most fundamental spatial assumption at play in broken-windows policing and CPTED is the division between legitimate and illegitimate users of space.

Indeed, as with interstate borders at the national scale, the inscription of security into the built environment at the community- and neighborhood-level is above all aimed at distinguishing between risky and risk-free circulations. These forms of spatial security thus tie in with an overall effort to pacify at-risk spaces and populations, and contain or eliminate risky ones.

Oscar Newman insisted that urban design 'operates more in the area of "influence" than control' (Newman 1972: 207). But what about those geographies of security that are aimed at completely removing certain populations, not just from particular communities or urban settings but from society in general? What about geographies of security that are geared towards monitoring and controlling people's movements in a far more authoritarian fashion? Some forms of spatial design, most notably prisons and detention centers, do not limit themselves to promoting security by means of 'a setting conducive to realizing the *potential* of mutual concern' (Newman 1972: 207 original emphasis). It is to these quintessentially authoritarian geographies of security that we will now turn.

Warehousing 'risky' populations

Rates of incarceration in the US are staggering. According to the Bureau of Justice Statistics (Department of Justice 2009: 2) in 2008, the US correctional population, that is to say, those in prison, jail, on parole, or on probation totaled 7.3 million. This means that by the end of 2008, one in every 31 adults was under correctional supervision. Those under community supervision (70 percent or 5,095,200) made up the bulk of the correctional population, while inmates of federal penitentiaries, state prisons and local jails accounted for 30 percent (or 2,304,100). And incarceration rates are highly racialized: about 36 percent of the prison and jail population was black, 34 percent was white and 20 percent was Hispanic. What is more, Black males are still six and a half times more likely to end up in jail than white males.

The US correctional population has been on the increase since the early 1970s and has been soaring since the beginning of the 1980s. Jonathan Simon (2000) speaks of a long-standing tendency towards 'hyper-incarceration'. And Stephen Graham even goes as far as to argue that:

> the trend towards hyperincarceration in the US can best be understood as a process of state warfare *within* the US homeland. This war targets entire racial and social classes and their urban districts; meanwhile, the nation becomes an unsurpassed 'penal democracy'.
>
> (Graham 2010: 110; see also James 2007)

By and large, the rise of hyper-incarceration is a direct consequence of the war on drugs, which has led not only to quantitative changes, but also to a sweeping qualitative realignment of incarceration. In fact, the overall field of crime control has shifted from penal-welfarism to the so-called penal state. Penal welfarism consisted of a variety of therapeutic, educational, and welfare programs based on the belief that offenders can ultimately be reintegrated into society. In the penal state, on the other hand, the prison loses its reformist and welfarist trappings and turns into a means for managing a surplus population by completely excluding it from society (see Garland 2001; Wacquant 2001a, 2001b; Beckett and Sasson 2000; Peck 2003; Corva 2008; Simon 1993, 1999, 2007). In short, prisons have turned from correctional institutions to 'waste management prisons' (Simon 2007: 142).

In the penal state, the security of society is supposed to trump the welfare of the offender. But warehousing an increasingly high number of high-risk individuals in waste management prisons and eventually releasing them back into the community without providing them with the necessary social support to prevent them from re-offending, produces even more insecurity. In fact, the penal state constantly (re)produces a permanent criminal underclass, which, in turn, leads to ever more incarceration. This criminal underclass is more likely than not black, as African Americans have made up the majority of inmates since the late 1980s (Wacquant 2001b: 96).

Loïc Wacquant suggests that the prison and the hyperghetto now constitute two increasingly intertwined sites for the confinement of a racialized and gendered criminal underclass, considered to pose a risk to ordinary (white, middle-class) society:

> [They] contribute to the ongoing *reconstruction of the 'imagined community' of Americans* around the polar opposition between praiseworthy 'working families' – implicitly white, suburban, and deserving – and the despicable 'underclass' of criminals, loafers, and leeches, a two-headed antisocial hydra personified by the dissolute teenage 'welfare mother' on the female side and the dangerous street 'gang banger' on the male side – by definition dark-skinned, urban, and undeserving.
>
> (Wacquant 2001b: 120 original emphasis)

The hyperghetto and the prison are instruments for controlling a 'risky' population. But at the same time they also constitute risky spaces that, due to the very fact that they warehouse a risky population, need to be constantly controlled and targeted by a variety of different tactics and technologies, ranging from seemingly benign design features to the deployment of paramilitary police units. In fact, most US prisons now have so-called Special Response Teams which, like their ghetto counterparts, are modeled on military Special Forces (Simon 1999).

Wacquant's account (2001b) of the meshing between prison and hyperghetto once again highlights liberalism's division between those that can be governed through the promotion of freedom and those that need to be governed in a more authoritarian fashion. In the United States, African Americans in general (and young African American males in particular) have long been, and still are, construed as impervious to liberal government or even as a threat to the liberal order. And the prison and the hyperghetto are two closely entwined sites for the implementation and (re)production of this distinction.

Detention, deportation and 'extraordinary rendition'

However, African Americans are not the only illiberal population subject to authoritarian control in general and spatial incapacitation in particular. The recent increase in the detention of immigrants is an egregious case of the use of highly authoritarian practices against a particularly vulnerable population that is now also increasingly cast as posing a threat to national security. According to a recent Amnesty International report on US immigration detention:

> In just over a decade, immigration detention has tripled. In 1996, immigration authorities had a daily detention capacity of less than 10,000. Today more than 30,000 immigrants are detained each day, and the number is likely to increase even further. They include asylum seekers, torture survivors, victims of human trafficking, longtime lawful permanent residents, and the parents of US citizen children.
>
> (Amnesty International USA 2009)

Detention differs from criminal incarceration in that detained immigrants are not necessarily guilty of any crime (except perhaps immigration misdemeanors) and have not been sentenced by a court. This is why it is often called 'administrative detention'. Immigrants and asylum seekers are often detained in regular jails and prisons, but compared to regular inmates they have little access to the criminal justice system to fight their detention and/or deportation. The United Nations High Commissioner for Refugees defines detention as:

> confinement within a narrowly bounded or restricted location, including prisons, closed camps, detention facilities, or airport transit zones, where freedom of movement is substantially curtailed, and where the only opportunity to leave this limited area is to leave the territory.
>
> (United Nations 1993: 3)

But sometimes there is no opportunity to leave the territory. If their country of origin does not let them return or if there is no repatriation agreement, immigrants are theoretically condemned to indefinite detention.

Although US Immigration and Customs Enforcement (ICE) documented an average detention period of 37 days for 2007, individual immigrants and asylum seekers are often detained for months or even years, while their eligibility to remain in the US is being assessed. The aforementioned Amnesty International report (Amnesty International USA 2009), moreover, states that: '[i]ndividuals who have been ordered deported may languish in detention indefinitely if their home country is unwilling to accept their return or does not have diplomatic relations with the United States'.

Detention played only a minor role in US immigration policy through the first half of the twentieth century. And the practice of immigration detention was slowly wound down in the 1950s. In 1954, the closure of the Ellis Island immigration center marked the end of the last federal detention facility for immigrants (Simon 1998: 579). However, in the wake of a massive influx of undocumented migrants from both Cuba and Haiti, immigration detention was reintroduced. In the spring of 1980, almost 100,000 Cubans arrived on the Florida coast from the Cuban port city of Mariel, in what became known as the Mariel boatlift. About a year earlier, a steady flow of 'boatpeople' from Haiti brought 15,000 undocumented immigrants to Florida's shores. The Haitian immigrants in particular were commonly seen as 'economic' rather than 'political' refugees. The Immigration and Naturalization Service[5] (INS) responded to what was then widely seen as an immigration crisis by opening the Krome Detention Center outside Miami in 1981 (Simon 1998: 579). As Reagan's Attorney General, William French Smith (cited in Dunn 1996: 46), put it, 'Detention of aliens seeking asylum was necessary to discourage people like the Haitians from setting sail in the first place.' This policy of deterrence is still firmly entrenched today (Dow 2004: 7–9).

The 1980s and 1990s saw a massive expansion of the detention regime, as immigration policy become more and more intertwined with the wars on crime and drugs. The 1986 Anti-Drug Abuse Act led to a massive increase of the prison population, which was mainly due to the stiff new mandatory sentences put in place by the Act. At the same time, the INS launched its Alien Criminal Apprehension Program (ACAP), 'which entailed devoting more resources to locating aliens doing time in prisons and jails in order to apprehend and deport them more efficiently' (Dow 2004: 163).

According to Jonathan Simon, the rise of immigration detention has targeted two particular 'risky' populations: first of all, the detention regime is aimed at so-called 'criminal aliens', 'defined as noncitizens whether or not they legally reside in the United States, who have committed certain specified categories of criminal offenses in the United States or have lied about their criminal record prior to immigration' (Simon 1988: 581). Up to the early 1980s, 'aliens' were only deportable for crimes of 'moral turpitude' and deportation could always be, and frequently was, waived by a state court. Throughout the 1980s and 1990s, a number of federal laws broadened the scope of the detention/deportation regime by lowering the threshold of criminality and abolishing state court waivers. Hence, today, both legal residents and undocumented immigrants are deportable and subject to 'mandatory detention', even for crimes considered mere misdemeanors by most states, and even when they have already served their criminal sentences (Amnesty International USA 2009; Dow 2004). The second target of the detention regime is the general flow of immigrants and asylum seekers into the United States. As noted above, the regime was reintroduced in response to large numbers of refugees from Cuba and Haiti, and was greatly expanded with the passage of the Illegal Immigration Reform and Responsibility Act in 1996. This Act mandated the increased use of detention against asylum seekers and gave immigration inspectors wide-ranging authority to deport asylum seekers through a process known as expedited removal (Dow 2004: 9). According to Matthew Sparke, through the Illegal Immigration Reform and Responsibility

Act, 'INS agents were freshly empowered as sovereign subjects – indeed, as quasi-sovereigns – able to make final decisions about admission' (Sparke 2006: 170).

After the attacks on 11 September 2001, thousands of suspected terrorists and terrorist sympathizers were picked up and detained and/or deported. Exact numbers are hard to come by, because then Attorney General Ashcroft sought not only to control the flow of people, but also the flow of information.

The detention/deportation of immigrants suspected of having terrorist ties became the domestic equivalent of other more widely publicized detention and removal programs. The military detention center at Guantánamo Bay was used to spatially incapacitate, and keep in legal limbo, so-called unlawful combatants; while the so-called Extraordinary Rendition Program[6] was devised to ship terror suspects to secret detention facilities or authoritarian states that are less queasy about the use of harsh interrogation techniques. One critic even went as far as to suggest that extraordinary rendition amounts to the 'outsourcing of torture' (Mayer 2005).

As immigration policy was harnessed to the fight against terrorism, the distinction between immigrants and terrorists became increasingly blurred. Indeed, immigration has become securitized (see Bigo 2002; Huysmans 2006). In a *Military Review* article, William S. Lind even equated immigration with fourth-generation warfare. He warned that '[i]n Fourth Generation war, invasion by immigration can be at least as dangerous as invasion by a state army' (Lind 2004: 13). He further contended that:

> America, with a closed political system (regardless of which party wins, the Establishment remains in power and nothing really changes) and a poisonous ideology of multiculturalism, is a prime candidate for the homegrown variety of Fourth Generation war, which is by far the most dangerous kind.
>
> (Lind 2004: 14)

In 2008, a new immigration-control program called 'Secure Communities' was trialed in 14 jurisdictions across the United States. The goal of this program was to identify and deport 'criminal aliens' through improved biometrical information-sharing between local and federal enforcement agencies and prison authorities (Immigration and Customs Enforcement 2011b). According to the 'Secure Communities Standard Operating Procedures' (Immigration and Customs Enforcement 2009):

> The Secure Communities (SC) initiative makes the removal of aliens convicted of serious criminal offenses from the United States a priority. The SC initiative's three main objectives are: (1) identify aliens in federal, state, and local custody charged with or convicted of serious criminal offenses who are subject to removal and at large aliens convicted of a serious criminal offense who are subject to removal; (2) prioritize enforcement actions to ensure apprehension and removal of aliens convicted of serious criminal

offenses; and (3) transform criminal alien enforcement processes and systems to achieve lasting results.

(Immigration and Customs Enforcement 2009: 3)

Under the Obama administration, the program was greatly expanded. As of December 2011, 'Secure Communities' was operational in 2,027 jurisdictions in 44 states. The Immigration and Customs Enforcement Agency (ICE), moreover, expects the program to cover the entire nation by 2013 (Immigration and Customs Enforcement 2011a).

'Secure Communities' centers on the interoperability between FBI and ICE biometrical databases. Whenever somebody is booked into a jail or prison in one of the participating jurisdictions, their fingerprints are not just submitted to the FBI criminal database but also to ICE, which can then check them against their own immigration violation database. If there is a 'match', ICE can put a so-called 'detainer' on the person. This means that he or she can be held for an additional 48 hours, so that ICE agents can interview the person and decide whether or not to deport him or her. This often results in further periods of detention before the actual removal occurs (Immigration and Customs Enforcement 2011b). However, these so-called criminal aliens are not necessarily convicted of any crime, because 'illegal immigrants can be removed before the criminal case is complete' (Immigration and Customs Enforcement 2011c). According to the ICE website, 'There are a variety of reasons that the local arrest may not result in a criminal conviction. However, all of those removed are guilty of an immigration violation, and removed pursuant to the Immigration and Nationality Act' (Immigration and Customs Enforcement 2011c).

The decision whether or not to immediately deport a person is, moreover, based on the person's individual risk-profile which comprises his or her criminal history, previous immigration violations, etc. (Immigration and Customs Enforcement 2009, 2011c). In brief, 'Secure Communities' is a governmental program that targets the doubly illiberal population of 'criminal aliens' in the name of homeland security.

The violence of detention

The organization now known as ICE has long been one of the most secretive federal agencies (Dow 2004). For instance, a recent article in the *New York Times* (Bernstein 2010) reports that ICE has repeatedly sought to cover up deaths in detention. The *New York Times* and the American Civil Liberties Union (ACLU) have obtained documents showing that 107 immigrants have died in ICE custody since October 2003, after responsibility for what was formerly known as the INS was transferred to the Department of Homeland Security (Bernstein 2010).

A strikingly similar cover-up concerning the alleged suicide of three Guantánamo inmates on 9 June 2006 is reported in an article in *Harper's Magazine* (Horton 2010a). After a six-month investigation Scott Horton, an attorney

and international law expert, came to the conclusion that the deaths were probably the result of torture or even homicide. His article draws on the testimony of
former staff sergeant Steve Hickman, who was on night guard-duty when the
alleged suicides happened. Hickman's testimony is further corroborated by a
number of members of his unit. The deaths occurred in a secret facility within
the Guantánamo prison camp, called Camp No, which is run either by the CIA
or Joint Specials Operations Command (Horton 2010a). The day after the deaths
happened, the camp went into complete lockdown and then Guantánamo Bay
commander, Rear Admiral Harry Harris, declared the deaths suicides and even
went so far as to call them an 'act of asymmetrical warfare waged against us'. A
US Naval Criminal Investigative Service report supported Harris's account.
Moreover, the Justice Department failed to investigate the claims made by
whistleblower Steve Hickman, even after President Obama's inauguration
(Horton 2010a).

What is more, Horton (2010b) pointed out that 'when President Obama, on
January 22nd, issued an executive order shutting down the black sites, the secret
prisons, that order was very carefully tailored so that it was only CIA black sites
that were closed'. In 2010, there were still a number of 'black sites' in both
Afghanistan and Iraq, but instead of being operated by the CIA, they were now
run by Joint Special Operations Command (JSOC) (Horton 2010b). JSOC is a
highly secretive military agency that operates outside the regular military chain
of command. It forms part of the overall United States Special Operations
Command (USSOCOM) and is officially described as the 'joint headquarters
designed to study special operations requirements and techniques; ensure interoperability and equipment standardization; plan and conduct joint special operations exercises and training; and develop joint special operations tactics' (cited
in GlobalSecurity.org 2005). Yet, apparently JSOC not only plans covert operations, but also executes them.

The CIA and secretive military agencies such as JSOC, as well as the INS
and its successor agency ICE, have regularly sought to operate outside the confines of enforceable law in what is best described as a 'space of exception'.
Indeed, the examples above underscore the point that Guantánamo Bay, the
network of secret CIA- and JSOC-run prisons, the extraordinary rendition
system and the detention of immigrants, should be read as symptomatic of a
routine use of emergency powers against particular populations.

Today, immigrants are held 'in the INS's [now called ICE] service processing
centers; in local jails, in facilities owned by private prison companies and in
Bureau of Prisons facilities, including federal penitentiaries' (Dow 2004: 9).
Moreover, a recent article suggests that the Immigration and Customs Enforcement Agency (ICE) also detained undocumented immigrants 'in 186 unlisted
and unmarked subfield offices, many in suburban office parks or commercial
spaces revealing no information about their ICE tenants – nary a sign, a marked
car or even a US flag' (Stevens 2010: 13). This amounts to running a secret
detention regime. At a police and sheriffs conference in August 2008, James
Pendergraph, then executive director of ICE's Office of State and Local

Coordination, went as far as to boast about ICE's capacity to make people disappear, 'If you don't have enough evidence to charge someone criminally but you think he's illegal, we can make him disappear' (cited in Stevens 2010: 13). What is more, ICE frequently moves detainees from one facility to another – often in the middle of the night, without allowing them to contact either their families or their attorneys – by means of the federal interagency transportation network run by the Justice Prisoner and Alien Transportation System (JPATS) (Dow 2004: 27).

Immigrants are turned into quintessentially illiberal subjects who are, on the one hand, coercively excluded from liberal society and, on the other, are expected to function as cheap and (due to their legally precarious status) easily disciplined and exploited labor. Just as immigrants are both included in society through their economic exclusion and excluded from society through detention/ deportation, so detention centers also exist both within and outside state territory. Whilst they are located within the territory, they only serve to warehouse illiberal subjects in order to remove them from the territory (see Schinkel 2009).

Many commentators see undocumented immigrants as exemplars of what Agamben (1995) calls 'homines sacri', and detention centers as manifestations of Agamben's figure of the camp (see, for example, Edkins and Pin-Fat 2005; Schinkel 2009). For Agamben, the camp is not just a historical fact, but also 'the hidden matrix and *nomos* of the political space in which we are still living' (Agamben 1995: 166):

> *The camp is the space that is opened when the state of exception begins to become the rule.* In the camp, the state of exception, which was essentially a temporary suspension of the rule of law on the basis of a factual state of danger, is now given a permanent spatial arrangement, which as such nevertheless remains outside the normal order.
>
> (Agamben 2005: 169 original emphasis)

Agamben observes that:

> [in] the system of the nation state, the so-called sacred and inalienable rights of man show themselves to lack every protection and reality at the moment in which they can no longer take the form of rights belonging to citizens of a state.
>
> (Agamben 2005: 126)

This observation nicely encapsulates the situation of immigrants and unlawful combatants. Since immigrants in general are non-citizens they enjoy far less rights than citizens. But so-called unlawful combatants and stateless immigrants enjoy almost no rights at all, and can be detained indefinitely.

Conclusion

Geographies of security seek not only to protect a national territory from foreign threats but also to secure an imaginary, predominately white middle-class, homeland from risky circulations that are both local and global. But such supposed security comes at a hefty price. Amy Kaplan (2003) notes that the very concept of homeland security renders the life of those who do not belong very insecure indeed:

> The notion of the homeland contributes to making the life of immigrants terribly insecure. It plays a role in policing and shoring up the boundaries between the domestic and the foreign. Yet it does this not simply by stopping foreigners at the borders, but by continually drawing those boundaries everywhere throughout the nation, between Americans who can somehow claim the United States as their native land, their birthright, and immigrants who look to homelands elsewhere, who can be rendered inexorably foreign.
>
> (Kaplan 2003: 87)

The same applies to those domestic as well as foreign spaces and populations that are held to pose a threat to the homeland. In attempting to pacify risky spaces and populations for the sake of (re)producing a liberal capitalist order, governmentalities of security ultimately lead to the increasing insecurity of the those spaces and populations. This is the often disavowed authoritarian and violent underbelly of liberalism that becomes manifest in prisons and detention facilities.

Yet, we should note that liberal authoritarianism and violence is not so much a case of American Exceptionalism, as an inherent part of liberalism's tendency to govern through freedom and the concomitant distinction between those that can be governed through the promotion of freedom and those that cannot. Historically, this is borne out by the distinction between European metropolises and colonial peripheries and, currently, by the fact that, in spite of some differences, the detention/deportation regime in place in the European Union is by no means more 'liberal' than the American one (see Schinkel 2009; Welch and Schuster 2005a, 2005b).

5   Organizing security

Dreams of omnipotence through omniscience

Both warfighting and policing rely on intelligence. In order to catch a criminal, their whereabouts have to be known; likewise, one has to know the location of enemy forces in order to destroy them. This may seem all too obvious, but the effective production and timely exploitation of intelligence is one of the key challenges facing both military and law-enforcement organizations. Armies and police forces strive to render their opponents as visible as possible, while trying to keep their own operations and capabilities invisible. French philosopher, Paul Virilio, has the following to say about the relationship between visibility and invisibility in contemporary war:

> Thus, alongside the 'war machine', there has always existed an ocular (and later optical and electro-optical) 'watching machine' capable of providing soldiers, and particularly commanders, with a visual perspective on the military action under way. [...] If what is perceived is already lost, it becomes necessary to invest in concealment what used to be invested in simple exploitation of one's available forces – hence the spontaneous generation of the new Stealth weapons.
>
> (Virilio 1989: 3–4)

Yet, armies and police forces not only try to keep their adversaries under constant surveillance, while trying to keep their own capabilities hidden from view, but sometimes also seek to exaggerate their capabilities in order to deter potential or actual opponents from committing crimes or launching military operations in the first place.

In fact, efforts to identify, track and target dangerous circulations are always contoured by complex interrelations between visibility and invisibility. And this has enormous consequences for the ways in which security is organized.

For quite a while now, the US armed forces have tried to couple a 'war machine' with a 'watching machine'. The Pentagon's concept of 'network centric warfare' (NCW), for instance, which first emerged in an article by Vice Admiral Arthur K. Cebrowski and John Gartska (1998), aims to attain and exploit so-called information superiority (see also Alberts *et al.* 1999; Department of Defense 2005; Dillon 2002). Information superiority is defined as 'a state that is achieved when a competitive advantage is derived from the ability to exploit a superior information position' (Alberts *et al.* 1999: 34). To put it simply, network-centric warfare is geared towards seeing and knowing more than the enemy as well as being able to rapidly and decisively act on that superior knowledge:

> We define NCW as an information superiority-enabled concept of operations that generates increased combat power by networking sensors, decision makers, and shooters to achieve shared awareness, increased speed of command, higher tempo of operations, greater lethality, increased survivability, and a degree of self-synchronization. In essence, NCW translates information superiority into combat power by effectively linking knowledgeable entities in the battlespace.
>
> (Alberts *et al.* 1999: 2)

Network centric warfare is marked by four interrelated themes:

1   A shift from individual platforms (tanks, bombers, battleships, etc.), to networked forces in order to increase information sharing.
2   A shift in focus from individual actors to information sharing amongst nodes in the military network, in order to 'enhance the quality of information and shared situational awareness'.
3   Shared situational awareness, in turn, is supposed to enable the overall military network to constantly adapt to changes in the battlespace.
4   Ultimately, this should lead to a dramatic improvement in 'mission effectiveness' (Command and Control Research Program 2009; see also Alberts *et al.* 1999; Department of Defense 2005; Dillon 2002).

The underlying assumption is that success in contemporary warfare pivots on producing timely and accurate information about the battlespace and on effectively managing the flows of this information. As Michael Dillon notes:

> Information has been embraced as the new principle of formation for all military systems, initiating a whole-scale re-thinking of the very basis of military organization, doctrine, force requirements, procurement policies, training and operational concepts. Military formations no longer simply rally around the flag, they form up, mutate and change around information networks.
>
> (Dillon 2002: 73)

In short, for proponents of network-centric warfare, omniscience can be translated into omnipotence through the perpetual (re)formation of the war machine around the imperatives of the watching machine.

Yet, some critics of network-centric warfare argue that since the concept focuses too much on technology, it ultimately fails to address questions concerning the ability of human decision-makers and organizations to process vast quantities of information under stress and to tight deadlines (see, for example, Mandeles 2005). The critique of Thomas X. Hammes (2006) goes even further. In his book on fourth-generation warfare, he contends that network-centric warfare and similar concepts are circumscribed by the dominant paradigm of conventional, firepower-centered, high-tech warfare and completely fail to ask the question as to what future warfare will actually look like. Drawing from a number of Pentagon publications[1] issued during the 1990s and early 2000s, Hammes succinctly summarizes the military's focus on technology as well as its failure to come to terms with the new fourth-generation reality of warfare:

> Essentially, DOD [Department of Defense] transformation guidance for the future ignores the success of 4GW in the last five decades. Instead, supposed future enemies will ignore the past and willingly fight America in a high-technology, fast-moving campaign that reinforces all our strengths while avoiding our weaknesses. Perhaps the most disturbing aspects of all these official publications are that they are so inwardly focused and that that focus is not open for discussion. It has already been defined. It is technology. These publications simply disregard any action taken by an intelligent, creative opponent to negate our technology. In fact, they seem to reduce the enemy to a series of inanimate targets to be serviced. He who services the most targets the fastest must win.
>
> (Hammes 2006: 9)

Things have, however, changed since the publication of Hammes' book in 2006. As we saw in Chapter 2, the United States is now widely held to be pitted against violent non-state actors who are organized along tribal and/or religious lines and who tend to hide and operate amongst civilian populations. Stephen Graham suggests that 'the institutional battles now being waged [...] over how to respond to counterinsurgency operations within large urban areas are amongst the most important within US military politics' (Graham 2010: 153; see also Hills 2004). Indeed, the complexity and chaos of cities is widely held to negate US dominance, because the density of the urban environment interferes with air- and space-based tracking and targeting capabilities. Moreover, the urban environment provides insurgents with plenty of opportunities to hide amongst the 'clutter of concealment' (Graham 2010: 154, 157–60):

> Opposition forces will camouflage themselves in the background noise of the urban environment. Within the urban environment, it is not the weapon itself but rather the city which maximizes or mutes an arm's effectiveness. In claustrophobic alleys and urban canyons, civilians are impossible to control or characterize as friendly or not. Weapons hidden beneath a cloak, in a child's carriage, or rolled in a carpet, can get past security personnel undetected.
>
> (Van Konynenberg 1997; cited in Graham 2010: 159)

In fact, what RAND analysts call the 'urbanization of insurgency' has led to a flurry of research programs geared towards reclaiming the dreams of omnipotence through technologically-driven omniscience by rendering cities of the global south transparent to the US military gaze (Taw and Hoffman 1994; Graham 2010: 160).

But alongside attempts to lift the 'fog of war' of insurgency through the application of technology, US military strategy has also shifted towards population- and culture-centric warfare (see Department of the Army 2007; Gompert *et al.* 2009; Kilcullen 2005; Long 2006; McFate 2005a, 2005b; McFate and Jackson 2005, 2006; Nagl 2005; Ucko 2009: 174). This has led to a growing demand for human knowledge about societies, in and from which dangerous circulations are held to emerge. Fighting enemies that operate amongst civilian populations is now considered to require thorough knowledge, not only about one's opponents but also about all aspects of the societies in which they operate. The 2010 'Quadrennial Defense Review' (Department of Defense 2010a: 52) thus views the development of 'foreign language skills and regional and cultural knowledge' as a pivotal component of future US warfighting capabilities. Moreover, the current *Counterinsurgency Field Manual* (Department of the Army 2007: 40) also stresses again and again that 'successful conduct of COIN operations depends on thoroughly understanding the society and culture within which they are being conducted'.

The 'watching machine' is thus not only supposed to monitor and track targets but also to provide information about foreign societies and cultures in order to identify dangerous circulations; while the 'war machine' is no longer merely concerned with servicing inanimate targets, but also with providing services for civilian populations. This adds a whole new layer of complexity to the ways in which the armed forces are organized.

A changing security environment

The challenges faced by security organizations become even more daunting when we look at the supposed fusion of crime and war, and the concomitant erosion of the boundaries between domestic and international security. Recent events across the border in Mexico have spurred discussions about the rise of non-state warmaking entities and the increasing fusion of crime and conflict. In a special issue of *Small Wars and Insurgencies* specifically dedicated to the Mexican 'drug wars', most of the contributors assert that the Mexican state is facing a 'narco-insurgency' that to a certain extent has already spilled over into the United States (see, above all, Bunker 2010; Bunker and Sullivan 2010). Mexico is said to be embroiled in a violent conflict amongst cartels as well as between cartels and state security agencies, and may ultimately turn into a failed state (see Bunker 2010; Bunker and Sullivan 2010; United States Joint Forces Command 2008). Law enforcement expert Robert Bunker argues that Mexican:

> gang, cartel, and mercenary groups can translate a higher percentage of their economies (group revenue) into 'criminal-insurgent' activities based on

diplomacy-corruption (plata) and military-like (plomo) capabilities than the nation-state 'law enforcement' capabilities needed to counter them.

(Bunker 2010: 21)

This has led to a situation in which the Mexican state 'is no longer able to govern entire sectors within its sovereign territory and, instead, these areas have been taken by a narco-insurgency and lost to the influence of criminal-based entities'. Moreover, Bunker goes as far as to contend that Mexico's 'narco-insurgency' can quickly spread and mutate into a threat of hemispheric proportions (Bunker 2010: 10, 21–6). On 8 September 2010, US Secretary of State Hillary Clinton (2010) made similar claims about the situation in Mexico – much to the chagrin of Mexican officials: 'This is a really tough challenge. And these drug cartels are now showing more and more indices of insurgency; all of a sudden, car bombs show up which weren't there before'.

According to Bunker (2010: 24) and other security pundits, the Mexican 'narco-insurgency' is merely one front in a global conflict 'over humanity's new forms of social and political organization' – that is to say, a multi-scalar conflict over the maintenance of a global liberal order and the interstate system in which this order is embedded (see also van Creveld 2008; Sullivan 2005; Manwaring 2005, 2008; Bunker and Sullivan 2010; Bunker and Begert 2008). The current global threat environment and the corresponding shifts in conflict have been framed in numerous ways. But most discourses of (in)security now share a concern over violent non-state actors that are held to pose a severe threat to the global liberal order.

Violent non-state actors

According to John Sullivan, states are now threatened by a variety of 'privatized violent actors' (Sullivan 2005: 74–6; see also Mair 2003), which he breaks down into five ideal types: *terrorists*, *criminals* (organized crime), *rebels* (insurgents), *warlords* (and pirates), and *private military companies (PMCs)*.

Robert Cassidy (2006a: 10), moreover, argues that such non-state actors rely on a mode of warfare that differs markedly from the conventional, state-centric Western way of war (see also Peters 1994; Tucker 1998; Keegan 1993). In contrast to the Western style of war, which is mainly fought by professional soldiers, 'Eastern warfare' is supposed to center on a warrior ethos:

> These barbaric warriors, unlike Western warrior soldiers, do not play by the rules, do not respect conventions, and do not comply with unpleasant orders. Warriors have always been around, but with the rise of professional soldieries their importance was eclipsed. Now, thanks to the confluence of fragmented former empires, stateless insurgents, and the diminution of the warrior ethos in parts of the postmodern West, the warrior thug has returned to the fore, with more financing, arms, and brutality than since the fourteenth century.

(Cassidy 2006a: 10)

By constructing an overly simplistic dichotomy between Eastern and Western warfare, Cassidy merely echoes the overdetermined division between safe, liberal, Western forms of life and their dangerous illiberal and often 'Orientalized Others'. Cassidy thus racializes asymmetrical warfare.

In Chapter 2, we have already encountered Hammes's much more measured concept of fourth-generation warfare (4GW), which is defined as an 'evolved form of insurgency' that 'uses all available networks – political, economic, social, and military – to convince the enemy's political decision makers that their strategic goals are either unachievable or too costly for the perceived benefit' (Hammes 2006: 2). The idea of fourth-generation warfare closely resembles what RAND Corporation researchers John Arquilla and David Ronfeldt (2001) call 'netwar' (see also Arquilla and Ronfeldt 1993, 2000; Arquilla 2007). Netwar is defined as 'an emerging mode of conflict (and crime) at societal levels, short of traditional military warfare, in which the protagonists use network forms of organization and related doctrines, strategies, and technologies attuned to the information age' (Arquilla and Ronfeldt 2001: 6). A network form of organization and a capacity for 'swarming' are two defining features of this mode of conflict. Netwar can be waged by a vast spectrum of actors, ranging from transnational terrorist groups and crime syndicates to NGO activists. In terms of their organizational design netwar actors exhibit flat, decentralized and non-hierarchical structures based on dense communications (Arquilla and Ronfeldt 2001: 9). These organizational structures tend to make netwar actors highly adaptable and flexible.

Netwarriors are, moreover, able to engage in 'swarming', which Arquilla and Ronfeldt define as follows:

> Swarming is a seemingly amorphous, but deliberately structured, co-ordinated, strategic way to strike from all directions at a particular point or points, by means of a sustainable pulsing of force and/or fire, close-in as well as from stand-off positions. This notion of 'force and/or fire' may be literal in the case of military or police operations but metaphorical in the case of NGO activists, who may, for example, be blocking city intersections or emitting volleys of emails and faxes.
>
> (Arquilla and Ronfeldt 2001: 12)

Despite Arquilla and Ronfeldt's distinction between 'good' and 'bad' forms of netwar, they tend to conflate protest, crime and terrorism. By highlighting what emerging forms of protest and crime have in common and by lumping these phenomena together, they intimate that protest, crime and terrorism all require an increasingly militarized response – or rather a response that cuts across the traditional police/military divide. They argue that the spread of netwar poses a challenge to the nation-state insofar as netwar protagonists operate in the interstices of institutional remits, 'striking where lines of authority crisscross and the operational paradigms of politicians, officials, soldiers, police officers and related actors get fuzzy and clash' (Arquilla and Ronfeldt 2001: 14).

In the last chapter we saw that governmentalities of security seek to control dangerous circulations by configuring territorial space in such a way that risk-free flows can be facilitated and risky flows can be interdicted. Divisions between risky and risk-free circulations are thus enacted and inscribed in space through geographies of security. However, the management of circulations across both domestic and international space also requires a reconfiguration of what we may call organizational space. Borders between different organizations serve to control the flow of information, personnel and resources between them and thereby help maintain an organizational identity (see Marx 2005). Security agencies are particularly reluctant to share their information with other organizations. In order to maintain operational security and make sure that their methods and informants do not become compromised, these organizations tend to surround themselves with a number of institutional firewalls. On the other hand, intelligence that is not acted upon risks becoming outdated and useless. And the aforementioned distinction between licit and illicit flows can only be made on the basis of solid intelligence that is also acted upon.

Since practitioners of netwar exploit the institutional boundaries between security agencies, most notably the distinction between the police and the military, states face a considerable challenge. Arquilla and Ronfeldt (2001) therefore suggest that states themselves adopt certain features of netwar. Above all, they recommend effective interagency approaches:

> It is not necessary, desirable, or even possible to replace all hierarchies with networks in governments. Rather, the challenge will be to blend these two forms skillfully, while retaining enough core authority to encourage and enforce adherence to networked processes. By creating effective hybrids, governments may become better prepared to confront the new threats and challenges emerging in the information age, whether generated by ethnonationalists, terrorists, militias, criminals, or other actors.
>
> (Arquilla and Ronfeldt 2001: 16)

Indeed, what Arquilla and Ronfeldt prescribe is that states should adopt some of the organizational features of their opponents in order to combat them more effectively. Ironically, the celebrated democratic potential of distributed networks can thus lead to a strengthening of state power and may ultimately result in de-democratization. For, in democratic states, the clearly delineated fields of activity of specific agencies ensure at least a modicum of democratic accountability. The creation of interagency ties and the concomitant erosion of the boundaries between police and military operations can, however, severely undermine this accountability.

Confronted with what is now widely problematized as an increasingly complex and uncertain global security conjuncture, security organizations are supposed to become able to produce more accurate and timely information about present and future threats, communicate this information more efficiently and speedily, and better adapt to a constantly changing threat environment. In short, security organizations must become genuine 'learning organizations' capable of (re)channeling flows of information through organizational space, in order to produce actionable intelligence on, and preemptively intervene in, a complex and constantly changing environment. This ultimately comes down to designing both inter-organizational and extra-organizational boundaries in such a way that flows of information can be effectively managed, while maintaining enough secrecy and operational security so that intelligence sources and intelligence-gathering methods are not put at risk. And this redesign of security organizations is now supposed to increasingly cut across the traditional boundaries between the police and the military, private and public actors and civilian and military domains.

The militarization of policing and the 'policization' of warfighting

In Chapter 3, we saw that the erosion of the boundaries between the military and the police has many facets: technology transfers from the military to the police, the proliferation of paramilitary units, the increasing role of military advisors in counter-narcotics, riot control and counterterrorism, and above all, domestic applications of military doctrine (see Balko 2006; Kraska and Kappeler 1997; Kraska 1999; Parenti 1999; Stamper 2011; Warren 2002, 2004). Political scientist, Robert Warren (2002, 2004) for instance, shows that during the 1990s, urban space became increasingly militarized through the formulation and application of MOUT (Military Operations on Urbanized Terrain) doctrine. Traditionally, urban warfare has not played a very prominent role in US military strategy: air strikes, rather than the deployment of ground troops, were regarded as the prime weapon against enemy cities. As Stephen Graham (2007: 121) puts it: 'Cities were seen as targets, not battlefields'. Since the end of the Cold War, however, the US military stepped up its efforts to design effective MOUT doctrine. RAND Corporation researcher, Sean J. A. Edwards gives three particular reasons for the increasing likelihood of US involvement in urban warfare: 'continued urbanization and population growth; a new, post-Cold War U.S. focus on support and stability operations; and a number of new political and technological incentives for U.S. adversaries to resort to urban warfare' (Edwards 2000: xi). Indeed, the last 20 years saw a massive proliferation of publications on urban warfare, with cities of the global south emerging as current and future battlefields (see Davis 2006). Originally, MOUT doctrine was meant to be applied solely outside the United States and other industrialized nations, but events such as the 1992 L.A. Riots, the 1993 World Trade Center and the 1995 Oklahoma City bombings spurred discussions about possible domestic urban operations. At an urban warfare conference in 2000, one speaker, for instance, maintained that MOUT doctrine 'will prove invaluable when we have to conduct urban operations in the streets of America' (cited in Warren 2004: 219).

According to Robert Warren (2004), the highly militarized response to protests against a World Trade Organization meeting in Seattle in November 1999 has provided a blueprint for domestic crowd control. Indeed, military doctrine and tactics are now regularly used to police crowds at protests, demonstrations or large-scale sports events (see Democracy Now 2011a; Graham 2010, 2012; Stamper 2011; Warren 2002, 2004). The emergency powers and paramilitary practices that are now routinely used for purposes of domestic crowd control include restricting the movement of people in cities; locking down and barricading at-risk sites; using non-lethal, and sometimes even lethal, weapons; but also 'preemptive arrests; harassing independent media; deploying military personnel and air and naval defense; and conflating political protesters with violent anarchists and terrorists to delegitimize them' (Warren 2004: 222).

Efforts to pacify at-risk and risky spaces and populations in America's cities have been informed by military doctrine since the 1960s. As previously noted, community policing, which is now widely touted as an effective approach to policing risk societies, bears a close resemblance to counterinsurgency-style pacification. The author of a 2006 RAND report *On 'Other War': Lessons from Five Decades of RAND Counterinsurgency Research* (Long 2006) draws very explicit parallels between community policing and counterinsurgency-style pacification:

> [P]acification is best thought of as a massively enhanced version of the 'community policing' technique that emerged in the 1970s (encouraged in part by RAND research). Community policing is centered on a broad concept of problem solving by law enforcement officers working in an area that is well-defined and limited in scale, with sensitivity to geographic, ethnic, and other boundaries. Patrol officers form a bond of trust with local residents, who get to know them as more than a uniform. The police work with local groups, businesses, churches, and the like to address the concerns and problems of the neighborhood.
>
> (Long 2006: 53)

Counterinsurgency-style pacification is here cast as community policing for special cases, or as the author puts it, as 'an expansion of this concept to include greater development and security assistance' (Long 2006: 53). Expeditionary counterinsurgency is thus viewed as a mere expansion of domestic policing. Or rather, policing at-risk and risky populations and spaces in the homeland is just a more or less toned-down variant of counterinsurgency-style pacification.

Both community policing and counterinsurgency operations also place similar demands on organizational design, because the identification and targeting of criminal and/or insurgent activities amongst everyday circulations requires close ties between a variety of different organizations. In both fields, knowledge about the local populace is seen as a prerequisite for gaining their trust and cooperation. Moreover, in order to enable staff, who interact with local communities on an almost daily basis, to make their voices heard and to allow for a more lateral flow of information, both community policing and counterinsurgency are said to require more decentralized command and control structures:

One of the most important specific aspects of organizational change relevant to community policing is a flattened organizational structure. Community policing departments are often less hierarchical, supporting management's dispersion of decision-making authority to the lowest organizational level and holding those individuals accountable for the outcomes.

(Scheider and Chapman 2003)

Local commanders have the best grasp of their situations. Under mission command, they are given access to or control of the resources needed to produce timely intelligence, conduct effective tactical operations, and manage IO [Information Operations] and civil-military operations. Thus, effective COIN operations are decentralized, and higher commanders owe it to their subordinates to push as many capabilities as possible down to their level.

(Department of the Army 2007: 47)

Both domestic and expeditionary efforts to pacify at-risk and risky spaces and populations thus call for less hierarchical command and control structures, and for close collaboration with community-level organizations.

The privatization of security

The supposed need for pacification campaigns has also created massive business opportunities for private security providers. P. W. Singer argues that the rise of what he calls Privatized Military Firms (PMFs) is primarily related to the end of the Cold War and its 'effect on the supply and demand of military services [which] created a "security gap" that the private market rushed to fill' (Singer 2003: 49). The end of the Cold War led to the massive demobilization of armies across the world, and has thus created a vast pool of unemployed soldiers, while also flooding the global arms market with decommissioned weaponry. The end of the Cold War, moreover, led to the decline in external support for states in the global south, many of which imploded and plunged into violent conflicts that were now no longer controlled and managed by the Cold War balance of power. So PMFs could draw from a vast supply of trained soldiers and decommissioned weaponry, and found ready employment in an increasing number of conflicts around the world.

But Singer (2003: 64) also mentions two longer-term trends that influenced the rise of PMFs: First, as we have already seen, the nature of warfare has changed considerably over the last few decades; it is now marked by growing levels of diversification, technologization, civilianization and criminalization:

In 'high-intensity warfare,' that is, the large-scale military operations carried out by western powers, combat has become more technological and more civilianized. At the same time, in the majority of conflicts carried out in the developing world, it has become messier and criminalized. What is interesting is that both involve the monopoly of power being taken away from public professionals.

(Singer 2003: 64)

The diversification, technologization, civilianization and criminalization of contemporary war have opened up very lucrative business opportunities for private security entrepreneurs across the whole spectrum of contemporary warfare.

Second, a neoliberal rationality of privatization and deregulation, aimed at imposing market relations upon many sectors previously controlled by the state, also played a major part in the rise of PMFs:

> In the United States in the 1990s, hundreds of billions of dollars worth of formerly governmental activities were taken over by private companies. This move was pushed from the left by the Clinton administration's 'national performance review' and from the right by the pro-privatization Republican majority in Congress. That political trends toward privatization would then cross into the realm of security should not be so shocking. In fact, many of the first targets of privatization were national defense manufacturing industries.

(Singer 2003: 67)

Patterns of privatization, combined with rapid economic globalization, have also led many private corporations to set up shop in unstable regions. In line with a neoliberal rationality based on the professed superiority of market solutions, this has in turn increased the demand for private protection (see also Duffield 1999).

The privatized military industry has seen steady growth over the last decade. For instance, US war efforts in Afghanistan and Iraq have relied heavily on military contractors who provide services icluding logistics, intelligence-gathering, guarding embassies and host-nation dignitaries, training Iraqi and Afghan police and military forces as well as assisting in drone strikes and targeted assassinations of suspected militants (see Scahill 2009a, 2009b, 2009c, 2010).

PMFs are not at all capital-intensive. The labor input is relatively cheap because the industry primarily employs ex-soldiers whose expensive training has already been paid for by the state. Moreover, PMFs frequently function as virtual companies. This means that they do not maintain many permanent employees, but rather hire them on an ad-hoc basis. But the most significant advantage of the industry lies in the fact that the outsourcing of military services creates structural dependencies that grow each time a client decides to farm out particular military functions. By outsourcing vital security functions, 'the client loses expertise and capabilities and becomes more reliant on the PMF' (Singer 2003: 78). As a consequence, the global market in military services is booming:

> Thus, the privatized military industry is still in its relative infancy, but it appears that the true boom lies shortly ahead. The reason for this optimism is that the potential client base is only now being tapped, meaning that the market is far from saturated.

(Singer 2003: 79–80)

Although state militaries will remain the primary users of private military services, multinational corporations, Non-Governmental Organizations and Inter-Governmental Organizations are also likely to employ the services of PMFs, if they are not already doing so (Singer 2003: 80–3; see also Duffield 1999).

The trend towards privatization is also manifest in the domestic sphere. In the US, the private security industry has seen tremendous growth since the 1990s. According to Singer, 'The amount spent on private security is 73 percent higher than that spent in the public sphere, and three times as many persons are employed in private forces as in official law enforcement agencies'. The privatization of domestic security ranges from local rent-a-cops to privately-run prisons, and even includes the deployment of private paramilitary forces to guard nuclear weapons facilities (Singer 2003: 69). Above all, private security providers play an increasingly prominent role in guarding the internal borders that separate the white, middle-class, suburban homeland from risky spaces and populations. Singer quotes a defense analyst who summarizes this trend very succinctly, 'You already see more and more people hiring private security firms to keep the Third World away from suburban America' (cited in Singer 2003: 69).

Singer (2003: 73), however, argues that PMFs 'are far different from the security guards that work at local shopping malls':

> The identifying marker of the privatized military industry is their offer of services traditionally falling within the domain of national militaries (combat operations, strategic planning, military training, intelligence, military logistics, and information warfare). [...] From offering training in special-forces tactics to providing armed units designed to repel guerrilla attacks, both their services and their impact is definitively military in nature.
>
> (Singer 2003: 73)

Yet, given the increasing blurring between policing and warfighting, the difference between domestic private security providers and what Singer calls privatized military firms is not as clear-cut as he makes it out to be. Of course, there is a considerable difference between a private rent-a-cop at the local shopping mall and the member of a private special operations team working in a foreign war zone, just as there is a considerable difference between a beat cop and a SWAT operative. Yet we should not mistake this difference for any fundamental distinction between domestic public safety and foreign defense. This difference rather reflects different positions on an overall transversal continuum of insecurity and risk: the more insecure an environment is held to be, the more militarized are those responsible for securing it.

The most famous (or rather infamous) private military contractor is the North Carolina-based company Blackwater, which, following a series of scandals has been re-branded as XE Services. Founded in 1997 by two ex-Navy SEALs, Eric Prince and Al Clark, XE (pronounced *zi*) provides a wide range of services to the State Department, the Pentagon, the CIA and a number of domestic police departments. The company consists of an opaque web of divisions, subsidiaries and spin-offs that offer products ranging from military and police training to intelligence-gathering, logistics, target acquisition, and tactical teams (Scahill 2007).

Shortly after New Orleans was struck by Hurricane Katrina, on 29 August 2005, Blackwater personnel arrived in the city. Under a contract with the Department of Homeland Security, Blackwater was deployed to protect government facilities in a city that was widely held to be in the grip of complete chaos. The company officially claimed that it was part of the general disaster relief effort. But investigative journalist Jeremy Scahill (2007: 389) shows that 'its men on the ground told a different story':

> Some patrolled the streets in SUVs with tinted windows and the Blackwater logo splashed on the back; others sped around the French Quarter in an unmarked car with no license plates. They wore khaki uniforms, wraparound sunglasses, beige or black military boots, and had Blackwater company IDs strapped to their bulging arms. All of them were heavily armed – some with M-4 automatic weapons, capable of firing nine hundred rounds per minute, or shotguns. [...] In an hour-long conversation in the French Quarter, four Blackwater troops characterized their work as 'securing neighborhoods' and 'confronting criminals.' They all carried M-4 assault weapons and had guns strapped to their legs. Their flak jackets were covered with pouches for extra ammunition. 'This is a totally new thing to have guys like us working CONUS [Continental United States],' another Blackwater contractor said. 'We're much better equipped to deal with the situation in Iraq'.
>
> (Scahill 2007: 389–90)

The deployment of heavily-armed Blackwater contractors to hurricane-stricken New Orleans, chimes with a general trend towards the 'securitization' of disaster relief efforts (see Fassin and Pandolfi 2010; Calhoun 2010). This is based on the assumption that the collapse of governmental structures in the aftermath of natural disasters poses a significant security problem, which is said to manifest itself in widespread looting. Those left behind after Hurricane Katrina were widely viewed as a threat 'to be contained, targeted and addressed as a means of protecting the property of the largely white suburban and exurban populations who had escaped in their own cars' (Graham 2010: 25; see also Graham 2006). Reporting from New Orleans, Christian Parenti wrote:

> It seems the rescue effort is turning into an urban war game: An imaginary domestic version of the total victory that eludes America in Baghdad will be imposed here, on New Orleans. It's almost as if the Tigris – rather than the Mississippi – had flooded the city. The place feels like a sick theme park – Macho World – where cops, mercenaries, journalists and weird volunteers of all sorts are playing out a relatively safe version of their militaristic fantasies about Armageddon and the cleansing iron fist.
>
> (Parenti 2005: 1)

Initial reports about a steadily deteriorating security situation and hordes of black youths looting and shooting their way across a devastated city, have since proved to be exaggerations at best and outright lies at worst (see Solnit 2010). Yet, by scrambling to secure both private property and government facilities, Blackwater and other private contractors stood to profit massively from unfounded concerns over security (see Scahill 2007: 396). According to Jeremy Scahill (2007: 395), 'By June 2006, [Blackwater] had raked in some $73 million from its Katrina work for the government – about $243,000 a day'.

But it was in Iraq where Blackwater was at its most controversial. On 16 September 2007, Blackwater employees opened fire at Baghdad's Nisour Square, killing 17 Iraqi civilians, including women and children. According to statements by 12 Iraqi witnesses, a number of Iraqi investigators and an American official, the contractors (who were escorting a convoy of US State Department vehicles) acted disproportionately and opened fire without provocation (see Glanz and Rubin 2007; Scahill 2007: 1–9; Singer 2007). The *New York Times* reported that:

> [a] deadly cascade of events began when a single bullet apparently fired by a Blackwater guard killed an Iraqi man whose weight probably remained on the accelerator and propelled the car forward as the passenger, the man's mother, clutched him and screamed. The car continued to roll toward the convoy, which responded with an intense barrage of gunfire in several directions, striking Iraqis who were desperately trying to flee.
>
> (Glanz and Rubin 2007: 1)

Jeremy Scahill (2007, 2009a, 2009b, 2010) documents a number of deadly incidents involving Blackwater employees. But what became known as the 'Nisour Square Massacre', propelled the hitherto virtually unknown company into global notoriety and caused a major diplomatic spat between the United States and the Iraqi regime it had put in place after the 2003 invasion.

Losing hearts and minds

Many defense analysts have since argued that the use of private contractors can severely undermine counterinsurgency efforts to win the hearts and minds of the local population (Singer 2007). When Blackwater founder Eric Prince was summoned to testify before Congress on 2 October 2007, he was confronted with mounting evidence that Blackwater's behavior in Iraq had hampered the US counterinsurgency campaign:

> 'It does appear from some of the evidence here that Blackwater and other companies sometimes, at least conduct their missions in ways that lead exactly in the opposite direction that General Petraeus wants to go,' Democrat John Tierney told Prince. 'That doesn't mean you're not fulfilling your contractual obligations.' Tierney then read numerous comments from U.S. military officials and counterinsurgency experts raising questions about Blackwater's

actions having a blowback effect on official U.S. troops. Tierney quoted Army Col. Peter Mansoor: 'If they push traffic off the roads or if they shoot up a car that looks suspicious, they may be operating within their contract, but it is to the detriment of the mission, which is to bring people over to our side.' He quoted retired Army officer Ralph Peters: 'Armed contractors do harm COIN – counterinsurgency efforts. Just ask the troops in Iraq'.

(Scahill 2007: 23)

In fact, the use of private military contractors in counterinsurgency campaigns seems to militate against the current field manual's demands for establishing 'unity of command':

Where possible, COIN leaders achieve unity of command by establishing and maintaining the formal command or support relationships discussed in FM 3–0. Unity of command should extend to all military forces supporting a host nation. The ultimate objective of these arrangements is for military forces, police, and other security forces to establish effective control while attaining a monopoly on the legitimate use of violence within the society. Command and control of all U.S. Government organizations engaged in a COIN mission should be exercised by a single leader through a formal command and control system.

(Department of the Army 2007: 56)

Even if they are under contract to US government organizations, armed civilian contractors cannot be easily integrated into the formal command and control system because, in practice, private contractors are more likely to obey their corporate bosses than military leaders. What is more, the very existence of armed civilians may ultimately undermine the objective of 'attaining a monopoly on the legitimate use of violence' (Department of the Army 2007: 56). Indeed, they can be detrimental to counterinsurgency's overarching goal of establishing 'effective governance by a legitimate government' (Department of the Army 2007: 37). Armed contractors may also set a precedent for local warlords and militias who sometimes seek to re-brand themselves as security firms. This has happened in Afghanistan, where local security contractors, which are alleged to have ties with warlords and even the Taliban, have been on the rise since the Taliban was toppled (see Roston 2009, 2010; Tierney 2010).

The *Counterinsurgency Field Manual* does acknowledge the need for establishing proper control over private contractors:

When under contract to the United States, contractors should behave as an extension of the organizations or agencies for which they work. Commanders should identify contractors operating in their AO [Area of Operations] and determine the nature of their contract, existing accountability mechanisms, and appropriate coordination relationships.

(Department of the Army 2007: 65)

Yet, as the scandal surrounding the so-called Host Nation Trucking (HNT) contract shows, the trend towards farming out both military and non-military activities is often marked by a complete lack of transparency, accountability and oversight, which can severely hamper counterinsurgency efforts. Indeed, Afghan corruption seems to be at least partly fueled by the US-led counterinsurgency campaign, as funds earmarked for reconstruction and development end up filling the coffers of corrupt Afghan politicians and businessmen (see Wilder 2009a, 2009b; Laquement 2010; Choharis and Gavrilis 2010). Or worse still, US and NATO monies sometimes wind up in the war chests of warlords or even the Taliban. This seems to have been the case with the HNT contract, which has been investigated by US Congress (see Roston 2009, 2010; Tierney 2010). In order to free up military personnel for counterinsurgency and combat duties, the Department of Defense has outsourced its Afghan supply chain to local logistics firms and made them responsible for protecting their cargo. Roughly 70 percent of all resources provided to US troops in the field are thus supplied through the HNT contract, which is worth about $2.16 billion. Under the contract, local truckers are responsible for their own security on one of the most challenging supply chains in the history of warfare. Therefore, private logistics providers frequently pay protection money to local strongmen. According to the report of the House Subcommittee on National Security and Foreign Affairs (Tierney 2010: 3), 'This arrangement has fueled a vast protection racket run by a shadowy network of warlords, strongmen, commanders, corrupt Afghan officials, and perhaps others'.

On the one hand, empowering both public and private host-nation actors to act on their own behalf and in their own interests, is perfectly in line with the precepts of counterinsurgency doctrine. Outsourcing certain activities to host-nation actors can play an important role in establishing a viable private sector and hence in furthering economic development. This may indeed bolster the overall legitimacy of the campaign, insofar as foreign forces can present themselves as boosting the economic wellbeing of the local population. On the other hand, handing out lucrative contracts without proper oversight may fuel corruption and ultimately undermine the political legitimacy of both the host-nation government and the overall counterinsurgency campaign.

The outsourcing of central state functions to private corporations, is indicative of what Foucault called 'the introduction of economy into political practice' (Foucault 1991b: 92). In fact, an economic rationality has entered into the provision of security. Private actors have become a sort of security enabler for government agencies, because they appear to offer a number of clear advantages. First of all, the use of private contractors can be more cost-effective than the deployment of state security personnel. Yet it can also be more expensive, especially when the political fallout of scandals is factored in. Second, the deployment of PMFs involves less political risk because, for the time being, military casualties elicit much stronger public reactions than the deaths of private contractors. Third, the use of PMFs leaves a lighter footprint and affords government agencies a higher degree of plausible deniability. Given the current budgetary constraints, we will thus likely see an expansion of private involvement, especially in small-scale covert operations that are supposed to stay off the public radar.

On the other hand, due to poor oversight and the absence of accountability, the actions of private contractors can, and do, severely hamper counterinsurgency efforts. Events in both Iraq and Afghanistan have shown that contractors rarely act within the confines of a general unity of effort and that their actions even undermine the overall objectives of a campaign. Moreover, the fact that the goals of PMFs are sometimes at odds with the overall military mission is compounded by the, often fraught, relations between military and civilian governmental agencies. Above all, the increasing use of military contractors has created a downward spiral of dependency, because outsourcing erodes more and more skill sets within the US armed forces and this, in turn, requires even more outsourcing:

> In conclusion, the U.S. government is in a terrible predicament today when it comes to private military contractors and counterinsurgency operations, and it is a predicament of its own making. It has over-outsourced to the point that it is unable to imagine carrying out its most basic operations without them. At the same time, the use of contractors appears to be hampering efforts to actually win the counterinsurgency campaign on multiple levels.
>
> (Singer 2007: 17–18)

Plugging cultural knowledge into the US military

According to the 2006 *Counterinsurgency Field Manual* (Department of the Army 2007: 36), success in counterinsurgency rests on differentiating between an active minority supporting the insurgency, an active minority opposing it, and a neutral or passive majority that can swing either way. The main objective of the so-called population-centered, or 'hearts and minds' variant of counterinsurgency, is to convince the passive majority to throw in their lot with the counterinsurgents. This is supposed to be achieved through the provision of security and development backed by a consistent information strategy (Department of the Army 2007). Moreover, in adopting a *divide and rule* approach, counterinsurgent forces also frequently aim to map and exploit already existing social antagonisms. Thus, counterinsurgents seek to make more or less finely grained distinctions within the targeted population between those that can be won over through various non-lethal ways and those hardliners that need to be taken out by force.

In order to make these distinctions and calibrate the use of firepower accordingly, soldiers and marines are said to require a thorough understanding of a host-nation's culture and society. Apart from acting as soldiers, policemen, relief workers, and spin doctors, soldiers and marines are also supposed to perform as amateur social scientists, capable of producing knowledge not only about the insurgents, but also about all aspects of the society in which they operate (Department of the Army 2007). In brief, the targeted population has to be made intelligible so that it can be targeted more discriminately.

Historically, foreign populations have not figured very prominently in US military strategy. The US armed forces have always prioritized the paradigm of conventional war while ignoring types of conflicts that are fought in the midst of foreign populations (see Cassidy 2006a: 99–126). However, as noted in Chapter 2, almost 60 years ago President John F. Kennedy tried to shift the focus of US military strategy from conventional firepower-centered to counterinsurgency warfare – a strategic realignment in which the social sciences also played a major part.

When counterinsurgency doctrine experienced a renaissance at the beginning of the twenty-first century, a combination of security and development directed at foreign populations remained at the heart of the doctrine (Clemis 2009). However, as insurgencies are now no longer viewed as the outcome of a super-power struggle for hegemony in the Third World, but rather as conflicts along ethnic, cultural and religious fault lines, there has emerged a growing need for more contextual analyses of specific cultures, tribes, religious sects, etc (Clemis 2009; Heuser 2007). When, after two initially successful invasions, the United States saw itself challenged by tribal insurgencies in both Iraq and Afghanistan, and when US armed forces became aware that they lacked the most fundamental linguistic and cultural tools for understanding the operational environment, so-called 'culture-centric warfare' seemed to offer a solution to their woes (see Clemis 2009; Kipp *et al.* 2006; McFate 2004, 2005a, 2005b; McFate and Jackson 2005, 2006; Renzi 2006). And social scientists, most notably anthropologists, were quickly heralded as invaluable tools for designing and implementing military programs aimed at pacifying recalcitrant non-Western populations.

In *Military Review*, anthropologist Montgomery McFate (2005a: 28) bemoaned what she saw as anthropology's 'brutal process of self-flagellation' and demanded that it should once again shoulder its responsibilities as a 'warfighting discipline':

> Once called 'the handmaiden of colonialism,' anthropology has had a long and fruitful relationship with various elements of national power, which ended suddenly following the Vietnam War. The strange story of anthropology's birth as a warfighting discipline, and its sudden plunge into the abyss of postmodernism, is intertwined with the U.S. failure in Vietnam. The curious and conspicuous lack of anthropology in the national-security arena since the Vietnam War has had grave consequences for countering the insurgency in Iraq, particularly because political policy and military operations based on partial and incomplete knowledge are often worse than none at all.
> (McFate 2005a: 24)

From 2005, the US military has actively sought to plug socio-cultural knowledge into both doctrine and force structure. The new *Counterinsurgency Field*

Manual, whose chapter on intelligence was co-authored by McFate, is peppered with terms, such as 'social networks', 'roles and statuses', 'social norms', 'taboo', 'culture', 'identity', 'narratives', 'myths', 'beliefs', 'ideologies', etc. which one would hardly suspect to find in a military field manual (Department of the Army 2007: 79–135). What is more, the manual even seems to espouse a mild form of cultural relativism. It explicitly seeks to enlighten soldiers and marines that:

> American ideas of what is 'normal' or 'rational' are not universal. To the contrary, members of other societies often have different notions of ration- ality, appropriate behavior, level of religious devotion, and norms concern- ing gender. Thus, what may appear abnormal or strange to an external observer may appear as self-evidently normal to a group member. For this reason, counterinsurgents – especially commanders, planners, and small- unit leaders – should strive to avoid imposing their ideals of normalcy on a foreign cultural problem.
>
> (Department of the Army 2007: 27)

Due to the identified need for specific socio-cultural knowledge in counterinsur- gency, and the conspicuous lack thereof in campaigns in Iraq and Afghanistan, the military establishment decided to launch the so-called Human Terrain System (HTS) in 2005:

> This system is being specifically designed to address cultural awareness shortcomings at the operational and tactical levels by giving brigade com- manders an organic capability to help understand and deal with 'human terrain' – the social, ethnographic, cultural, economic, and political elements of the people among whom a force is operating.
>
> (Kipp *et al.* 2006: 9)

The Human Terrain System seeks to embed five- to nine-person Human Terrain Teams (HTTs) into military units. According to the 'Human Terrain Handbook' (Finney 2008: 2), these teams are 'composed of individuals with social science and operational backgrounds that are deployed with tactical and operational mil- itary units to assist in bringing knowledge about the local population into a coherent analytical framework'. The first HTT was fielded in Afghanistan in 2006. Several other teams were deployed to both Afghanistan and Iraq in 2007 (Ucko 2009). They combine social network analysis with the geo-spatial analysis of human and physical geography, in order to identify and track elements of the populations, so that they can be targeted either by kinetic or non-kinetic means, depending on their level of dangerousness.

But plugging cultural knowledge into the military machine is by no means uncontroversial, and the military-social science machine does not always operate smoothly. Anthropologist David Price (2007, 2009) disclosed that the definitions of the basic social science terms provided in the manual's chapter on intelligence are based on what he calls 'pilfered scholarship'. He contends that the manual 'borrowed' terms, phrases, and even entire paragraphs from a large number of unacknowledged sources and that the 'effect of such non-attributions is devastating to the manual's academic integrity [...] – claims that the military hoped to bolster with the republication of the Counterinsurgency Field Manual at a top academic press'[2] (Price 2009: 64).

What is more, a number of anthropologists quickly began to criticize what they saw as 'the weaponization of anthropology' (see Feldman 2009; González 2007, 2009a, 2009b; González *et al.* 2009; Sahlins 2009). In 2007, a group of anthropologists set up the Network of Concerned Anthropologists to provide a common platform for collective action against the creeping militarization of their discipline (González *et al.* 2009). Moreover, in October 2009, the American Anthropological Association's Commission on the Engagement of Anthropology with the US Security and Intelligence Communities (CEAUSSIC) issued its 'Report on the Army's Human Terrain System Proof of Concept Program' which came to the conclusion that:

> [i]t appears clear that the exigencies of military units operating in a battle space while actively at war are fundamentally incompatible with the Code of Ethics of the AAA, but also with any sort of responsible effort of social scientific research. So far, three HTT social scientists have in fact been killed, a stark reminder that battle zones are first and foremost battle zones and not research spaces. We suggest that anthropology needs to understand its relationship to the military and to such goals as the 'cultural preparation of the environment' from a different vantage point of collaboration.
>
> (Albro *et al.* 2009: 53)

On the other hand, some military personnel have not been particularly eager to have social scientists participate in counterinsurgency operations either. One of the most vocal critics of the new fad of culture-centric warfare is retired Army Lieutenant Colonel Ralph Peters, who in his influential article, 'The Human Terrain of Urban Operations' (2000), argued that future conflicts will increasingly be fought amongst the populations of major cities in the global south. Although he agrees on the important role of socio-cultural knowledge in counterinsurgency operations, Peters suggests that too strong a focus on cultural issues may place undue restrictions on the use of firepower. What is more, he goes as far as to state that 'it's immoral to throw away the lives of our troops in repeated attempts to validate somebody's doctoral thesis' (Peters 2007: 1). Ironically, while some social scientists argue that their engagement with the military can restrict the indiscriminate use of firepower and thereby both improve and humanize unconventional modes of warfare, Peters maintains that the participation of social scientists could severely hamper the ability of the armed forces to do what they do best, namely warfighting (for the 'humanization' argument see Kilcullen 2007a; McFate 2007; Sewall 2007).

Yet, the actual on-the-ground production and deployment of socio-cultural expertise has also proved highly problematic. David Ucko (2009: 165), for instance, dismisses the Human Terrain System as a stopgap measure intended to provide a quick and cheap fix to 'the absence of an equivalent capability within the existing force structure'. This stopgap measure may further erode these capabilities and thus create a general structural dependency feeding the insatiable demand for more outsourcing. Ucko therefore demands that the military should rather seek to improve the linguistic and cultural abilities of its own specialist civil affairs personnel. He further notes that Human Terrain Teams had to be 'placed at the brigade level rather than at the battalion or company level, where they might have had a greater impact', because the military was unable to find enough 'qualified civilian volunteers'. Last, but not least, he states that teams deployed in Afghanistan and Iraq were often poorly trained, and thus produced knowledge of 'varied quality' and that 'the managerial practices and protocols governing their use and activity in a war zone were at times undefined' (Ucko 2009: 166).

Despite all efforts to boost cultural knowledge and awareness within the US military, US soldiers on the ground sometimes still displayed breathtaking cultural insensitivity and ignorance. For instance, in February 2012, local Afghan workers discovered that US soldiers were incinerating copies of the Qur'an alongside waste documents. This sparked massive protests and violence across Afghanistan, and may have been a severe blow to US and NATO's struggle for the hearts and minds of the Afghan people (Graham-Harrison 2012; North 2012).

In spite of the contested and contradictory nature of the counterinsurgency-related production and deployment of socio-cultural knowledge, there clearly is an ongoing attempt to strategically inscribe civilian socio-cultural expertise into the military exercise of power and violence. The overall strategic role of this knowledge in counterinsurgency operations is to differentiate between elements of host-nation populations so that they can be targeted more effectively. According to proponents of the HTS, the human terrain maps produced by HTTs are only meant to be used for benign ends, such as tailoring social programs to particular groups and areas, or providing the host-nation government with demographic data. But as the information is fed into a central database that can also be accessed by Special Forces, the CIA, or host-nation security services, the human terrain maps could also be put to more iniquitous uses (see Kipp *et al.* 2006; González 2009b).

In counterinsurgency, socio-cultural knowledge is ultimately deployed to sort members of targeted populations into risk slots, so that both lethal and non-lethal modes of targeting can be adapted accordingly. As Marshall Sahlins puts it:

> The principal role of academics in the service of counterinsurgency is to develop the human intelligence (HUMINT) that will allow a triage between those elements of the population to be attacked (or assassinated) and those it would be better not to – in brief, sophisticated targeting.
>
> (Sahlins 2009: vi)

Socio-cultural knowledge thus serves the biopolitical purpose of facilitating a triage within populations that have already been singled out by the 'global triage of liberal rule' (Dillon and Reid 2009). The objective of biopolitics, namely promoting species-life and securing it from threats arising from within species-life itself, ultimately entails 'modes of discrimination exercised at the level of the biological life of individuals and populations which are explicitly as well as implicitly racialized' (Dillon and Reid 2009: 133). However, liberal biopolitics cannot openly profess to privilege some aspects of the species over others on the basis of race:

> Liberal biopolitics had therefore somehow to elide the ways in which all biopolitically driven regimes, including those at one time of liberal imperialism itself, are disposed to favour some aspects of the species over others, as a necessary consequence of seeking to promote the life of the species.
>
> (Dillon and Reid 2009: 49)

In other words, liberal governance can no longer triage between 'safe' and 'dangerous' species-life purely on racial grounds. Yet, the notion of culture, even if it remains implicitly racialized, is not nearly as politically suspect as the category of race. As Brad Evans (2010: 427) observes, 'Racism is not what it used to be. Cultural fitness has now replaced biological heritage to contour the new lines of political struggle'.

Some critics have remarked that the deployment of cultural knowledge in counterinsurgency operations is based on a new form of Orientalism (see Gregory 2008; Feldman 2009; Kienscherf 2010). Greg Feldman (2009: 92), for instance, holds that insofar as counterinsurgency 'divides occupied peoples into either modern or regressive' elements and 'depicts those living in geopolitically sensitive areas as in need of a U.S. presence to pacify and develop their countries', it ultimately constitutes an Orientalist, and hence also neo-imperial, project. In its classical sense, Edward Said's (1979) term 'Orientalism' denotes the complex and ambiguous historical relationship between the production of knowledge about the Orient and the imperial project of establishing occidental control over spaces and populations construed as Oriental. McFate's (2005a: 24) demand that anthropology should reclaim its erstwhile role as a 'warfighting discipline' thus amounts to saying that the discipline of anthropology should once again turn into a machine for the production of Orientalist discourse – something anthropologists have struggled against for many decades.

Insofar as it constantly (re)produces not only the dividing line between 'us' and 'them' but also seeks to place 'them' on a scale of dangerousness, knowledge about the 'Other' becomes just one element in a complex machine geared towards establishing governmental control over foreign populations:

> The emphasis on cultural difference – the attempt to hold the Other at a distance while claiming to cross the interpretive divide – produces a diagram in which violence has its origins in 'their' space, which the cultural turn endlessly partitions through its obsessive preoccupation with ethno-sectarian

division, while the impulse to understand is confined to 'our' space, which is constructed as open, unitary, and generous.

(Gregory 2008: 11)

The military deployment of cultural knowledge thus juxtaposes an Orientalist space, which is construed as illiberal, violent and crisscrossed by multiple divisions, with an occidental space that is by default liberal, unitary, and peaceful. Moreover, as we saw in Chapter 4, through the establishment of geographies of security, the conceptual production and mapping of endlessly partitioned, internally divided and inherently dangerous spaces and populations bleeds into the actual physical division of these spaces and populations (see also Gregory 2010).

Conclusion

One of the primary functions, if not the primary function, of the state (namely the provision of security) is currently undergoing dramatic changes. In response to problematizations of threat that increasingly cluster around notions of the proliferation of violent non-state actors in ungoverned spaces and an increasing fusion of war and crime, state security agencies are trying to transform themselves into networked entities that increasingly cut across many traditional boundaries. Indeed, in the current global security conjuncture, the separation between internal public safety and external defense, held to be a hallmark of the modern state, is widely viewed as irrelevant. Hence, the boundaries between security organizations are being eroded to improve the management of information flows not only within and between separate organizational spaces, but also between security organizations and their environment, and to ultimately translate improved information capabilities into more effective and, above all, more targeted preemptive action.

Military technologies are being deployed along the US–Mexico border to monitor, track and target the flows of drugs and immigrants. Paramilitary units, modeled on and trained by military special operations forces, are operating both along the border and in domestic urban 'hot spots' to quickly interdict risky circulations. At the same time, pacification and stabilization activities in the midst of civilian populations, at home and abroad, require increasingly specialized skill sets that exceed the capabilities of the armed forces. As a consequence, both the police and the military are scrambling to fill these gaps with civilian contractors of various stripes, ranging from private security personnel to social scientists.

This complex concatenation of military and police organizations, public and private agencies and civilian and military actors, generates a host of contradictions. Above all, different organizations do not always subscribe to ideas of 'unity of effort' and are not that easily subsumed under a 'unity of command'. In spite of ever more intricate linkages, individual organizations often seek to maintain their own distinct identities and hence often wind up working against, as much as with one another. In short, despite all efforts to transform security organizations from bureaucracies to networks, the dream of omnipotence through omniscience will remain as elusive as ever.

6 Legitimizing security

Introduction

Governmentalities of security invariably entail attempts to legitimize their design and deployment. They produce their own legitimacy. Governmentalities of security are designed and deployed in response to what is now increasingly problematized as 'global circulations of insecurity'. Above all, governmentalities of security tend to take the form of domestic *and* expeditionary programs of pacification that target spaces and populations from which risky circulations are held to emerge, as well as spaces and populations deemed to be put at risk by dangerous circulations. Both at-risk and risky spaces and populations are thus cast as the primary referent objects of governmentalities of security. Contemporary liberal governmentalities of security, moreover, legitimize themselves in moral terms. They purport to protect and promote 'good' circulations and secure vulnerable populations, while interdicting 'bad' circulations and eliminating evil-doers, such as terrorists, insurgents, war criminals, drug traffickers, etc.

Governmentalities of security are, moreover, an exercise in state-making, as they seek to constantly produce and reproduce the hallmark of sovereignty, namely 'the *monopoly of the legitimate use of physical force* within a given territory' (Weber 1919: 1 original emphasis). Domestically, sovereignty and the overall legitimacy of the US state are reproduced through a combination of para-militarized policing and increasingly '*restrictive* welfare measures' (Wacquant 2009b: 83 original emphasis). Internationally, the US seeks to establish sovereignty and legitimacy for governments (following its intervention in, or establishment of, regime change) through a combination of para-militarized security and development efforts. We should note that in both cases, security tends to be the predominant force. But neither the sovereignty of the United States, nor the sovereignty of governments targeted by interventions, are ends in themselves. Attempts to (re)produce sovereignty, rather, serve to stabilize a global liberal capitalist order as well as the corresponding interstate system.

The biopolitics of human (in)security

The post-Cold War period has witnessed a conceptual shift from traditional state-centered security to so-called human security (United Nations 2003; see also De Larrinaga and Doucet 2008; Duffield 2008, 2010; Hettne 2010; Makaremi 2010; Manwaring 2005; Stern and Ojendal 2010; Voelkner 2010). Human security is broadly defined as a system of processes for protecting 'people from critical (severe) and pervasive (widespread) threats and situations' and for 'creating political, social, environmental, economic, military and cultural systems that together give people the building blocks of survival, livelihood and dignity' (United Nations 2003: 4). Whereas in the post-World War II era discourses of security centered primarily on the territorial integrity of sovereign states, the discourse of human security takes people, or even human life itself, as its referent object.

Today, there are numerous conceptualizations of human security. Some of them seek to address a broad range of economic, social, political and cultural insecurities, while others are limited to the elemental insecurities of violence and abuse (Buzan and Hansen 2009: 202–5; Voelkner 2010: 134). Yet, generally speaking, human security constitutes a response to problematizations of insecurity that cluster around global circulations of threat. As the United Nations Commission on Human Security puts it:

> Today's global flows of goods, services, finance, people and images spotlight the many interlinkages in the security of all people. We share a planet, a biosphere, a technological arsenal, a social fabric. The security of one person, one community, one nation rests on the decisions of many others – sometimes fortuitously, sometimes precariously.
>
> (United Nations 2003: 2)

Human insecurities are viewed as 'bad' globalized circulations that need to be interdicted so that 'good' global circulations can be facilitated. Moreover, global circulations of insecurity, such as terrorism, crime and drugs, are increasingly said to originate in 'dysfunctional states that have formal sovereignty but lack the capacities to safeguard the welfare of their citizens and thereby put the stability of other states at risk' (Chandler 2010: 5).

Mary Kaldor (Kaldor and Beebe 2010: 37), one of the most vociferous proponents of human security, states that '"bad neighborhoods," like the Horn of Africa, the Upper Nile, the Middle East, the Caucasus, and Central Asia', provide breeding grounds for violence which could spread into the world's 'good neighborhoods', 'through refugees and displaced persons, through transnational criminal activities; and through polarizing activities' (see also Glasius and Kaldor 2005; Kaldor 1999). There is a considerable overlap between Kaldor's global distribution of 'bad neighborhoods' and the Pentagon's 'arc of instability' that stretches from Africa through the Middle East all the way to Central and Southeast Asia. Thomas Barnett's (2004) idea of the 'Gap' is even more extensive and also includes wide swathes of Central America and the Caribbean. Yet the fundamental logic remains the same: a division of the globe into an integrated metropolitan system of stable states, on the one hand, and a kind of peripheral global borderlands marked by failed and failing states, violence, crime and corruption, on the other (see Dalby 2007). What is more, 'bad' circulations held to originate from these global borderlands are regarded as major threats not only to individuals and local communities but also to Western states and even the whole world. In fact, a human security agenda is now frequently presented as a 'response to the narrative of global chaos' (Makaremi 2010: 108).

> A number of contemporary global crises have their roots in forty to sixty fragile countries. As these states have experienced prolonged conflict or misrule, networks of criminality, violence, and terror have solidified, providing an ever expanding platform that threatens the entire globe.
> (Ghani and Lockhart 2008: 23; cited in Chandler 2010: 5)

What is problematized by human security is not so much state sovereignty per se, but the sovereignty and autonomy of particular illiberal states. What is more, despite its critique of narrow state-centric approaches to security, the human security agenda remains tied to the state, because the state is viewed 'as vital for providing the public goods that constitute human security' (Duffield 2008: 149; see also Voelkner 2010). Indeed, according to the United Nations Commission on Human Security (United Nations 2003: 2), the 'state remains the fundamental purveyor of security'. If states fail to provide for the security of their people or even become a threat to their own populations, they may turn into targets of intervention. The logic of human security may thus be deployed to legitimize intervention in the internal affairs of nominally sovereign states. Indeed, the portrayal of mainly non-Western populations as helpless victims in need of protection from their own incapable or even predatory governments constitutes the rationale behind growing demands for 'coercive external management of crisis situations by Western institutions' (Chandler 2006b: 40). This, in turn, allows powerful Western states to frame their military interventions as humanitarian, ethical and ultimately as legitimate. In this respect, the discourse of human security resembles human rights discourse. Human security builds on the human rights framework and seeks to expand it beyond its narrowly legalistic confines. However, despite the conceptual differences surrounding the notion of law, both the human security and the human rights agenda ought to be read as attempts to secure humanity (by externalizing rationalities and practices of (re)producing internal order) from threats that emerge from within itself. Discourses of human rights and human security thus call for global police operations in the name of humanity. Appeals to the rights and the security of global society serve to deflect criticism of intervention, because '[t]he consensus rules that anything done in the name of human rights is right, and any criticism is not just wrong but tantamount to supporting murder, torture and rape' (Sellars 1999: 11; cited in Chandler 2006b). Yet actual efforts to police global society are, in practice, nothing but more or less coercive (and sometimes outright military) interventions in the affairs of nominally sovereign states that, more often than not, are located in the post-colonial global south. As a consequence, interventions in the name of human rights and/or security often bear a close resemblance to imperial police operations which were, after all, also frequently mounted with the professed aim of protecting and developing local populations.

The rights and the security of human beings are supposed to trump state sovereignty – states forfeit their claims to sovereignty when they are no longer able to protect their populations. Yet, the discourse of human rights and human security does not so much mark the end of state sovereignty per se, as the demise of the principle of equal sovereignty. After the end of World War I, Western policy-makers sought to shift international relations from the doctrine of 'might is right' towards international law, 'in an attempt to contain the threat of war between the Great Powers as well as anticipated anticolonial revolt' (Chandler 2006b: 124). Efforts to base the relations between states on international law instead of military power and dominance required all states to be treated as equal members of the international community. After the end of World War II, sovereign equality became enshrined in the United Nations Charter, which unequivocally states that '[t]he Organization is based on the principle of the sovereign equality of all its Members' (United Nations 1945). However, international law, sovereign equality and the principle of non-intervention have come under attack from human rights and security advocates as well as from powerful Western states, most notably the United States. Indeed, demands for the global enforcement of human rights and human security are fundamentally at odds with the principles of sovereign equality and non-intervention:

> The crucial issue, then, is to face up to the necessity which enforcing these principles would impose to breach systematically the principles of sovereignty and non-intervention. [...] The global society perspective, therefore, has an ideological significance which is ultimately opposed to that of international society.
>
> (Shaw 1994: 134–35; cited in Chandler 2006b: 128)

Today, the principle of sovereignty is widely viewed as providing a legal cover, 'a cloak of impunity', for human rights violators (Urquhart 2000; cited in Chandler 2006b: 128–29). Yet, although many human rights theorists now claim to be involved in a 'struggle against sovereignty', they merely question the sovereignty of non-Western states – 'states that are judged to lack Western democratic credentials' (Robertson 1999: xviii; cited in Chandler 2006b: 129). Geoffrey Robertson makes a strong case for the abolition of the principle of sovereign equality:

> The reality is that states are not equal. There can be no 'dignity' or 'respect' when statehood is an attribute of the governments which presently rule Iraq and Cuba and Libya and North Korea and Somalia and Serbia and the Sudan.
>
> (Robertson 1999: 129; cited in Chandler 2006b: 129)

Interestingly, the majority of states (whose claim to statehood Robertson puts into question) are post-colonial states. This intimates that the attack on sovereign equality amounts to a quasi-imperial project that seeks to undermine the sovereignty of weak states while bolstering that of strong ones. In fact, Max Boot even goes so far as to declare:

> [M]ost of the world's nations do not have Westphalian legitimacy in the first place. They are highly artificial entities, mostly created by Western officials in the twentieth century. [...] There is no compelling reason, other than an unthinking respect for the status quo, that the West should feel bound to the boundaries it created in the past. There is even less reason why the West should recognize the right of those who seize power within those borders to do whatever they want.
>
> (Boot 2000: 129)

Ironically, the discourses of human rights and security may ultimately mark a return to the old principle of 'might is right' insofar as powerful states, or coalitions of powerful states, can legitimize interventions in weak states by claiming that the latter pose a threat both to their own populations and the entire globe. Indeed, these interventions can and often do occur, even if they are not sanctioned by international law; and are widely held to be legitimate even if they are not legal. The practice of militarized humanitarian interventionism, moreover, exacerbates existing inequalities between developed and developing nations. As Chandler puts it, '[t]he more the concept of human rights militarism is allowed to gain legitimacy, the greater the inequalities become between the enforcing states and the rest of the world' (Chandler 2006b: 187).

What is at stake in the discourse of human security is the defense of global society against forms of deviant, abnormal life. The logic of human security is deeply biopolitical in that it seeks to promote certain forms of species-life and protect them from threats emerging from within species-life itself (De Larrinaga and Doucet 2008; Duffield 2008). Human security is, in fact, based on a distinction 'between the tolerant and right-honoring zone of liberal civil society's "inside" and the intolerant, right-violating "outside" against which it perpetually wars' (Medovoi 2007: 62). What is more, securing humanity from 'the intolerant, right-violating "outside"' that, in fact, emerges from within humanity 'prepares the ground for the emergence of a sovereign power that claims the globe as its field of operation' (De Larrinaga and Doucet 2008: 534). If global sovereignty ever emerged, it would be unlikely to flow from any single state, but would rather be something akin to Hardt and Negri's (2000: xii) 'Empire' – 'a decentered and deterritorializing apparatus of rule that progressively incorporates the entire global realm within its open expanding frontiers'. Although there is a clear tendency towards global sovereignty, 'Empire' is not so much a fact as a possibility that has been opened up by increasing efforts to make a biopolitical distinction between 'good' and 'bad' circulations on a planetary scale. What is more important than the possibility of global sovereignty is thus the fact that the biopolitics of human security can provide powerful states with the apparent, albeit often contested, legitimacy to *provisionally* execute global sovereignty in the name of all of humanity.

If certain states are unable to provide security for their populations, and fail to protect (or even violate) their citizens' human rights, other more powerful states are held to have a moral duty to intervene, protect the targeted population and develop the host-nation's capacities so that it may eventually be able to secure its own population. In practice, the discourse of human security both legitimizes *and* entails not so much a form of 'Empire' as a biopolitical mode of imperialism. This form of imperialism is as much driven by limited national geopolitical ambitions as by the unlimited aim of securing humanity from its own inherent threats. What is important to note, is that the biopolitical goal of securing global humanity is much more than an ideological smokescreen for national geopolitical interests. Rather, in a global security environment thought to be marked by the multi-scalar circulation of threats, biopolitics and geopolitics are increasingly viewed as completely entangled. Securing the US homeland means pacifying the globe. But pacifying the globe takes forever, and is ultimately impossible. Since its objectives are boundless, biopolitical imperialism's campaigns of pacification thus tend to be both spatially and temporally indeterminate.

Biopolitical pacification

Counterinsurgency doctrine forms a concrete program of biopolitical imperialism insofar as it is presented as a therapy for particular pathologies of insecurity and danger within delimited areas. Counterinsurgency doctrine is held up as an effective remedy for the global spread of violence and instability. General David Petraeus, one of the chief architects of US counterinsurgency strategy, told Mary Kaldor that counterinsurgency and human security are pretty much the same because both cluster around the 'two key principles' of providing security and vital services to the population and separating 'the reconcilables from the irreconcilables' (cited in Kaldor and Beebe 2010: 68). Although she comes out in support of the US military's move towards counterinsurgency, Mary Kaldor maintains that significant differences remain between counterinsurgency and human security:

> In counterinsurgency, human security, or population security, is a tactic, not a strategy. The end goal is not the security of Afghans or Iraqis – that is a means to an end. The end goal is the defeat of America's enemies, a point that General Petraeus and others frequently repeat.
>
> (Kaldor and Beebe 2010: 73)

In effect, Kaldor argues that counterinsurgency is not biopolitical enough because it remains an instrument of US geo-strategy.

Yet, most proponents of counterinsurgency doctrine suggest that in the face of global circulations of violence and instability, US geo-strategic goals largely overlap with the pursuit of human security. For instance, in the 'Introduction to the University of Chicago Press Edition' of the *Counterinsurgency Field Manual*, Sarah Sewall (2007: xlii), director of Harvard's Carr Human Rights Center, argues that with the disappearance of the stabilizing framework of the Cold War, the major security challenge for the United States now consists in 'buttressing multiple failing state structures to legitimize the interstate system'. This requires (re)building the capacities of fledgling states through a combination of military and civilian means:

> U.S. unwillingness to govern other nations is, in this account, a fatal national flaw. The field manual stresses the importance of effectively employing nonmilitary power. It is not a responsibility that can be left to a beleaguered host nation. Counterinsurgents must harness the ordinary administrative functions to the fight, providing personnel, resources, and expertise.
>
> (Sewall 2007: xxxviii)

Hence, the United States has to get into the business of governing nations that are deemed unable to govern themselves.

At present, so-called ungoverned spaces – also often referred to as 'failed', 'failing', or 'weak' states – and their unruly populations, are amongst some of the most significant referent objects of both human security and US national security (Kilcullen 2005, 2009; Sewall 2007). The 2002 US National Security Strategy (United States Government 2002: 1) declared that 'America is now less threatened by conquering states than we are by failing ones'. US Secretary of State Condoleezza Rice (2005) stated that ungoverned spaces posed a greater risk to US national security than traditional 'Great Power' rivalry:

> Today [...] the greatest threats to our security are defined more by the dynamics within weak and failing states than by the borders between strong and aggressive ones. Weak and failing states serve as global pathways that facilitate the spread of pandemics, the movement of criminals and terrorists, and the proliferation of the world's most dangerous weapons. Our experience of this new world leads us to conclude that the fundamental character of regimes matters more today than the international distribution of power.

The 2010 'Quadrennial Defense Review' (QDR) (Department of Defense 2010a: 32), which will be the chief blueprint for US military planning and budgetary allocations for the next couple of years, asserts that 'the changing international environment will continue to put pressure on the modern state system, likely increasing the frequency and severity of the challenges associated with chronically fragile states'. In this environment, the US military can no longer simply rely on its formidable conventional arsenal but must develop the capabilities to mount a series of low intensity operations across the global south:

> The wars we are fighting today and assessments of the future security environment together demand that the United States retain and enhance a

whole-of-government capability to succeed in large-scale counterinsurgency (COIN), stability, and counterterrorism (CT) operations in environments ranging from densely populated urban areas and mega-cities, to remote mountains, deserts, jungles, and littoral regions. [...] Accordingly, the U.S. Armed Forces will continue to require capabilities to create a secure environment in fragile states in support of local authorities and, if necessary, to support civil authorities in providing essential government services, restoring emergency infrastructure, and supplying humanitarian relief.

(Department of Defense 2010a: 43)

Counterinsurgency is viewed as particularly significant in this context, because it cuts across the divide between civilian assistance and military intervention and is designed to address especially problematic cases of state failure. Indeed, as previously noted, counterinsurgency combines what Duffield (2010) calls 'the liberal way of development' with what Dillon and Reid (2009) call 'the liberal way of war'. The liberal way of development seeks to foster 'adaptive patterns of household and communal self-reliance in the global south' (Duffield 2010: 55–6, 68), while the liberal way of war (Dillon and Reid 2009) is aimed at securing global life itself from those 'patterns of self-reliance' that are viewed as a threat to global (liberal) life.

Counterinsurgency is supposed to rid particular regions of 'forms of radical autonomy and emergence [that] are deemed to be a risk to the system as a whole', while establishing and promoting modes of 'adaptive self-reliance' that are viewed as safe (Duffield 2010: 68). The latter task is often relegated to Nongovernmental and Intergovernmental Organizations (NGOs and IGOs) that are expected to operate under the military umbrella of what the *Counterinsurgency Field Manual* (Department of the Army 2007: 56–8) calls 'unity of effort':

All organizations contributing to a COIN operation should strive, or be persuaded to strive, for maximum unity of effort. Informed, strong leadership forms the foundation for achieving it. Leadership in this area focuses on the central problems affecting the local populace. A clear understanding of the desired end state should infuse all efforts, regardless of the agencies or individuals charged with their execution.

(Department of the Army 2007: 57)

Counterinsurgency's reliance on a deeply biopolitical problematization of security and danger, as well as its commitment to eradicating risky forms of life while promoting safe ones, is best illustrated by the writings of Former Senior Counterinsurgency Advisor to General Petraeus, David Kilcullen. He argues that international terrorist groups, most notably al-Qaeda, 'opportunistically exploit existing breakdowns in the rule of law, poor governance, or pre-existing conflict. Terrorist infection is thus part of the social pathology of broader societal breakdown, state weakness, and humanitarian crisis' (Kilcullen 2009: 35). Although Kilcullen (2009) makes a number of points about terrorism in general, much of his discussion centers on al-Qaeda, which he considers to be at the heart of a globalized insurgency against the West (Kilcullen 2005; see also Kilcullen 2010). What he calls the 'accidental guerrilla syndrome' (2009) sets in with the 'infection' of ungoverned spaces by al-Qaeda. It then proceeds to the 'contagion phase', in which al-Qaeda uses these safe havens to spread propaganda and launch terrorist attacks. In the 'intervention phase' external forces, most likely Western powers led by the United States, decide to take military action. This leads to the so-called 'rejection phase', in which the local population rejects the foreign intervention and enters into alliance with al-Qaeda (Kilcullen 2009: 35–8):

> Again, I use medical analogy advisedly here. The *rejection* phase looks a lot like a social version of an immune response in which the body rejects the intrusion of a foreign object, even one (such as a pin in a broken bone or a stent in a blocked blood vessel) that serves an ultimately beneficial purpose.
> (Kilcullen 2009: 38)

Kilcullen's use of medical tropes is highly illustrative. Indeed, processes of state failure are often presented in terms of pathology (McFalls 2010: 318). For medical tropes shift the terms of debate, from the political to the ultimately technocratic terrain of fixing social pathologies through the outside intervention of agents whose superior expertise and superior values are taken for granted (McFalls 2010: 318–19). Any debate about whether or not to intervene in the first place is thereby effectively forestalled – the only debate that is still possible is one about the 'how' of intervention. This also holds true for Kilcullen's (2009) *The Accidental Guerrilla*. Even though Kilcullen acknowledges that outside interventions may well exacerbate processes of radicalization, he fails to question the utility of intervention per se. He merely concerns himself with devising politico-military instruments that do not feed the 'accidental guerrilla syndrome'. In fact, Kilcullen takes the necessity of outside intervention for granted, because he assumes that something has to be done about 'terrorist infection'. However, he does not ask the question as to whether or not the initial 'infection' might have been an 'immune response' to earlier Western interference.

Kilcullen's arguments about the growth of cancerous terror cells in ungoverned spaces are profoundly biopolitical. In his analysis of the 'technical armature and rhetoric of counterinsurgency' in Iraq, Derek Gregory (2010: 277) suggests that '[t]he emphasis on danger, or on what Foucault called "dangerousness", is vital to the development of a martial biopolitics'. What Gregory calls 'martial biopolitics' is nothing but the sum total of practices of pacification aimed at securing humanity from threats that emanate from within it (Dillon and Reid 2009). These threats are inevitably problematized in terms of pathologies and therapies:

> Every account of life is therefore contoured by its allied discourse of danger, every account of order is contoured by an account of the disorder which

threatens it. The biopolitics of liberal rule and war differs only in the account that it gives of ordered and disordered life and is self-endangering. To employ a medical term which therefore fits this condition of rule precisely, the emergency of emergence requires a form of global triage. Global triage specifies who gets what treatment, where, when and how. Some of that treatment – a lot of that treatment – is directly and indirectly lethal.

(Dillon and Reid 2009: 89–90)

Counterinsurgency is thus envisaged as a specific therapeutic program for the actual implementation of 'global triage'. This is exactly what Kilcullen (2009) suggests. He contends that the 'accidental guerrilla syndrome' can be countered by way of a global therapeutic strategy aimed at extending stable governmental structures into ungoverned spaces while disrupting terrorist networks – what he calls 'counterinsurgency plus' (see also Kilcullen 2005, 2010). This professedly benevolent strategy, however, inevitably entails the killing of both actual and suspected insurgents and terrorists as well as, potentially, scores of innocent civilians.

Legitimizing expeditionary pacification

Outwardly benevolent attempts to stabilize ungoverned spaces inevitably entail the effective establishment and the public denial of quasi-imperial forms of rule over foreign populations. But any intent to rule foreign populations has to be denied for the sake of the political legitimacy of both the intervention itself and the host-nation government on whose behalf the intervention is said to occur. Narratives of political legitimacy thus form an integral part of the immanent operational logic of counterinsurgency. In order to be effective, counterinsurgents have to actively produce and tactically deploy legitimacy. The primary aim of counterinsurgency is, after all, 'to foster development of effective governance by a legitimate government' (Department of the Army 2007: 37). Legitimacy is supposed to derive from the host-nation government's (and to a lesser extent the counterinsurgents') capability to provide security to the population:

And sometimes, the ability of a state to provide security – albeit without freedoms associated with Western democracies – can give it enough legitimacy to govern in the people's eyes, particularly if they have experienced a serious breakdown of order.

(Department of the Army 2007: 37)

The support of the majority of the targeted population is seen as vital to the success of the overall campaign. In order to win the support of the population, counterinsurgency efforts have to be cast as legitimate, the fact of foreign occupation has to be downplayed and the use of firepower has to be finely calibrated. As the *Counterinsurgency Field Manual* (Department of the Army 2007) stresses again and again:

COIN is fought among the populace. Counterinsurgents take upon themselves responsibility for the people's well-being in all its manifestations.
[...] Effective COIN programs address all aspects of the local populace's
concerns in a unified fashion. Insurgents succeed by maintaining turbulence
and highlighting local grievances the COIN effort fails to address. COIN
forces succeed by eliminating turbulence and helping the host nation meet
the populace's basic needs.

(Department of the Army 2007: 55)

Since the local population and their support are viewed as the center of gravity
of counterinsurgency operations, soldiers and marines have to take all necessary
precautions not to alienate the populace. One particular concern for the authors
of the field manual is the indiscriminate use of firepower and what is euphemisti-
cally called 'collateral damage'. The field manual thus enjoins soldiers and
marines to avoid 'unnecessary' civilian casualties:

Any use of force generates a series of reactions. There may be times when
an overwhelming effort is necessary to destroy or intimidate an opponent
and reassure the populace. Extremist insurgent combatants have to be killed.
In any case, however, counterinsurgents should calculate carefully the type
and amount of force to be applied and who wields it for any operation. An
operation that kills five insurgents is counterproductive if collateral damage
leads to the recruitment of fifty more insurgents.

(Department of the Army 2007: 45)

What is more, the field manual lays out a number of 'paradoxes of counterinsurgency operations' to underscore the fact that 'the conduct of COIN is counterin-
tuitive to the traditional U.S. view of war' (Department of the Army 2007:
47–51). Statements such as: 'Sometimes, the more you protect your force, the
less secure you may be'; 'Sometimes, the more force is used, the less effective it
is'; or 'The more successful a counterinsurgency is, the less force can be used
and the more risk must be accepted' are meant to hammer home the point that
the most powerful military machine on earth has to accept major risks to its own
soldiers in order to win the support of foreign populations and prevail against
unconventional enemies (Department of the Army 2007: 48–9).

On 1 August 2010, after he took over as commander of ISAF and American
forces in Afghanistan from General Stanley McChrystal, who resigned (or was
sacked) following a controversial article in *Rolling Stone* magazine (see Hastings 2010), General David Petraeus (2010) issued a 'Counterinsurgency
Guidance' to his troops (and the general public). This document echoes many of
the themes already present in the field manual. The first two guiding principles
focus on the Afghan population:

Secure and serve. The decisive terrain is the human terrain. The people are
the center of gravity. Only by providing them security and earning their trust
and confidence can the Afghan government and ISAF prevail.

Live among the people. We can't commute to the fight. Position joint bases and combat outposts as close to those we're seeking to secure as is feasible. Decide on locations with input from our partners and after consultation with local citizens and informed by intelligence and security assessments.

(Petraeus 2010: 1)

The guidelines, published in the wake of the release of the 'Afghan War Diary'[1] which documents numerous cases of 'collateral damage', also stress the need for strict rules of engagement to avoid civilian casualties:

Fight hard and fight with discipline. Hunt the enemy aggressively, but use only the firepower needed to win a fight. We can't win without fighting, but we also cannot kill or capture our way to victory. Moreover, if we kill civilians or damage their property in the course of our operations, we will create more enemies than our operations eliminate. That's exactly what the Taliban want. Don't fall into their trap. We must continue our efforts to reduce civilian casualties to an absolute minimum.

(Petraeus 2010: 2)

Practices of counterinsurgency range from the most benevolent governmental efforts 'to structure the possible field of action of others' (Foucault 2000c: 341) to the most lethal use of violence. The choice of these practices hinges on the level of risk assigned to particular individuals, communities and spaces. The level of risk or illiberality is, in turn, based on various attempts to produce knowledge about the targeted population (see Chapter 5 for one such attempt).

As previously noted, success in counterinsurgency is said to depend on the strategic articulation of security, development and information operations. For instance, the NATO-run International Security Assistance Force (ISAF) mission in Afghanistan is described as follows:

ISAF, in support of the Government of the Islamic Republic of Afghanistan, conducts operations in Afghanistan to reduce the capability and will of the insurgency, support the growth in capacity and capability of the Afghan National Security Forces (ANSF), and facilitate improvements in governance and socio-economic development, in order to provide a secure environment for sustainable stability that is observable to the population.

(International Security Assistance Force 2010)

NATO presently employs a so-called 'Shape-Clear-Hold-Build-Transition' approach. Prior to any military operation, NATO forces first seek to 'shape' the perceptions of specific audiences through information operations. For example, NATO troops have sometimes informed the local population about future assault plans to garner their support and minimize casualties. Before mounting Operation Moshtarak (which means 'together' in the local Dari language) in

Afghanistan's Helmand province, NATO forces and Afghan government officials told local residents about the imminent attack and tried to persuade them to switch their allegiances to the counterinsurgent forces (British Broadcasting Corporation 2010; Gardner 2010). During the 'clear' phase, counterinsurgents attempt to rid a targeted area from insurgents through major offensive operations. Once an area is cleared, NATO forces adopt a defensive posture to 'hold' the cleared area and prevent the insurgents from re-infiltrating. This includes the establishment of geographies of security (see Chapter 4), including a raft of often highly oppressive population control measures, such as perimeter defenses, travel restrictions, ID cards, and intensive infantry patrols. During the next phase NATO forces aim to consolidate their position and permanently stabilize the area by 'building' local institutions and establishing a functioning local civil society. In the 'transition phase', 'more long-term development activities replace the stabilization initiatives' and control is supposed to be transferred to local authorities (Thruelsen 2010: 261–2; Department of Defense 2010a, 2010b: 12–13).

The long-term stability of targeted countries and regions is, above all, deemed to pivot on the establishment of legitimate governmental structures:

> The primary objective of any COIN operation is to foster development of effective governance by a legitimate government. Counterinsurgents achieve this objective by the balanced application of both military and non-military means. All governments rule through a combination of consent and coercion. Governments described as 'legitimate' rule primarily with the consent of the governed; those described as 'illegitimate' tend to rely mainly or entirely on coercion.
>
> (Department of the Army 2007: 37)

Counterinsurgents are thus urged to actively produce the legitimacy of the host-nation government, by providing security and helping build the governmental capacities necessary for a regime to be considered legitimate in the eyes of the population. However, the very process of what may be called legitimacy-building also serves to produce the legitimacy of the intervention itself, for counterinsurgency operations also have to legitimize themselves vis-à-vis the local population and domestic, as well as international, audiences. In short, the potential end product of a successful mission, namely a legitimate and stable government, is what provides legitimacy to a counterinsurgency campaign. The irony is, that counterinsurgency aims to externally and also coercively establish governments that 'rule primarily with the consent of the governed' (Department of the Army 2007: 37). The professed objective of bolstering the capacities of the host-nation government to become more responsive to, and more representative of, its population hinges on the disavowal of the military and political power of the intervening force. Counterinsurgents have to deny any imperial intentions, at the same time as they seek to massively interfere in the internal affairs of a nominally sovereign nation.

To put it bluntly, in order to be successful counterinsurgents must not be seen as imperial masters. In a way, counterinsurgency appears as an extreme version of those post-1990s international state-building practices that David Chandler (Chandler 2006a) dubbed 'Empire in Denial'. Chandler argues that Western state-building practices impose far-reaching and highly invasive forms of outside regulation on non-Western nations, while at the same time denying the West's power. He further contends that, 'the drive to extend these forms of regulation stems from the evasiveness brought about by the problems of legitimizing power rather than the desire to exercise power more effectively' (Chandler 2006a: 191). Yet, the very act of legitimizing power by denying it can also help exercise it more effectively.

The problematic of producing both the legitimacy of the host-nation government and of the intervention itself, is at the heart of counterinsurgency. In line with the logic of human security, legitimacy is considered to derive from the fact of protection: governments are seen as legitimate if they can protect their population. The inability to protect, in turn, is seen as warranting outside intervention. Yet the very act of mounting a military operation on behalf of a beleaguered government or of establishing a government in the wake of an invasion, may undermine the very legitimacy of the regime in question because its population may come to regard this government as incapable, at best, or at worst, as the puppet of foreign powers. This is compounded by the fact that counterinsurgency operations frequently rely on oppressive population control measures that have not changed much since the era of Western imperialism (see Chapter 4). Indeed, a lack of political legitimacy, combined with the fact of foreign occupation, may give rise to widespread resentment, which can ultimately provide fertile breeding grounds for further violence.

According to the logic of counterinsurgency, legitimacy is not something that precedes the actual act of intervening but is supposed to be produced through the politico-military instruments deployed on the ground. Counterinsurgency has to engineer both its own legitimacy and the political legitimacy of the host- nation government – a process that entails an intricate, and mostly impossible, balancing act between empowering the host-nation and imposing quasi-imperial rule. Erring on either side will, and often does, undermine the political legitimacy of the host-nation government as well as the legitimacy of the overall campaign.

Counterinsurgency aims to pacify risky spaces and populations and reintegrate them into a global liberal order by providing security, development and good governance to targeted populations. In fact, one of the primary aims of counterinsurgency is to secure the local population, even if attempts to do so may harm some of its members. Discourses of human security furnish the legitimacy of expeditionary counterinsurgency campaigns. But counterinsurgency operations are not just about the security of targeted populations, they are also aimed at the annihilation of those circulations that are seen as putting not only the local population, but also the United States itself (and even the entire globe) at risk.

Legitimizing domestic pacification

Pacification efforts in domestic crime hot spots follow a similar logic. They seek to secure at-risk communities by immobilizing risky circulations. Over the last three decades, attempts to justify the expansion of policing and the constant stiffening of sentences have drawn on both victims of crime and a whole demonology of criminals. The use of para-militarized practices of pacification against particular domestic spaces and populations has been, and continues to be, legitimized through figurations of predatory criminals, helpless victims and a fearful public. In fact, both expeditionary and domestic pacification are now driven by a 'one-sided perspective focusing on condemnation and punishment', on the one hand, and appeals to the plight of actual and potential victims, on the other (Chandler 2006b: 67).

During the 1970s, views of crime and criminals changed significantly. Crime is now longer seen as the effect of need or deprivation, but as a problem of personal discipline and moral hygiene. In short, the perspective on crime shifted from a socio-political focus to a purely moral one. This also transformed the view of the offender:

> The recurrent image of the offender ceased to be that of the needy delinquent or the feckless misfit and became much more threatening – a matter of career criminals, crackheads, thugs, and predators – and at the same time more racialized.
>
> (Garland 2001: 102)

In the US media, violent criminals are frequently cast as urban underclass black or Latino males, while their victims are portrayed as white middle-class females (Gilliam and Iyenger 2000; Herbert and Brown 2006; Madriz 1997; Russell 1998; Wacquant 2001b, 2009b). Representations of crime, criminals and victims are thus both informed by, and ultimately reinforce, racial, class and gender divisions.

Loïc Wacquant (2009b: 83 original emphasis) notes that in the wake of the urban riots in the 1960s, 'the diffusion of racialized images of urban destitution went hand in hand with rising resentment toward public aid which bolstered (white) demand for *restrictive* welfare measures centered on deterrence and compulsion'. This has turned 'the ghetto poor into social leeches, if not veritable "enemies" of American society' (Waquant 2009b: 83) and legitimized the use of pacification practices that combined the para-militarized provision of 'security' with increasingly coercive forms of welfare-cum-workfare. Indeed, entangled discourses of crime, immorality and welfare dependency served to justify the design and deployment of domestic governmentalities of security that are modeled on expeditionary counterinsurgency-style pacification to target 'populations deemed dispossessed, deviant, and dangerous – chief among them the black (sub)proletariat of the big cities'. The ensuing reconfiguration of crime control resulted in a 'triple reduction': first, policing has been primarily geared towards 'the visible delinquency of the lower class'; second, it has predominantly targeted 'the retail sales and consumption of drugs in segregated black and Latino neighborhoods'; third, it has problematized drugs and drug-related crime as a security threat that could only be dealt with through para-militarized policing and ever tougher sentencing (Wacquant 2009b: 152–3).

Criminologist David Garland (2001: 53–73) argues that since the 1970s, crime control has shifted from what he calls 'penal-welfarism' – an institutional arrangement 'combining the liberal legalism of due process and proportionate punishment with a correctionalist commitment to rehabilitation, welfare and criminological expertise' (Garland 2001: 27) – to a criminology of control. Penal-welfarism hinged on the assumption that criminal behavior is an effect of social causes, such as poverty and racism, and that criminals can ultimately be corrected and reintegrated into society, 'both through professional management within the carceral system and through the expansion of social entitlement programs' (Corva 2008: 178). Under the new criminology of control, most of the institutional arrangements of penal-welfarism and the state-run criminal justice system remain in place but are deployed according to a different rationality. As noted in Chapter 3, the deployment of police forces and their interaction with the public has shifted from reactive, emergency response policing towards more proactive community-oriented approaches, as well as to more intensive, so-called 'quality-of-life' strategies. According to Garland (2001: 169), 'policing has become "smarter", more targeted, more attuned to local circumstances, more responsive to public pressure, more willing to work with the community and to emphasize prevention'. The police now increasingly partner with other non-state agencies, such as private corporations and community organizations. Indeed, Garland notes that one of the most significant changes in the field of crime control is the formation of a new 'apparatus of prevention and security', which centers around the management of risk (Garland 2001: 170). This apparatus seeks to regulate the supply-side of crime by way of 'minimizing criminal opportunities, enhancing situational controls, and channeling conduct away from criminogenic situations' (Garland 2001:170–1). The sector of crime-prevention, with its new specialists (crime prevention advisors, inter-agency coordinators, systems analysts, risk managers, etc) and new forms of expertise (environmental criminology, identification of hot spots, risky activities and populations-at-risk) marks an extension of crime control beyond the state, because it aims to expand and guide the social control efforts of private citizens, corporations and communities (Garland 2001: 171). At the same time, there has been a proliferation of para-militarized policing, the rise of mass incarceration and a general increase in state 'punitiveness' (see Kraska and Kappeler 1997; Kraska 1999; Peck 2003; Simon 1999; Simon 2000; Simon 2007; Wacquant 2001a, 2001b, 2009b):

> The political culture of crime control now takes it for granted that the state will have a huge presence, while simultaneously claiming this presence is never enough. The paradoxical outcome is that the state strengthens its punitive forces and increasingly acknowledges the inadequate nature of this sovereign strategy. Alongside an increasingly punitive sentencing structure, one

also sees the development of new modes of exercising power by which the state seeks to 'govern at a distance' by forming alliances and activating the governmental powers of non-state agencies.

(Garland 2001: 173)

Contemporary crime control is thus torn between reaffirming the myth of a sovereign state capable of providing security within its territory, and attempts to reactivate non-state crime control through 'responsibilizing' communities, private businesses and individuals (see Garland 1996; Garland 2001). On the one hand, state intervention in crime control has steadily increased; while on the other hand, the state has seemingly relinquished responsibility for crime control through outsourcing law enforcement capabilities, or through efforts to (re)activate modes of informal social control. However, sovereign practices often go hand-in-glove with practices of responsibilization. Moreover, practices of societal responsibilization do not necessarily undermine the state's capacity to provide security. In reality, the police and local communities rarely co-produce security as equal partners (see Herbert 1999; Sadd and Grinc 1994). Rather, the police seek to enlist members of a targeted community 'as their "eyes and ears", to become in effect, auxiliary police officers gathering the sorts of intelligence that those in uniform cannot hope to acquire' (Herbert 1999: 154). In short, community policing seeks to mobilize members of the public not as partners, but as local human intelligence assets.

As previously noted, both expeditionary counterinsurgency operations and domestic programs of community policing seek to enlist the help of targeted communities as well as other actors to re-establish formal and informal modes of social control that would safeguard the community's long-term security. In fact, the contemporary field of crime control is best conceptualized as the domestic deployment of practices of pacification that target specific spaces and populations, in order to re-integrate them into the liberal order, and to contain and/or eliminate risky circulations held to emerge from within these spaces and populations.

The state has indeed constantly expanded its 'punitive forces' while acknowledging the inadequacy of its sovereign strategy (Garland 2001: 173). But this is not as paradoxical as it seems, especially if we conceptualize sovereignty not as given, but as something that needs to be performed. Rationalities and practices of security are aimed at state-making; they constantly produce and re-produce sovereignty, both materially and symbolically. In fact, this is what Foucault (2003: 15) meant by characterizing political power as a 'continuation of war by other means'. Historically, states emerged through the production of a monopoly over the means of violence within a given territory, that is to say, through the pacification of a given territory and population (see Giddens 1987; Tilly 1985, 1992; Weber 1919). But the monopoly over the means of violence has to be perpetually reproduced through continuous pacification by means of both government and violence. However, neither the (re)production of sovereignty nor the (re)activation of informal non-state control are ends in themselves, but are tactically deployed to stabilize a liberal capitalist order in which 'good' circulations can flow freely both within and across state territory. This means that 'bad' circulations need to be interdicted not just within the state's territory, but also to an ever larger extent globally. For, insecurity is increasingly problematized in terms of globalized circulations that affect both local communities and the inter-state system as much as states themselves.

Failing states, failing cities, global chaos

Even though the concepts and terms vary, contemporary problematizations of insecurity are more often than not multi-scalar. They seek to locate and target insecurities across global, national, regional and local scales. Indeed, problematizations of insecurity, and prescribed responses to them, frequently encompass both 'failing' states and 'failing' cities and communities, providing a complex map of local and regional insecurities that are nonetheless viewed as connected up into global circulations of threat.

Unsurprisingly, figurations of these circulations of threat are highly amorphous as global terrorists, local insurgents, transnational drug traffickers, local gang members as well as illegal immigrants, are all held to embody particular aspects of global circulations of threat. This trend is, for instance, borne out by narratives about the financing of insurgent and terrorist activities through illegal means, such as the trade in illicit goods and people smuggling (Kan 2009). Here, the global circulation of violence from (primarily but not only) ungoverned spaces of the global south is seen as inextricably intertwined with the circulation of illicit goods, above all drugs, and 'illegal' people (including not only suspected criminals or terrorists, but also refugees and victims of people smugglers). According to Paul Rexton Kan (2009: 94), Associate Professor of National Security Studies at the US Army War College, 'The drug trade and warfare have been pushed into a closer relationship by the lack of the overarching global superpower competition, asymmetrical nature of contemporary wars, changes in the patterns of the drug trade, and increasing pace of globalization'. Kan predicts that in the future, more and more conflicts will therefore be fuelled by the drug trade. This will likely give rise to an even larger number of well-financed and hence also well-armed non-state war-making entities:

> [I]nternal or intrastate war is increasingly a misleading moniker. The emergence of organized violence no longer needs to anchor political authority in conventional, bureaucratic, or consent-based structures like the nation-state. The drug trade is speeding this process along. It too is neither dependent on nor bound by the nation-state and has over its history been less and less subject to a variety of local, national, and international enforcement capabilities.
>
> (Kan 2009: 115)

For Kan, the increasingly close link between the drug trade and unconventional warfare poses a significant challenge for Western states because it requires a response that cuts across the traditional distinction between domestic public safety and international security, and ranges from the local to the global. What Kan does not mention is the fact that US security agencies, above all the CIA, have also been complicit in the international drug trade. During the Cold War, the CIA frequently cooperated with, and provided support to, a host of individuals and organizations involved in the international drug trade, including 'Corsican syndicates, Nationalist Chinese irregulars, Lao generals, Afghan warlords, Haitian colonels, Panamanian generals, Honduran smugglers, and Nicaraguan Contra commanders' (McCoy 2003: 16). These drug traffickers served as irregulars in many CIA covert operations across the hot spots of the Cold War, and were regularly involved in both counterinsurgency and so-called proinsurgency operations aimed at toppling allegedly pro-Soviet regimes (McCoy 2003: 11–18). Arguably, CIA collaboration with known drug traffickers and criminals was a contributing factor to the long-term instability of regions, such as Central Asia, Southeast Asia and Central America. It thus stands to reason that US Cold War covert operations in many ways contributed to the close link between drug trafficking and irregular warfare identified by Kan.

Local, national, regional and global effects of 'bad' circulations are said to crystallize in major cities of, primarily but not only, the global south. According to Stephen Graham (2010: 53), 'the obsession with "failed states" as the key security threats to US interests is, in fact, morphing into a concern with "failed" cities'. Undoubtedly, the rapid growth of megacities in the global south (where more and more people are effectively cut off from economic growth and formal labor markets and are thus pushed into the shadow economy) does give cause for concern. But instead of addressing the underlying causes of global insecurities held to emerge from these urban sprawls, most notably structural economic as well as political inequalities, a growing number of security experts merely diagnose such cities as 'feral' and prescribe paramilitary pacification (for a critique of this reductive view, see Graham 2010: 54n; Davis 2004, 2006; Wacquant 2008). In his article on 'Feral Cities', which was published in the *Marine Corps University Journal*, Richard Norton (2010; see also 2003) defines a feral city as follows:

> A feral city is a metropolis in a nation-state where the government has lost the ability to maintain the rule of law within the city's boundaries. These cities nevertheless remain connected to the greater international system through such avenues as trade and communication. The most immediately recognizable example of such a city is present-day Mogadishu, Somalia.
>
> (Norton 2010: 51)

Although huge swathes of their slum-dwelling populations are delinked from licit economic circulations, feral cities are viewed as connected to global networks, so that the risky circulations of terrorism, crime, drugs and disease that are held to emerge from them are deemed to spread across the wider region and even the entire globe.

Norton (2010: 56) places cities on a continuum of ferality in five categories:

1   governance
2   economy
3   services
4   security
5   civil society.

Healthy cities are color-coded 'green', those that show some signs of a feral condition, 'yellow' and those that 'are in the process of becoming feral', 'red' (see also Bunker and Sullivan 2011: 765–70). The feral city construct is another glaring example of a sliding scale of dangerousness that is mapped upon a binary opposition between friend and enemy, liberal and illiberal, risky and risk-free, or feral and healthy. Indeed, Norton seeks to risk-profile entire cities and/or particular communities, so that modes of targeting can be adapted according to their level of ferality.

In practice, 'cities are considered patchworks of colors – mosaics of health – with ferality variances possible in their zones, neighborhoods, and enclaves' (Bunker and Sullivan 2011: 766). As a consequence, although the feral city construct is primarily applied to the global south, it could easily be transferred to what are perceived as pockets of the global south in major US cities. In fact, similar diagnostic tools are deployed to identify 'failing' communities; so-called crime hot spots, within US cities. Indeed, if the current economic climate worsens, due to the ongoing economic crisis and the concomitant imposition of austerity measures, both distribution conflicts and illicit economic activity in US and European cities could well turn them into something akin to feral cities. This, in turn, might lead to a further escalation of domestic paramilitary pacification activities.

Enemies of humanity

The provision of both global and domestic security is legitimized by, *and* seeks to enact, a rationality of risk management geared towards identifying, categorizing and targeting individuals, populations and spaces that are deemed to be either at-risk or risky. What is at work in the legitimization of liberal governmentalities of security, is a combination of a sliding scale of dangerousness with a fundamental division between 'friend' and 'enemy'. But the enemy is not a 'just enemy' (justus hostis) – an opponent one encounters on more or less equal grounds – but the 'unjust enemy' of peace and humanity, who: 'we despise and seek either to transform into a more acceptable life-form or to annihilate' (Prozorov 2006: 83, 84). Liberal governmentalities of security are thus set to conduct a biopolitical triage between risk-free and risky circulations, while sub-dividing risky circulations into different levels of risk. The actual degree of authoritarianism and violence used in targeting risky circulations is supposed to be adjusted to the perceived level of risk, and ranges from more or less coercive modes of government to the use of lethal force.

With their references to 'bad neighborhoods', war criminals, genocidaires, and human rights violators, liberal proponents of a human rights-based cosmopolitanism (such as Mary Kaldor) produce their own Manichaean distinctions between 'good' liberal cosmopolitans and their 'evil', illiberal Others (Kaldor 1999, 2003; Glasius and Kaldor 2005; Kaldor and Beebe 2010). Ironically, this distinction can easily be colonized by more insidious racialized discourses and hence runs the risk of collapsing back into, and reproducing, the particularistic identity-driven conflicts castigated by liberal analysts. In a similar vein, domestic discourses on crime control are also fraught with references to a vast array of illiberal subjects, ranging from illegal aliens to domestic narco-terrorists. This intense focus on perpetrators and their victims obscures social, economic and political inequalities (which are frequently reinforced by governmentalities of security) and casts the actual deployment of governmentalities of security as well-intentioned, benign and morally inevitable (Walters 2004: 248).

Ultimately, the illiberal subject positions targeted by liberal governmentalities of security are empty placeholders that can be filled, depending on the political conjuncture, with a variety of categories: immigrants, criminals, terrorists, insurgents or the undeserving poor. What all these categories have in common is that they operate within the fundamental Manichaeism of a biopolitical division between 'good' and 'bad' circulations. And this Manichaeism now increasingly operates across local, national, regional and global scales.

Conclusion

The problematic of liberal violence

On 2 May 2011, the global mediascape was abuzz with news about Osama Bin Laden's death. Bin Laden, who was widely believed to have masterminded the 9/11 attacks, had eluded US intelligence agencies for almost a decade. However, by the beginning of 2010 there was growing evidence that he was hiding in a compound in Abbottabad, Pakistan, a well-to-do garrison town about 60 kilometers east of Islamabad. Plans to kill or capture Bin Laden were hatched straight-away. At first, US military and intelligence officials formulated a plan to bomb the compound. But President Obama wanted proof that Bin Laden was really inside, so plans for a much riskier helicopter raid were drawn up instead. On 2 May 2011, members of the Naval Special Warfare Development Group, better known as SEAL Team Six (a highly secretive special operations unit) raided the compound and killed Bin Laden as well as one of his sons, his courier and at least one other person, most probably the courier's brother (see, for example, Walsh *et al.* 2011). Official US accounts of what happened during the raid are ambiguous and almost impossible to verify. In fact, there are still many unanswered questions surrounding the events. The most important of these is whether Bin Laden could have been taken alive. Were the US commandos instructed to assassinate Bin Laden, or was he killed because he resisted attempts to capture him?

The targeted killing of suspected terrorists and insurgents has become a widely used tactic in the global war on terror. The Obama administration has massively increased the use of unmanned aerial vehicles (UAVs – better known as drones) to target not only Taliban militants in Afghanistan (as well as in Pakistan's tribal belt, which is widely believed to be a key sanctuary for Taliban fighters) but also suspected terrorists in Yemen and Somalia. Only very few of the targets are as high profile as Bin Laden. In fact, many of the drone attacks in Afghanistan and Pakistan, for instance, have targeted mid-level Taliban operatives, in an attempt to deplete the overall insurgent network.

A number of commentators have debated the ethics, legality and effectiveness of targeted killing as a security practice (Bell 2005; Byman 2006; Gordon 2006; Grayson 2012; Hafez and Hatfield 2006; Kasher and Yadlin 2005; Statman

2004). Drone attacks are never as targeted as they are made out to be. They inevitably cause civilian casualties. This led some counterinsurgency experts to point out that drone attacks may hamper efforts to win the hearts and minds of the local population, and hence even further destabilize targeted areas (see, for example, Kilcullen and McDonald Exum 2009; Matulich 2012). Yet, these experts do not oppose the use of drone strikes per se, as long as they are part of a comprehensive population-centric strategy:

> Counterinsurgency (COIN) strategy provides for use of drones for efforts in 'clearing' insurgents but states clearly that these hinge on the ability of a host nation to 'hold and build' upon these efforts. By implementing an uncohesive COIN effort in the FATA [Federally Administered Tribal Areas] and NWFP [North West Frontier Province] the US risks further militarising the local population and leaving an unwilling Pakistani Army to deal with the more challenging population-centric objectives of COIN.
>
> (Matulich 2012: 1)

Targeted killings, through drone strikes or otherwise, are a mere tactic aimed at eradicating so-called 'irreconcilables', whereas counterinsurgency seeks to strategically combine lethal action against terrorists and insurgents with a host of non-lethal efforts to permanently stabilize a targeted area. Even though the US strategic focus may recently have shifted from population-centric pacification campaigns towards enemy-centric direct action, acts of targeting dangerous individuals are still part and parcel of governmentalities of security that seek not only to eradicate dangerous circulations, but also to promote safe ones.

So far, targeted killing has been used only outside the United States and primarily against non-US citizens. Yet apparently, President Obama has also signed off on a secret CIA 'hit list' of US citizens who are suspected of terrorist activities and who may thus be killed without due legal process (Miller 2010; Greenwald 2010). For instance, on 30 September 2011 Anwar al-Awlaki, a US citizen and an alleged top al-Qaeda operative, was killed by a drone strike in Yemen (Democracy Now 2011c). So, even if targeted killings are a security practice primarily used abroad, the inclusion of US citizens points to a much more complex relation between 'inside' and 'outside'. What is more, in the 1960s, COINTEL-PRO actions allegedly also included the assassination of individual leaders of domestic oppositional groups. For instance, two lead members of the Black Panther Party were killed in their beds during a Chicago police raid organized by the state's attorney's office, and facilitated by an FBI informant, in December 1969 (Chomsky 1997: 18–19; Glick 1989: 63–4). An internal police investigation into the killings completely exonerated everyone who took part in the raid. However, it remains unclear if the police officers who killed the two Panthers at point blank range were, in fact, instructed to do so from higher up the chain of command.

Besides the use of torture, assassination is perhaps the most extremely illiberal security practice used by liberal regimes (see Rejali 2007 on liberal torture).

And, at least, when the killed individuals are as high profile as Osama Bin Laden, it is definitely one of the most widely publicized practices. Indeed, given the apparent ineffectiveness of assassinations in providing for sustainable security, the spectacular rhetoric of biblical retribution, which is such an integral part of these high-profile killings, is perhaps as important in accounting for these practices as the primarily administrative logic of security (see Grayson 2012). But although these practices definitely also partake of a wider cultural spectacle of retribution, they should still be understood as embedded within the biopolitical logic of liberal governmentalities of security. The liberal practice of targeted killing is invariably aimed at those presenting highly individualized illiberal threats, who are construed as completely intractable to other more 'liberal' ways of dealing with them. Indeed, the use of lethal force is not so much an exception to, but an integral part of, liberal governmentalities of security.

How to challenge liberal violence?

Kyle Grayson (2012: 36) suggests that what is at the heart of the debate about the liberal practice of targeted killing is a fundamental dilemma about liberalism itself: 'Is liberalism a good system that can produce bad outcomes or a bad system that can produce good outcomes?' This question can be rephrased as follows: Can liberalism still provide the grounds for challenging the increasing use of illiberal, and sometimes even lethal, practices of security in the name of liberalism?

First, governmentalities of security in general, and certain security practices (such as targeted killings) in particular, can be challenged in the name of effectiveness. In fact, the overall field of security is marked by contradictions and controversies. Security professionals often disagree on the priority of specific insecurities as well as on questions of tactics, operations and strategy. The aforementioned critique of drone attacks serves as a good example of tactical and operational differences, both amongst security professionals and between them and political decision-makers. However, critical accounts of the supposed (in) effectiveness of particular rationalities and practices of security completely tend to ignore the fundamental problematic at the heart of liberal security, namely the biopolitical division between 'good' and 'bad' circulations. Moreover, the very ineffectiveness of governmentalities of security in promoting sustainable security and their tendency to even reinforce existing insecurities, ultimately drives their perpetual (re)adjustment and expansion. For, if security is but a response to perceived insecurities, then the more that threats proliferate, the louder will be the calls for ever more security. Ultimately, critiques of the effectiveness of particular governmentalities of security are bound to be complicit in the search for ever more and better security.

Second, the expansion of governmentalities of security can be challenged in the name of peace. This critique is based on two interrelated assumptions: (1) that governmentalities of security are a mere extension of warfighting into hitherto civilian domains; and (2) that there is still a clear-cut difference between war and peace. This view implies a resurrection of the inside/outside binary, in order to be able to critique the militarization of security from a civilian position of peace. However, if war and peace are completely intermingled, and if security increasingly operates according to a 'logic' of pacification – waging 'savage wars of peace' (Kipling 1899) within a global homeland, then 'peace' can hardly offer a vantage point for the critique of liberal security. For, although global peace may indeed be desirable the, often violent, means of pacification deployed in pursuit of global peace and stability are clearly not.

Third, the expansion of governmentalities of security can be challenged in the name of the rule of law. If security hinged on declaring mere exceptions to the normality of the rule of law, we could just attempt to strengthen legal mechanisms to make it much harder or even impossible to declare a state of exception. However, if the use of emergency powers has become a routine technology of government, if the passage and enforcement of laws itself has become a security tactic, and if we can no longer distinguish between 'normality' and the 'exception', this is clearly not a viable option. What is more, challenging the expansion of security in the name of law also entails what Neocleous calls 'a form of legal fetishism' (2008: 73; see also 2000). Legal fetishism treats law as 'a mystical answer to the questions of power', while ignoring how law is bound up in relations of power and how it sometimes even serves as a mere tactic of power (2008: 73).

Last but not least, the expansion of governmentalities of security can be challenged in the name of the perhaps most cherished principle of liberalism – freedom. Doing so rests on the assumption that freedom and security have become unbalanced in favor of security, so that we have to somehow rebalance them. However, if liberty and security are completely wrapped up in one another, this is surely pointless. For, as shown in the course of this book, liberal security aims to promote the freedom of some circulations by interdicting others. To put it crudely, liberal security has so far primarily tended to ensure the freedom of well-to-do white people, while severely curtailing that of poor people of color, both domestically and globally.

Liberal security is increasingly set to respond to insecurities and threats that are held to circulate across local, national, regional and global levels. These insecurities and threats are, moreover, held to emanate from particular spaces and populations that more often than not also happen to be amongst the most deprived. The security solutions prescribed in response to these problems tend to take the form of pacification campaigns, targeting particular spaces and populations, in order to (re)integrate them into a global order, while containing and/or eradicating elements within these populations and spaces that are seen as threats to the global order. Contemporary liberal security thus marks both an externalization of domestic order maintenance, projecting rationalities and practices of liberal government onto the global level, and an internalization of external order building, re-importing colonial violence into the homeland. Authoritarian practices, or emergency powers, have been and continue to be used in, and by, liberal regimes in the name of securing liberal order. These authoritarian practices are no mere aberration, but have become a permanent feature of liberal rule, leading to what some critics have called a permanent state of exception. Yet, these authoritarian practices are not directed at all and sundry. They tend to target some more than others. In fact, liberal authoritarianism in general, and liberal violence in particular, tends to be aimed at individuals, populations and spaces that are seen as either recalcitrant to liberal rule or as threats to the liberal capitalist order. The actual degree of authoritarianism is, moreover, supposed to be adjusted to the perceived level of risk embodied by the targeted individuals, populations and spaces. However, liberalism's nuanced calculations of risk always tend to bleed into a much cruder friend/enemy binary.

Liberal rule is torn between a universalistic deterritorializing tendency of temporal development, of becoming-liberal, on the one hand, and a particularistic, reterritorializing tendency of spatial separation, on the other. Liberal rule constantly seeks to extend its fundamental promises of freedom (the rule of law and peace) to ever more populations and spaces, working towards 'a decentered and deterritorializing apparatus of rule that progressively incorporates the entire global realm within its open expanding frontiers' – that is to say, towards the becoming-liberal of the entire globe (Hardt and Negri 2000: vii). Yet at the same time, liberal rule constantly draws and redraws borders between those who can be ruled liberally, and those who either have to be rendered amenable to liberal rule or have to be violently excluded. The contradiction between the deterritorializing and the reterritorializing forces at play in liberal rule manifests itself in attempts to distinguish between those circulations that need to be promoted and those that need to be interdicted. As these 'bad' circulations are held to threaten processes at the local, national, regional and global level, the universal promotion of liberal rule entails both the externalization of internal forms of liberal government and the internalization of external forms of violence. Liberalism's tendency to project the hitherto domestic promotion of the processes of the population onto the global level encounters both resistance and the emergence of circulations that are seen as putting the processes of the population at risk. Consequently, attempts to include ever more populations and spaces in the liberal order, while violently excluding dangerous ones, inevitably reinforce existing divisions and engender new ones. Indeed, liberal governmentalities of security are constantly expanding to make the biopolitical distinction between 'good' and 'bad' circulations on an increasingly wider scale, potentially including the entire globe. The constant expansion of liberal security is geared towards (re)producing a liberal capitalist order, but it also ultimately reinforces the social, economic, political and cultural divisions this order invariably entails.

Liberal security can thus hardly be challenged on liberal grounds. After all, liberal governmentalities of security are deployed in the name of freedom, the rule of law and peace and with the express purpose of securing a liberal order. In fact, a critique of liberal security has to be a critique of liberalism itself. The expansion of liberal governmentalities of security can only be challenged if we constantly ask the following set of questions: Whose freedom and security do they seek to provide for and at what costs to others? On what fundamental economic, social, political and cultural inequalities is the provision of security based, and to what extent does it reproduce these inequalities?

In mapping US international and domestic governmentalities of security, this book has tried to address some of these questions, but has also raised a lot more. To what extent can the blurring of domestic and international security be traced back to the rationalities and practices of colonialism and imperialism? What were the relations between security at home and security in the colonies in, say, nineteenth-century Britain? To what extent were practices, designed for imposing order on foreign populations, deployed to pacify domestic working class militancy? What was the influence of rationalities and practices of colonial rule and violence on domestic policing?

There surely is a need for more research into the imperial history and political economy of liberal governmentalities of security. If we want to understand both the transversal character of liberal security and its inherent authoritarianism and violence, we have to look much more closely into the multiple historical transfers and transpositions of governmentalities of security between metropolitan and peripheral locales. In particular, we should closely examine how specific security practices have shaped and/or destroyed human lives, and how the design and deployment of these practices have related to broader issues of political economy and collective identity-formation. Thus, on the one hand, liberal security ought to be studied with a much broader historical and theoretical perspective, to take into account how it has been shaped by its colonial and imperial history and to understand how it has operated and continues to function within a much more general economy of power and domination; while on the other hand, we should attend to its actual effects on human lives on the ground. Bridging the sometimes seemingly insurmountable gap between sweeping theoretical accounts and in-depth empirical analyses may seem like a tall order, but doing so will be of utmost importance if we want to mount a meaningful challenge to the inherent violence of liberal security.

Notes

Introduction

1 We should note that narcotics, most notably opium and its derivatives, had circulated freely as lucrative global commodities, which were inextricably intertwined with the political economy of colonialism, until the current international drug prohibition regime was established at the beginning of the twentieth century (see McCoy 2003: 2–11). The fact that narcotics are now seen as a 'bad' global circulation is above all due to the political pressure brought to bear by moral crusaders and prohibitionists at the end of the nineteenth century (McCoy 2003: 9–11). There is thus nothing inevitable about the international prohibition regime. In fact, a decriminalization of drugs is long overdue. By all accounts, the war on drugs has proven an abysmal failure, and its economic, and above all human, costs have become unbearable (see McCoy 2005).

1 Liberal security and the biopolitics of global pacification

1 The term 'Third Generation Gangs' (3 GEN Gangs) was coined by US law enforcement official and security expert, John P. Sullivan (2008: 160–2, 162), in an attempt to model the evolution of violent street gangs by categorizing them according to their level of 'politicization, internationalization, and sophistication'. Whereas First Generation Gangs are thought to be predominantly turf-focused and only participate in criminal enterprise opportunistically and locally, Second Generation Gangs are seen as 'entrepreneurial and drug-centred' with 'a tendency for centralized leadership and sophisticated operations for market protection' (Sullivan 2008: 162). According to Sullivan, although most existing gangs belong to the first or second generation, Third Generation Gangs are currently in the process of evolving. They include gangs that 'have evolved political aims, operate or seek to operate at the global end of the spectrum, and employ their sophistication to acquire power, money and engage in mercenary or political activities' (Sullivan 2008: 163). For instance, Sullivan (2008: 163) contends that the originally Los Angeles-based gangs, Mara Salvatrucha (MS-13) and Eighteenth Street (Calle 18 or M-18), are currently transforming into Third Generation Gangs. He argues that they have already spread across North and Central America and that they pose significant challenges to politically weak Latin American states, such as Honduras and El Salvador, by undermining their legitimacy and monopoly over the means of violence. (Sullivan 2008: 165–6; see also Sullivan 1997; 2000; Bunker and Sullivan 2010, 2011)

2 Expeditionary pacification

1 In military terms, information operations (IO) are broadly defined as 'those actions taken to affect an adversary's information and information systems while defending one's own information and information systems' (Armistead 2004: 17; see also

Department of Defense 2003a: 10). In his foreword to *Information Operations*, which is used as a textbook for students at the Joint Forces Staff College (JFSC), Dan Kuehl, Professor for Information Resources Management at the National Defense University, suggests that:

> [T]he global information environment has become a battlespace in which the tech-
> nology of the information age – which is the aspect we all too frequently focus on
> – is used to deliver critical and influential content in order to shape perceptions,
> influence opinions, and control behavior. [...] This new battlespace is focused on
> the "wetware," that is, the "gray" matter in which opinions are formed and de-
> cisions made.
>
> (Kuehl 2004: xvii–xviii)

Information operations are located in the interstices between soft and hard power; they are not only envisioned as an integral part of any military operation (as a 'force multiplier', which allows for much tighter control over the battlespace) but also, if used early enough in a campaign, as a means of avoiding armed conflict (Armistead 2004:19). Thus, while information operations both overlap with and incorporate so-called international public information or public diplomacy (which are used, both in times of peace and in times of conflict, to control and manage international opinion) they also include, in a more narrow sense, military endeavors such as psychological operations (see also Brown 2003; Department of Defense 2003a).

2 In fact, the term 'subversive insurgency' referred to insurgencies inimical to US interests, whereas other insurgencies were not seen as subversive but as liberation movements (an example of 'good, non-subversive' insurgents, from a US perspective that is,
would be the Nicaraguan Contras). Michael McClintock's Instruments of Statecraft provides a profound and critical account of the dynamic of, and contradictions between, US
pro- and counterinsurgency efforts during the Cold War (McClintock 1992).

3 Hammes further suggests that Mao recognized the power of networks well before the
concept became fashionable in the West:

> Mao strove to develop both the internal and external networks to support his
> revolution. Internally, the networks provided a way to move information to his
> followers and a way to keep those followers under close observation for security
> reasons. [...] Internationally, Mao built networks to neutralize, as much as feas-
> ible, support for the Nationalists. [...] Long before we conceived of our "modern,"
> wired, interconnected society, Mao had established an entire insurgency based on
> that principle. Using mission-type orders for most day-to-day operations, he
> reserved all major strategic decisions to himself – and also used the network to
> ensure that none of his subordinates could accumulate enough power to depose
> him.
>
> (Hammes 2006: 53–5)

Mao's use of networks entailed both the decentralization and centralization of command. Command was decentralized to ensure that subordinates could flexibly respond to the constantly changing situation on the ground, whereas overall control over the revolutionary movement was centralized to give Mao himself a panoptic vantage point.

4 As Douglas Blaufarb puts it:

> No other serious strategist has taken such a position. In Spain and Russia against
> Napoleon, in South Carolina against the British, in Arabia against the Turks, guer-
> rillas fought as auxiliaries, supporting a regular army. Mao insisted that it was
> possible for guerrillas to fight and win on their own, but that the process would
> inevitably be a lengthy one.
>
> (Blaufarb 1977; 4–5)

5 There seems to be a deep-seated cultural fascination with elite units, with the heroic hands-on warrior-types, who often defy discipline and institutional protocol to get the job done. We just have to think of the heroic role of Special Forces units and individual heroes with Special Forces backgrounds in popular culture. But, not only popular culture is obsessed with commando-style elites; national leaders are as well. McClintock (1992: 180) maintains that '[e]lite units provided their civilian leaders with a kind of heroic relief from the base reality of waging war'. He underscores this point by quoting from Eliot A. Cohen's book *Commandos and Politicians*:

> Elite units appeal to the romantic's conception of war because they present to him a picture not complicated by the thousands of dreary tasks required to field an army or fight a war. The unit's tasks seem heroic, for they require hand-to-hand combat rather than mere button-pushing. The requirements demanded of the unit's members are heroic, for they emphasize stamina, coolness under fire, and audacity – not technical virtuosity. The elite unit cultivates a romantic image through its eccentricities of dress and custom – colorful berets, special insignia, and so forth.
> (Cohen 1978: 40–1)

The appeal of the elite units thus consists in their romantic warrior image. They partake of the nomadic war machine rather than the bureaucratic state military, which is also borne out by their odd position within the chain of command and their disregard for military discipline.

6 Arguably, most of these points also apply to current counterinsurgency operations in Afghanistan. For instance, the recent *Rolling Stone* article, which led to the resignation, or rather sacking, of ISAF commander, General Stanley McChrystal, exposed severe tensions between the military and civilian agencies, most notably the Department of State (Hastings 2010). Moreover, the leaked cables of former US ambassador to Afghanistan, Karl W. Eikenberry, revealed strong concerns about the Afghan central government and NATO's ability to extend stable governmental structures into the Afghan countryside. Eikenberry indicated that Afghan President, Hamid Karzai, may not be 'an adequate strategic partner' and that much of the Afghan population regards the central government as unrepresentative and corrupt (Eikenberry 2009).

7 General Westmoreland was COMUSMACV until he was replaced by General Creighton Abrams on 1 July 1968.

8 Colonel Thomas X. Hammes is a retired marine who spent his active military duty on numerous infantry and intelligence assignments. Lieutenant Colonel John A. Nagl is a former Army officer who served as Operations Officer of Task Force I-34 Armor in Iraq from September 2003 to September 2004. He is now a fellow at the Center for a New American Security in Washington D.C.

9 General David Petraeus's other counterinsurgency-related assignments include his stint as head of US Central Command from October 2008 to July 2010 and his "demotion" to take General Stanley McChrystal's job as commander, International Security Assistance Force (ISAF) and US Forces Afghanistan (USFOR-A) in July 2010. Petraeus now serves as director of the Central Intelligence Agency (CIA).

10 CORDS stands for Civil Operations and Revolutionary Development Support and was a US program aimed at pacifying the Vietnamese countryside between 1967 and 1971.

11 The classical texts on counterinsurgency include Thompson's *Defeating Communist Insurgency: the Lessons of Malaya and Vietnam* (Thompson 2005); Galula's *Counterinsurgency Warfare: Theory and Practice* (Galula 1964); Trinquier's *Modern Warfare: A French View of Counterinsurgency* (Trinquier 1964); and Frank Kitson's *Low Intensity Operations* (Kitson 1971). These texts are mandatory reading at many US military academies.

3 Domestic pacification

1 Johnson's imagery of rugged individuals fighting crime without any institutional support is also a staple of police fiction. This is a clear instance of political rhetoric feeding on popular culture which, in turn, can feed back into cultural products.
2 The Anti-Drug Abuse Act set the same mandatory minimum sentence of five years for the possession of 5 grams of crack cocaine as for the possession of 500 grams of powder cocaine. The racist effects of these sentencing guidelines have been widely debated. The fact that African Americans are more likely to use the cheaper crack cocaine is well known. At the time of writing, these sentencing guidelines are being reviewed and are likely to be scrapped.

4 Geographies of security

1 The expression 'winning the hearts and minds of the people' is attributed to Sir Gerald Templar, who acted as British High Commissioner in Malaya during the so-called Malayan Emergency (Long 2006: 23). The British campaign against the Malayan National Liberation Army, from 1948 to 1960, is widely hailed as a model for successful counterinsurgency operations (most prominently by Nagl 2005). Alex Marshall (2010), however, argues that British imperial policing was not nearly as focused on the hearts and minds of the population as some of its contemporary adherents claim:

> In practice, British methods remained above all reliant upon the threat of the maximum use of force, and included such techniques as crowd control via the use of indiscriminate volley fire, ethnic displacement, mass floggings and torture, the poisoning of wells and burning of villages, the napalm area bombing of Malayan forests, and the creation of 'free fire' zones – all conducted under extremely permissive legal constraints.
>
> (Marshall 2010: 241)

2 The name of the official is Warren Reece, then coordinator of the Southwest Border High Intensity Drug-Trafficking Area Program and director of Operation Alliance (Dunn 1996: 200n).
3 The findings presented by Newman came out of a research project financed through funds allocated by the 1968 Safe Streets Act. In Chapter 3, we saw that this Act marked the beginning of what Jonathan Simon (Simon 2007) calls 'governance through crime'.
4 Parnaby remarks that Newman's focus on the need to maintain a positive environmental image in many ways anticipated Wilson and Kelling's 'broken-windows' theory (Parnaby 2006: 20 note 6). Katyal, however, laments that environmental design did not figure more prominently in Wilson and Kelling's theory (Katyal 2002: 1083).
5 The INS was part of the Justice Department up until 2003. When it was included in the Border and Transportation Security Directorate of the new Department of Homeland Security (DHS) in March 2003, it was split into a service (permanent residence, asylum, naturalization) branch and an enforcement and intelligence branch. The services functions of immigration policy are now conducted by the US Citizenship and Immigration Services (USCIS), while US Immigration and Customs Enforcement (ICE) is now in charge of enforcement and intelligence, including the detention regime.
6 Many commentators assume that extraordinary rendition was introduced by the Bush administration in direct response to the 9/11 attacks. However, in his inside account of US counterterrorism policy Richard Clarke (2004), former chair of the Counterterrorism Security Group within the US National Security Council, asserts that extraordinary rendition was first introduced under the Reagan administration and was widely practiced under Clinton. Indeed, he contends that the CIA regularly 'snatched' and secretly detained terror suspects during the 1990s and that, to his knowledge, all 'snatches' proposed by the CIA, Justice, or Defense from 1992 to 2001 were approved by the National Security Council (133–54).

5 Organizing security

1 The publications discussed are 'Joint Vision 2010', 'Joint Vision 2020', the Pentagon's 'Transformation Planning Guidance' as well as Vice Admiral Cebrowski's co-authored article 'Network-Centric Warfare' (Department of Defense 1996, 2000, 2003b; Cebrowski and Garstka 1998).
2 The top academic press Price refers to is the University of Chicago Press, whose 2007 edition of the manual made a number of best-seller lists.

6 Legitimizing security

1 The so-called 'Afghan War Diary' was released by whistle-blowing website Wikileaks in July 2010. The diary contains up to 92,000 internal US army documents about the Afghan war effort (Davies and Leigh 2010; Wikileaks 2010). Detailed scholarly analysis of these 'raw' internal messages could reveal to what extent the image of the war produced for public consumption matches US army personnel's perception and communication of the actual events on the ground. Moreover, it remains to be seen whether the heavily publicized 2009 shift towards counterinsurgency in Afghanistan was in itself just an attempt at garnering public support for an increasingly unpopular war. As the documents cover the period from 2004 to late 2009/early 2010, they could perhaps shed light on the question as to if, and how, the shift towards population-centered military operations, which occurred in 2009, was actually implemented on the ground.

References

Agamben, G. (1995) *Homo Sacer. Sovereign Power and Bare Life*; trans. D. Heller-Roazen, Stanford: Stanford University Press.

Agamben, G. (2005) *The State of Exception*; trans. K. Attell, Chicago: University of Chicago Press.

Ake, C. (1967) 'Political Integration and Political Stability: A Hypothesis', *World Politics* 19 (3): 486–99.

Alberts, D. S., Garstka, J. J. and Stein, F. P. (1999) Network Centric Warfare: Developing and Leveraging Information Superiority. Available online at: www.dodccrp.org/html4/research_ncw.html (accessed 7 September 2010).

Albro, R., Peacock, J., Fluehr-Lobban, C., Fosher, K., McNamara, L., Marcus, G., Price, D., Rush, L., Jackson, J., Schoch-Spana, M. and Low, S. (2009) 'AAA Commission on the Engagement of Anthropology with the US Security and Intelligence Communities (CEAUSSIC) Final Report on The Army's Human Terrain System Proof of Concept Program' (14 October 2009). Available online at: www.aaanet.org/issues/policy-advocacy/CEAUSSIC-Releases-Final-Report-on-Army-HTS-Program.cfm (accessed 9 March 2010).

Amnesty International USA (2009) 'Jailed Without Justice: Immigration Detention in the USA'. Available online at: www.amnestyusa.org/immigration-detention/immigrant-detention-report/page.do?id=1641033 (accessed 1 June 2009).

Amoore, L. (2008) 'Consulting, Culture, the Camp: On the Economies of the Exception'. In *Risk and the War on Terror*, Amoore, L. and De Goede, M. (eds.), London: Routledge, 112–29.

Amoore, L. (2009) 'Algorithmic War: Everyday Geographies of the War on Terror', *Antipode* 41 (1): 49–69.

Amoore, L. and De Goede, M. (2008) 'Introduction: Governing by Risk in the War on Terror'. In *Risk and the War on Terror*, Amoore, L. and De Goede, M. (eds.), London: Routledge, 3–19.

Aradau, C. and van Munster, R. (2007) 'Governing Terrorism through Risk: Taking Precautions, (un)Knowing the Future', *European Journal of International Relations* 13 (1): 89–115.

Aradau, C. and van Munster, R. (2008) 'Taming the Future: The Dispositif of Risk in the War on Terror'. In *Risk and the War on Terror*, Amoore, L. and De Goede, M. (eds.), London: Routledge, 23–40.

Armistead, L. (ed.) (2004) *Information Operations. Warfare and the Hard Reality of Soft Power*. Washington, D.C.: Brassey's.

Arquilla, J. (2007) 'The End of War as We Knew It? Insurgency, Counterinsurgency and

Lessons from the Forgotten History of Early Terror Networks', *Third World Quarterly* 28 (2): 369–86.

Arquilla, J. and Ronfeldt, D. (1993) 'Cyberwar is Coming!' *Comparative Strategy* 12 (2): 141–65.

Arquilla, J. and Ronfeldt, D. (2000) *Swarming and the Future of Conflict*, Santa Monica: Rand National Security Research Division (NSDR).

Arquilla, J and Ronfeldt, D. (2001) 'The Advent of Netwar (Revisited)'. In *Networks and Netwars. The Future of Terror, Crime, and Militancy*, Arquilla, J. and Ronfeldt, D. (eds.), Santa Monica: Rand National Defense Research Institute, 1–25.

Bacevich, A. J. (2008) 'The Petraeus Doctrine', *Atlantic Monthly (10727825)*, 17–20.

Bacevich, A. J. (2010) *Washington Rules: America's Path to Permanent War*, New York: Metropolitan Books.

Bakker, R. M., Raab, J. and Milward, H. B. (2011) 'A Preliminary Theory of Dark Network Resilience', *Journal of Policy Analysis and Management* 31 (1): 33–62.

Balko, R. (2006) *Overkill: The Rise of Paramilitary Police Raids in America*, Washington, D.C.: Cato Institute.

Barnett, T. (2004) *The Pentagon's New Map: War and Peace in the Twenty-first Century*, New York: Berkley Books.

Bauman, Z. and Galecki, L. (2005) 'The Unwinnable War: an Interview with Zygmunt Bauman', (1 December 2005). Available online at: www.opendemocracy.net/globalization-vision_reflections/modernity_3082.jsp (accessed 23 March 2012).

Bauman, Z. (2002) *Society under Siege*, Cambridge: Polity Press.

Beck, U. (1992) *The Risk Society*, London: Sage Publications.

Becker, A. and Schulz, G. W. (2011) 'Local Police Stockpile High-tech, Combat-ready Gear', *Center for Investigative Reporting* (21 December 2011). Available online at: http://americaswarwithin.org/articles/2011/12/21/local-police-stockpile-high-tech-combat-ready-gear (accessed 27 December 2011).

Beckett, K. and Herbert, S. (2008) 'Dealing with disorder – Social control in the post-industrial city', *Theoretical Criminology* 12 (1): 5–30.

Beckett, K. and Sasson, T. (2000) *The Politics of Injustice: Crime and Punishment in America*, Thousand Oaks, CA.: Pine Forge Press.

Bell, J. B. (2005) *Assassin: Theory and Practice of Political Violence*, New Brunswick, NJ: Transaction.

Benjamin, W. (1999) 'On the Concept of History'. Available online at: www.marxists.org/reference/archive/benjamin/1940/history.htm (accessed 12 March 2012).

Berger, D. (2006) *Outlaws of America: The Weather Underground and the Politics of Solidarity*, Oakland, CA: AK Press.

Berger, D. (ed.) (2010) *The Hidden 1970s: Histories of Radicalism*, New Brunswick, NJ: Rutgers University Press.

Berger, M. T. and Borer, D. A. (2007) 'The Long War: insurgency, counterinsurgency and collapsing states', *Third World Quarterly* 28 (2): 197–215.

Bernstein, N. (2010) 'Officials Hid Truth of Immigrant Deaths in Jail', *New York Times* (9 January 2010). Available online at: www.nytimes.com/2010/01/10/us/10detain.html (accessed 12 January 2010).

Bigo, D. (2002) 'Security and Immigration: Toward a Critique of the Governmentality of Unease', *Alternatives: Global, Local, Political* 27 (1): 63–92.

Bigo, D. (2008) 'Globalized (In)security: the Field and the Ban-Opticon'. In *Terror, Insecurity and Liberty: Illiberal practices of liberal regimes after 9/11*, Bigo, D. and Tsoukala, A. (eds.), New York: Routledge, 10–48.

Bigo, D. and Tsoukala, A. (2008) 'Understanding (In)security'. In *Terror, Insecurity and Liberty: Illiberal practices of liberal regimes after 9/11*, Bigo, D. and Tsoukala, A. (eds.), New York: Routledge, 1–9.

Blackstock, N. (ed.) (1988) *COINTELPRO: The FBI's Secret War on Political Freedom*, New York: Pathfinder Books.

Blaufarb, D. (1977) *The Counterinsurgency Era: U.S. Doctrine and Performance 1950 to the Present*, New York: The Free Press.

Boot, M. (2000) 'Paving the Road to Hell (Book review): The Failure of UN Peacekeeping', *Foreign Affairs* 79 (2): 143–8.

Bourdieu, P. (1990) *Sociology in Question*, London: Sage Publications.

Bratton, W. W. and Knobler, P. (1998) *Turnaround: How America's Top Cop Reversed the Crime Epidemic*, New York: Random House.

British Broadcasting Corporation (2010) 'Operation Moshtarak: Assault in Helmand Province', *BBC News* (13 February 2010). Available online at: http://news.bbc.co.uk/2/hi/south_asia/8500903.stm (accessed 15 February 2010).

Brown, R. (2003) 'Spinning the War: Political Communications, Information Operations and Public Diplomacy in the War on Terrorism'. In *War and the Media. Reporting Conflict 24/7*, Thussu, D. K. and Freedman, D. (eds.), London: Sage Publications, 87–100.

Brulliard, K. (2007) '"Gated Communities" For the War-Ravaged', *Washington Post*. Available online at: www.washingtonpost.com/wp-dyn/content/article/2007/04/22/AR2007042201419.html (accessed 1 February 2010).

Bullington, B. and Block, A. (1990) 'A Trojan horse – Anti-Communism and the War on Drugs', *Contemporary Crises* 14 (1): 39–55.

Bunker, R. J. (2005) 'Introduction and Overview: Why Response Networks?' In *Networks, Terrorism and Global Insurgency*, Bunker, R. J. (ed.), London, New York: Routledge, 1–19.

Bunker, R. J. (2010) 'Strategic Threat: Narcos and Narcotics Overview', *Small Wars & Insurgencies* 21 (1): 8–29.

Bunker, R. J. (2011a) 'Editor's note', *Small Wars & Insurgencies* 22 (5): 716–17.

Bunker, R. J. (2011b) 'Grand Strategic Overview: Epochal Change and New Realities for the United States', *Small Wars & Insurgencies* 22 (5): 728–41.

Bunker, R. J. and Begert, M. (2008) 'Overview: Defending Against Enemies of the State'. In *Criminal-States and Criminal-Soldiers*, Bunker, R. J. (ed.), London, New York: Routledge, xxvi–xlvi.

Bunker, R. J. and Sullivan, J. P. (2010) 'Cartel Evolution Revisited: Third Phase Cartel Potentials and Alternative Futures in Mexico', *Small Wars & Insurgencies* 21 (1): 30–54.

Bunker, R. J. and Sullivan, J. P. (2011) 'Integrating Feral Cities and Third Phase Cartels/Third Generation Gangs Research: The Rise of Criminal (Narco) City Networks and BlackFor', *Small Wars & Insurgencies* 22 (5): 764–86.

Bush, G. H. W. (2001) 'Address to the Nation, Washington D.C., 20 September 2001'. Available online at: www.presidentialrhetoric.com/speeches/09.20.01.html (accessed 15 November 2011).

Bush, G. H. W. (1988) 'Speech Accepting Nomination for President at the Republican Convention 18 August 1988'. Available online at: http://bushlibrary.tamu.edu/research/pdfs/rnc.pdf (accessed 27 October 2009).

Bush, G. H. W. (1989) 'Remarks at the International Drug Enforcement Conference in Miami, Florida 27 April 1989'. Available online at: http://bushlibrary.tamu.edu/research/public_papers.php?id=365&year=1989&month=4 (accessed 26 October 2009).

164   *References*

Butler, J. (2004) *Precarious Life: the Powers of Mourning and Violence*, London, New York: Verso.

Buzan, B. and Hansen, L. (2009) *The Evolution of International Security Studies*, Cambridge: Cambridge University Press.

Buzan, B., Wæver, O. and de Wilde, J. (1998) *Security: A New Framework for Analysis*, Boulder: Lynne Rienner.

Byman, D. (2006) 'Do Targeted Killings Work?' *Foreign Affairs* 85 (2): 95–111.

Cairo, H. (2006) 'The Duty of the Benevolent Master: From Sovereignty to Suzerainty and the Biopolitics of Intervention', *Alternatives: Global, Local, Political* 31 (3): 285–311.

Calhoun, C. (2010) 'The Idea of Emergency: Humanitarian Action and Global (Dis)Order'. In *Contemporary States of Emergency: The Politics of Military and Humanitarian Interventions*, Fassin, D. and Pandolfi, M. (eds.), New York: Zone Books, 29–58.

Campbell, D. (1998) *Writing Security: United States Foreign Policy and the Politics of Identity*. Minneapolis: University of Minnesota Press.

Carr Center for Human Rights Policy (2006) 'COIN FM Workshop Agenda'. Available online at: www.hks.harvard.edu/cchrp/programareas/workshops/february2006.php (accessed 24 November 2008).

Cassidy, R. M. (2006a) *Counterinsurgency and the Global War on Terror. Military Culture and Irregular War*, Westport, CT: Praeger Security International.

Cassidy, R. M. (2006b) 'The Long Small War: Indigenous Forces for Counterinsurgency', *Parameters: US Army War College* 36 (2): 47–62.

Cassidy, R. M. (2008) 'Counterinsurgency and Military Culture: State Regulars versus Non-State Irregulars', *Baltic Security & Defence Review* 10: 53–85.

Cebrowski, A., and Garstka, J. (1998) 'Network-Centric Warfare', *U.S. Naval Institute Proceedings* January 1998.

Celeski, J. (2006) 'Attacking Insurgent Space: Sanctuary Denial and Border Interdiction', *Military Review* 86 (6): 51–7.

Césaire, A. (1972) *Discourse on Colonialism*, New York: Monthly Review Press. Original edition, 1955.

Chandler, D. (2006a) *Empire in Denial: The Politics of State-building*, London: Pluto Press.

Chandler, D. (2006b) *From Kosovo to Kabul and Beyond: Human Rights and International Intervention*, London: Pluto Press. Original edition, 2002.

Chandler, D. (2010) *International Statebuilding: The Rise of Post-Liberal Governance*, London: Routledge.

Choharis, P. C. and Gavrilis, J. A. (2010) 'Counterinsurgency 3.0', *Parameters: US Army War College* 40 (1): 34–46.

Chomsky, N (1997) 'Introduction'. In *COINTELPRO: The FBI's Secret War on Political Freedom*, Blackstock, N. (ed.), New York: Pathfinder Press, 10–44.

Churchill, W. (2002) 'Preface'. In *The COINTELPRO Papers*, Churchill, W. and Wall, J. V. (eds.), Cambridge, MA: The Southend Press, x-xvi.

Churchill, W. and Wall, J. V. (eds.) (2002) *The COINTELPRO Papers: Documents from the FBI's Secret War against Dissent in the United States*, Cambridge, MA: South End Press.

Clarke, R. A. (2004) *Against all Enemies. Inside America's War on Terror*, New York: Free Press.

Clemis, M. (2009) 'Crafting Non-Kinetic Warfare: the Academic–Military Nexus in US Counterinsurgency Doctrine', *Small Wars & Insurgencies* 20 (1): 160–84.

Clinton, H. R. (2010) 'Remarks on United States Foreign Policy', *Speech at the Council of Foreign Relations* (8 September 2010). Available online at: www.state.gov/secretary/rm/2010/09/146917.htm (accessed 9 September 2010).

Cohen, E. A. (1978) *Commandos and Politicians: Elite Military Units in Modern Democracies*, Cambridge, Mass.: Harvard University Press.

Cole, R. Z. (2005) 'Drug Wars, Counterinsurgency, and the National Guard', *Military Review* 85 (6): 70–73.

Coleman, M. (2005) 'U.S. Statecraft and the U.S.–Mexico Border as Security/Economy Nexus', *Political Geography* 24 (2): 185–209.

Command and Control Research Program (2009) 'Network Centric Warfare', Office of the Assistant Secretary of Defense. Available online at: www.dodccrp.org/html4/research_ncw.html (accessed 5 September 2010).

Congressional Quarterly Incorporated (1971) 'Military Drug Abuse'. In *Congressional Quarterly Almanac*, Washington D.C.: CQ Press.

Congressional Quarterly Incorporated (1984) 'Major Crime Package Cleared by Congress'. In *Congressional Quarterly Almanac*, Washington, D.C.: CQ Press.

Congressional Quarterly Incorporated (1994) 'Lawmakers Enact $30.2 Billion Anti-Crime Bill'. In *Congressional Quarterly Almanac*, Washington D.C.: CQ Press.

Corva, D. (2008) 'Neoliberal Globalization and the War on Drugs: Transnationalizing Illiberal Governance in the Americas', *Political Geography* 27 (2): 176–93.

Côté-Boucher, K. (2008) 'The Diffuse Border: Intelligence-Sharing, Control and Confinement along Canada's Smart Border', *Surveillance & Society* (2). Available online at: http://library.queensu.ca/ojs/index.php/surveillance-and-society/article/view/3432 (accessed 6 January 2011).

Cozens, P., Hillier, D. and Prescott, G. (2001) 'Crime and the Design of Residential Property: Exploring the Theoretical Background (Part I)', *Property Management* 19 (2): 136–64.

Crandall, R. (2002) 'Clinton, Bush and Plan Colombia', *Survival* 44 (1): 159–72.

Crawshaw, M. (2007) 'Running a Country: The British Colonial Experience and its Relevance to Present Day Concerns', *The Shrivenham Papers* (3). Available online at: www.da.mod.uk/colleges/arag/document-listings/monographs/shrivenham_paper_3.pdf/view (accessed 28 July 2010).

Crowe, T. D. (2000) *Crime Prevention through Environmental Design*, Boston, MA: Butterworth-Heinemann.

Cunningham, D. (2003a) 'The Patterning of Repression: FBI Counterintelligence and the New Left', *Social Forces* 82 (1): 209–40.

Cunningham, D. (2003b) 'Understanding State Responses to Left- versus Right-Wing Threats – The FBI's Repression of the New Left and the Ku Klux Klan', *Social Science History* 27 (3): 327–70.

Dalby, S. (2007) 'The Pentagon's Imperial Cartography: Tabloid Realism and the War on Terror'. In *Violent Geographies: Fear, Terror and Political Violence*, Gregory, D and Pred, A (eds.), New York: Routledge, 295–308.

Davies, N and Leigh, D. (2010) 'Afghanistan War Logs: Massive Leak of Secret Files Exposes Truth of Occupation', *Guardian* (25 July 2010). Available online at: www.guardian.co.uk/world/2010/jul/25/afghanistan-war-logs-military-leaks (accessed 23 August 2010).

Davis, M. (1992) *City of Quartz: Excavating the Future in Los Angeles*, New York: Vintage Books.

Davis, M. (2004) 'The Urbanization of Empire', *Social Text* 22 (4): 9–15.

Davis, M. (2006) *Planet of Slums*, London: Verso.

De Goede, M. (2008) 'Risk, Preemption and Exception in the War on Terrorist Financing'. In *Risk and the War on Terror*, Amoore, L. and De Goede, M. (eds.), London: Routledge, 97–111.

De Larrinaga, M. and Doucet, M. G. (2008) 'Sovereign Power and the Biopolitics of Human Security', *Security Dialogue* 39 (5): 517–37.

De Larrinaga, M. and Doucet, M. G. (eds.) (2010a) *Security and Global Governmentality: Globalization, Governance and the State*, London: Routledge.

De Larrinaga, M. and Doucet, M. G. (2010b) 'Introduction: The Global Governmentalization of Security and the Securitization of Global Governance'. In *Security and Global Governmentality: Globalization, Governance and the State*, De Larrinaga, M. and Doucet, M. G. (eds.), London: Routledge, 1–19.

Dean, M. (2000) 'Liberal Government and Authoritarianism', *Economy & Society* 31 (1): 37–61.

Dean, M. (2002) 'Powers of Life and Death Beyond Governmentality', *Cultural Values* 6 (1/2): 119–38.

Democracy Now (2011a) 'Former Seattle Police Chief Norm Stamper on Paramilitary Policing From WTO to Occupy Wall Street', *Democracynow.org* (17 November 2011). Available online at: www.democracynow.org/2011/11/17/paramilitary_policing_of_occupy_wall_street (accessed 25 January 2012).

Democracy Now (2011b) 'The War at Home: Militarized Local Police Tap Post-9/11 Grants to Stockpile Combat Gear, Use Drones', *Democracynow.org* (27 December 2011). Available online at: www.democracynow.org/2011/12/27/the_war_at_home_militarized_local (accessed 27 December 2011).

Democracy Now (2011c) 'With Death of Anwar al-Awlaki, Has U.S. Launched New Era of Killing U.S. Citizens Without Charge?' *Democracynow.org* (30 September 2011). Available online at: www.democracynow.org/2011/9/30/with_death_of_anwar_al_awlaki (accessed 1 March 2012).

Department of Defense (1996) 'Joint Vision 2010'. (July 1996). Available online at: www.dtic.mil/jv2010/jvpub.htm (accessed 9 January 2009).

Department of Defense (2000) 'Joint Vision 2020. America's Military: Preparing for Tomorrow'. (May 2000). Available online at: www.dtic.mil/jointvision/jvpub2.htm (accessed 9 January 2009).

Department of Defense (2003a) 'Information Operations Roadmap'. (October 2003). Available online at: http://information-retrieval.info/docs/DoD-IO.html (accessed 23 August 2010).

Department of Defense (2003b) 'Transformation Planning Guidance'. (May 2003). Available online at: www.defenselink.mil/brac/docs/transformationplanningapr03.pdf (accessed 9 January 2009).

Department of Defense (2005) 'The Implementation of Network-Centric Warfare'. (January 2005). Available online at: www.oft.osd.mil/library/library_files/document_387_NCW_Book_LowRes.pdf (accessed 10 April 2008).

Department of Defense (2010a) 'Quadrennial Defense Review Report'. (February 2010). Available online at: www.defense.gov/QDR/ (accessed 1 May 2010).

Department of Defense (2010b) 'Report on Progress Toward Security and Stability in Afghanistan and United States Plan for Sustaining the Afghanistan National Security Forces', *Report to Congress* (April 2010). Available online at: www.defense.gov/pubs/pdfs/Report_Final_SecDef_04_26_10.pdf (accessed 29 July 2010).

Department of Justice (2009) 'Prisoners in 2008', *Bureau of Justice Statistics Bulletin.*

Available online at: http://bjs.ojp.usdoj.gov/index.cfm?ty=pbdetail&iid=1764 (accessed 1 April 2010).

Department of the Army (1963) 'FM 31–16 Counterguerilla Operations'. Available online at: http://cgsc.cdmhost.com/cdm4/document.php?CISOROOT=/p4013coll9& CISOPTR=278&REC=13 (accessed 11 November 2008).

Department of the Army (2007) *The US Army/Marine Corps Counterinsurgency Field Manual*, Chicago: University of Chicago Press.

Dillon, M. (2002) 'Network Society, Network-centric Warfare and the State of Emergency', *Theory Culture Society* 19 (4): 71–9.

Dillon, M. (2007) 'Governing through Contingency: The Security of Biopolitical Governance', *Political Geography* 26 (1): 41–7.

Dillon, M. and Neal, A. (eds.) (2008) *Foucault on Politics, Security and War*. London: Palgrave.

Dillon, M. and Reid, J. (2001) 'Global Liberal Governance: Biopolitics, Security and War', *Millennium – Journal of International Studies* 30 (1): 41–66.

Dillon, M and Reid, J. (2009) *The Liberal Way of War: Killing to make Life Live*, London: Routledge.

Dow, M. (2004) *American Gulag. Inside U.S. Immigration Prisons*, Berkeley, CA: University of California Press.

Downey, J. and Murdock, G. (2003) 'The Counter-Revolution in Military Affairs: The Globalization of Guerrilla Warfare'. In *War and the Media: Reporting Conflict 24/7*, Thussu, D. K. and Freedman, D. (eds.), London: Sage Publications, 70–86.

Downie, R. D. (1998) *Learning from Conflict. The U.S. Military in Vietnam, El Salvador, and the Drug War*, Westport, CT: Praeger.

Drabble, J. (2004) 'To Ensure Domestic Tranquility: The FBI, COINTELPRO, WHITE HATE and Political Discourse, 1964–1971', *Journal of American Studies* 38 (2): 297–328.

Drug Enforcement Administration (2009) 'DEA History in Depth, 1970–1975', Office of Public Affairs. Available online at: www.justice.gov/dea/history.htm (accessed 16 December 2011).

Drug Enforcement Administration (2011) 'DEA Fact Sheet', Office of Public Affairs. Available online at: www.justice.gov/dea/1107_fact-sheet.pdf (accessed 16 December 2011).

Dudley, M. (2007) 'Revisiting Cold War Ideology in the Secure City: Towards a Political Economy of Urbicide', *Theory and Event* 10 (2). Available online at: http://muse.jhu.edu/journals/theory_and_event/v010/10.2dudley.html (accessed 10 February 2012).

Duffield, M. (1999) 'Internal Conflict: Adaptation and Reaction to Globalisation', *The Corner House* (Briefing 12). Available online at: www.thecornerhouse.org.uk/resource/internal-conflict (accessed 2 September 2010).

Duffield, M. (2001) *Global Governance and the New Wars*, London: Zed Books.

Duffield, M. (2003) 'Social Reconstruction and the Radicalization of Development: Aid as a Relation of Global Liberal Governance'. In *State Failure, Collapse and Reconstruction*, Millikan, J. (ed.), Oxford: Blackwell, 291–312.

Duffield, M. (2005) 'Getting Savages to Fight Barbarians: Development, Security and the Colonial Present', *Conflict, Security and Development* 5 (2): 141–59.

Duffield, M. (2007) *Development, Security and Unending War: Governing the World of Peoples*, Cambridge: Polity.

Duffield, M. (2008) 'Global civil war: The Non-Insured, International Containment and Post-Interventionary Society', *Journal of Refugee Studies* 21 (2): 145–65.

Duffield, M. (2010) 'The Liberal Way of Development and the Development-Security Impasse: Exploring the Global Life-Chance Divide', *Security Dialogue* 41 (1): 53–76.

Dunn, T. J. (1996) *The Militarization of the U.S.–Mexico Border 1978–1992. Low-Intensity Conflict Doctrine Comes Home*, Austin, TX: Center for Mexican American Studies.

Edkins, Jenny and Pin-Fat, V. (2005) 'Through the Wire: Relations of Power and Relations of Violence', *Millennium – Journal of International Studies* 34 (1): 1–24.

Edkins, Jenny, Pin-Fat, V. and Shapiro, M. (eds.) (2004) *Sovereign Lives: Power in Global Politics*. London: Routledge.

Edwards, S. J. A. (2000) *Mars Unmasked. The Changing Face of Urban Operations*, Santa Monica, CA: Rand Arroyo Center.

Eikenberry, K. W. (2009) 'Two Classified Memos to Secretary of State Regarding COIN Strategy and Civilian Concern'. Available online at: http://documents.nytimes.com/eikenberry-s-memos-on-the-strategy-in-afghanistan (accessed 2 July 2010).

Eisenstadt, S. N. (1964) 'Modernization and the Conditions of Sustained Growth', *World Politics* 16 (4).

Emerson, R. (1960) *From Empire to Nation*, Boston: Beacon Press.

Epstein, C. (2008) 'Embodying Risk: Using Biometrics to Protect the Borders'. In *Risk and the War on Terror*, Amoore, L. and De Goede, M. (eds.), London: Routledge, 178–93.

Epstein, E. J. (1977) *Agency of Fear: Opiates and Political Power in America*. London: Verso.

Ericson, R. V. (2008) 'The State of Preemption: Managing Terrorism Risk through Counter Law'. In *Risk and the War on Terror*, Amoore, L. and De Goede, M. (eds.), London: Routledge, 57–76.

Ericson, R.V. and Haggerty, K. D. (1997) *Policing the Risk Society*, Oxford: Clarendon Press.

Ettlinger, N. and Bosco, F. (2004) 'Thinking Through Networks and their Spatiality: A Critique of the US (Public) War on Terrorism and Its Geographic Discourse', *Antipode* 36 (2): 249–71.

Evans, B. (2010) 'Foucault's Legacy: Security, War and Violence in the 21st Century', *Security Dialogue* 41 (4): 413–33.

Fassin, D. and Pandolfi, M. (2010) 'Introduction: Military and Humanitarian Government in the Age of Intervention'. In *Contemporary States of Emergency: The Politics of Military and Humanitarian Interventions*, Fassin, D. and Pandolfi, M. (eds.), New York: Zone Books, 9–25.

Federal Bureau of Investigation (1973) 'Trends in Urban Guerrilla Tactics', *FBI Law Enforcement Bulletin* (July 1973).

Federal Bureau of Investigation (1974) 'Training for the Future', *FBI Law Enforcement Bulletin* (March 1974).

Feely, M. and Simon, J. (1994) 'Actuarial Justice: The Emerging New Criminal Law'. In *The Futures of Criminology*, Nelken, D. (ed.), London: Sage Publications, 173–201.

Feldman, A. (2004) 'Securocratic Wars of Public Safety', *Interventions: The International Journal of Postcolonial Studies* 6 (3): 330–50.

Feldman, G. (2009) 'Radical or Reactionary? The Old Wine in the *Counterinsurgency Field Manual*'s New Flask'. In *The Counter-Counterinsurgency Manual or, Notes on Demilitarizing American Society*, Network of Concerned Anthropologists (eds.), Chicago: Prickly Paradigm Press, 77–93.

Filkins, D. (2008) 'Exiting Iraq, Petraeus Says Gains are Fragile', *New York Times* (21

August 2008). Available online at: www.nytimes.com/2008/08/21/world/middleeast/21general.html?ex=1219896000&en=2755b2f512f5992a&ei=5070&emc=eta1 (accessed 19 November 2008).

Finney, N. (2008) 'Human Terrain Team Handbook', (September 2008). Available online at: www.scribd.com/doc/8959317/Human-Terrain-Handbook-2008 (accessed 9 February 2010).

Foucault, M. (1978) *The History of Sexuality. Volume I: An Introduction*; trans. R. Hurley, New York: Vintage Books. Original edition, 1976.

Foucault, M. (1991a) *Discipline and Punish. The Birth of the Prison*; trans. A. Sheridan, Harmondsworth: Penguin. Original edition, 1975.

Foucault, M. (1991b) 'Governmentality'. In *The Foucault Effect: Studies in Governmentality*, Burchell, G., Gordon, C. and Miller, P. (eds.), Chicago: The University of Chicago Press, 87–104.

Foucault, M. (2000a) 'Interview with Michel Foucault'. In *Power*, Faubion, J. D. (ed.), New York: The New Press, 239–97.

Foucault, M. (2000b) 'Questions of Method'. In *Power*, Faubion, J. D. (ed.), New York: The New Press, 223–38.

Foucault, M. (2000c) 'The Subject and Power'. In *Power*, Faubion, J. D. (ed.), New York: The New Press, 328–48.

Foucault, M. (2000d) 'Truth and Power'. In *Power*, Faubion, J. D. (ed.), New York: The New Press, 111–33.

Foucault, M. (2003) *Society Must be Defended. Lectures at the College de France 1975–1976*; trans. D. Macey, New York: Picador.

Foucault, M. (2007) *Security, Territory, Population. Lectures at the College de France 1977–1978*; trans. G. Burchell, Houndsmill, Basingstoke: Palgrave Macmillan. Original edition, 2004.

Foucault, M. (2008) *The Birth of Biopolitics. Lectures at the College de France 1978–1979*; trans. G. Burchell, Houndsmill, Basingstoke: Palgrave Macmillan.

Fowler, M. C. (2005) *Amateur Soldiers, Global Wars. Insurgency and Modern Conflict*, Westport, Connecticut: Praeger Security International.

Friedmann, R. R. and Cannon, W. J. (2008) 'Homeland Security and Community Policing: Competing or Complementing Public Safety Policies', *Journal of Homeland Security and Emergency Management* 4 (4):1–20.

Galula, D. (1964) *Counterinsurgency Warfare: Theory and Practice*, Westport, Connecticut: Praeger Security International.

Gardner, F. (2010) 'Afghan Operation Moshtarak Places Success Over Surprise', *BBC News* (8 February 2010). Available online at: http://news.bbc.co.uk/2/hi/south_asia/8505179.stm (accessed 15 February 2010).

Garland, D. (1996) 'The Limits of the Sovereign State: Strategies of Crime Control in Contemporary Societies', *British Journal of Criminology* 36 (4): 445–71.

Garland, D. (2001) *The Culture of Control: Crime and Social Order in Contemporary Society*, Oxford: Oxford University Press.

Ghani, A. and Lockhart, C. (2008) *Fixing Failed States: A Framework for Rebuilding a Fractured World*, Oxford: Oxford University Press.

Giddens, A. (1987) *The Nation State and Violence*, Berkeley: University of California Press.

Gilliam, F. D. and Iyenger, S. (2000) 'Prime Suspects: The Influence of Local Television News on the Viewing Public', *American Journal of Political Science* 40 (3): 560–73.

Glanz, J. and Rubin, A. J. (2007) 'From Errand to Fatal Shot to Hail of Fire to 17 Deaths',

New York Times (3 October 2007). Available online at: www.nytimes.com/2007/10/03/world/middleeast/03firefight.html (accessed 6 September 2010).

Glasius, M. and Kaldor, M. (eds.) (2005) *A Human Security Doctrine for Europe*. London: Routledge.

Glick, B. (1989) *War at Home: Covert Action on U.S. Activists and What We Can Do About It*, Cambridge, MA: South End Press.

Glick, B. (1999) 'Preface: The Face of COINTELPRO'. In *The COINTELPRO Papers: Documents from the FBI's Secret Wars Against Domestic Dissent in the United States*, Churchill, W. and Wall, J. V. (eds.), Cambridge, MA: South End Press.

GlobalSecurity.org (2005) 'Joint Special Operations Command (JSOC)'. Available online at: www.globalsecurity.org/military/agency/dod/jsoc.htm (accessed 2 March 2010).

Gompert, D. C., Kelly, T. K., Lawson, B. S., Parker, M. and Colloton, K. (2009) *Reconstruction under Fire: Unifying Civil and Military Counterinsurgency*, Santa Monica, CA: RAND National Defense Research Institute.

González, R. J. (2007) 'Towards Mercenary Anthropology? The New US Army Counterinsurgency Manual *FM 3–24* and the Military–Anthropology Complex', *Anthropology Today* 23 (3): 14–19.

González, R. J. (2009a) *American Counterinsurgency: Human Science and the Human Terrain*, Chicago: Prickly Paradigm Press.

González, R. J. (2009b) 'Embedded: Information Warfare and the "Human Terrain"'. In *The Counter-Counterinsurgency Manual or, Notes on Demilitarizing American Society*, Network of Concerned Anthropologists (eds.), Chicago: Prickly Paradigm Press, 97–113.

González, R. J., Gusterson, H. and Price, D. (2009) 'Introduction'. In *The Counter-Counterinsurgency Manual, or Notes on Demilitarizing American Society*, Network of Concerned Anthropologists (eds.), Chicago: Prickly Paradigm Press, 1–20.

Gordon, A. (2006) '"Purity of Arms", "Preemptive War", and "Selective Targeting" in the Context of Terrorism: General, Conceptual, and Legal Analyses', *Studies in Conflict & Terrorism* 29 (5): 493–508.

Gordon, C. (1991) 'Governmental Rationality'. In *The Foucault Effect. Studies in Governmentality*, Burchell, G., Gordon, C. and Miller, P. (eds.), Chicago: University of Chicago Press, 1–51.

Gordon, C. (2000) 'Introduction'. In *Power*, Faubion, J. D. (ed.), New York: The New Press.

Graham-Harrison, E. (2012) 'Nato Apologise for Afghan Qur'an Burning', *Guardian* (21 February 2012). Available online at: www.guardian.co.uk/world/2012/feb/21/us-nato-apologise-afghan-quran-burning?INTCMP=ILCNETTXT3487 (accessed 24 February 2012).

Graham, S. (2006) '"Homeland" Insecurities? Katrina and the Politics of Security in Metropolitan America', *Space and Culture* 9 (1): 63–67.

Graham, S. (2007) 'War and the City', *New Left Review* 44 (March/April): 121–32.

Graham, S. (2010) *Cities under Siege: The New Military Urbanism*, London: Verso.

Graham, S. (2012) 'Olympics 2012 Security: Welcome to Lockdown London', *Guardian* (12 March 2012). Available online at: www.guardian.co.uk/sport/2012/mar/12/london-olympics-security-lockdown-london?INTCMP=SRCH (accessed 14 March 2012).

Grandin, G. (2010) 'Muscling Latin America', *The Nation* (8 February 2010): 9–13.

Gray, C. H. (1997) *Postmodern War: The New Politics of Conflict*, London: Routledge.

Grayson, K. (2012) 'The Ambivalence of Assassination: Biopolitics, Culture and Political Violence', *Security Dialogue* 43 (1): 25–41.

Green, J. and Mastrofski, S. D. (1987) *Community Policing: Rhetoric or Reality?*, New York: Praeger.

Greenwald, G. (2010) 'Obama Argues His Assassination Program is a "State Secret"', *Salon.com* (25 September 2010). Available online at: www.salon.com/2010/09/25/secrecy_7/ (accessed 1 March 2012).

Gregory, D. (2006) 'The Black Flag: Guantanamo Bay and the Space of Exception', *Geografiska Annaler Series B-Human Geography* 88B (4): 405–27.

Gregory, D. (2008) '"The Rush to the Intimate" – Counterinsurgency and the Cultural Turn', *Radical Philosophy* (150): 8–23.

Gregory, D. (2010) 'Seeing Red: Baghdad and the Event-ful City', *Political Geography* 29 (5): 266–79.

Grondin, D. (2010) 'The New Frontiers of the National Security State: The US Global Governmentality of Contingency'. In *Security and Global Governmentality: Globalization, Governance and the State*, De Larrinaga, M. and Doucet, M. G. (eds.), London: Routledge, 79–95.

Hafez, M. M. and Hatfield, J. M. (2006) 'Do Targeted Assassinations Work? A Multivariate Analysis of Israel's Controversial Tactic During Al-Aqsa Uprising', *Studies in Conflict & Terrorism* 29 (4): 359–82.

Haldeman, H. R. (1994) *The Haldeman Diaries: Inside the Nixon White House*, New York: P. G. Putnam's Sons.

Hammes, T. X. (2006) *The Sling and The Stone. On War in the 21st Century*, Minneapolis, MN: Zenith Press.

Hansen, B. (2000) *Critique of Violence: Between Poststructuralism and Critical Theory*, London: Routledge.

Hardt, M. and Negri, A. (2000) *Empire*, Cambridge, Mass.: Harvard University Press.

Hardt, M and Negri, A. (2004) *Multitude. War and Democracy in the Age of Empire*, London: Penguin.

Hastings, M (2010) 'The Runaway General', *Rolling Stone* (8–22 July 2010). Available online at: www.rollingstone.com/politics/news/17390/119236 (accessed 5 August 2010).

Hayden, T. (2007) 'The New Counterinsurgency', *The Nation* (24 September 2007: 18–24.

Herbert, S. (1999) 'The End of the Territorially-Sovereign State? The Case of Crime Control in the United States', *Political Geography* 18 (2): 149–72.

Herbert, S. and Brown, E. (2006) 'Conceptions of Space and Crime in the Punitive Neoliberal City', *Antipode* 38 (4): 755–77.

Hettne, B. (2010) 'Development and Security: Origins and Future', *Security Dialogue* 41 (1): 31–52.

Heuser, B. (2007) 'The Cultural Revolution in Counter-Insurgency', *Journal of Strategic Studies* 30 (1): 153–71.

Hills, A. (2004) *Future Wars in Cities*, London: Frank Cass.

Hilsman, R. (1967) *To Move a Nation. The Politics of Foreign Policy in the Administration of John F. Kennedy*, New York: Doubleday.

Hindess, B. (1998) 'Neo-liberalism and the National Economy'. In *Governing Australia: Studies of Contemporary Rationalities of Government*, Dean, M. and Hindess, B. (eds.), Cambridge: Cambridge University Press, 127–43.

Hindess, B. 2000. The Liberal Government of Unfreedom. Paper read at Conference on the Ethos of Welfare, Aug–Sep, at Helsinki, Finland.

Hindess, B. (2004) 'Liberalism –What's in a Name?' In *Global Governmentality:*

Governing International Spaces, Larner, W. and Walters, W (eds.), London: Routledge, 23–39.

Hindess, B. (2005) 'Politics as Government: Michel Foucault's Analysis of Political Reason', *Alternatives* 30 (4): 389–413.

Hoffman, F. G. (2007a) *Conflict in the 21st Century: The Rise of Hybrid Wars* Arlington: Potomac Institute for Policy Studies.

Hoffman, F. G. (2007b) 'Neo-Classical Counterinsurgency?' *Parameters: US Army War College* 37 (2): 71–87.

Hoover, J. E. (1970) 'Law Enforcement Faces the Revolutionary-Guerrilla Criminal', *FBI Law Enforcement Bulletin* (December 1970).

Hopper, L. J. and Droge, M. J. (2005) *Security and Site Design: A Landscape Architectural Approach to Analysis, Assessment, and Design Implementation*, Hoboken, NJ: John Wiley & Sons.

Horton, S. (2010a) 'The Guantánamo "Suicides": A Camp Delta Sergeant Blows the Whistle', *Harper's Magazine* (March 2010). Available online at: http://harpers.org/archive/2010/01/hbc-90006368 (accessed 20 March 2010).

Horton, S. 2010b. 'America's Secret Afghan Prisons': Investigation Unearths New US Torture Site, Abuse Allegations in Afghanistan. *Democracy Now* (2 February 2010). Available online at: www.democracynow.org/2010/2/2/americas_secret_afghan_prisons_investigation_unearths (accessed 3 February 2010).

House Un-American Activities Committee (1968) *Guerrilla Warfare Advocates in the United States: Report by the Committee on Un-American Activities*, House Report No. 1351, May 6, 1968, Washington, DC: US Government Printing Office.

Hsu, S. S. and Sheridan, M. B. (2009) 'Anti-Drug Effort at Border is Readied', *Washington Post* (22 March 2009). Available online at: www.washingtonpost.com/wp-dyn/content/article/2009/03/21/AR2009032102247.html (accessed 02/08/2010).

Hunt, R. A. (1995) *Pacification: The American Struggle for Vietnam's Hearts and Minds*, Boulder, CO: Westview Press.

Huntington, S. P. (1968) *Political Order in Changing Societies*, New Haven: Yale University Press.

Huysmans, J (2006) *The Politics of Insecurity: Security, Migration and Asylum in the EU*, London: Routledge.

Huysmans, J. (2011) 'Security Speech Acts and Little Security Nothings', *Security Dialogue* 42 (4–5): 371–83.

Immigration and Customs Enforcement (2009) 'Immigration and Customs Enforcement (ICE) Secure Communities Standard Operating Procedures (SOP)'. Available online at: http://trac.syr.edu/immigration/reports/234/include/securecommunitiesops93009.pdf (accessed 10 January 2012).

Immigration and Customs Enforcement (2011a) 'Activated Jurisdictions'. Available online at: www.ice.gov/doclib/secure-communities/pdf/sc-activated.pdf (accessed 10 January 2012).

Immigration and Customs Enforcement (2011b) 'Secure Communities'. Available online at: www.ice.gov/secure_communities/ (accessed 10 January 2012).

Immigration and Customs Enforcement (2011c) 'The Secure Communities Process'. Available online at: www.ice.gov/secure_communities/ (accessed 10 January 2012).

International CPTED Association (2009) 'Website of the International CPTED Association (ICA)'. Available online at: www.cpted.net (accessed 2 December 2009).

International Security Assistance Force (2010) 'Mission', *North Atlantic Treaty Organization*. Available online at: www.isaf.nato.int/mission.html (accessed 29 July 2010).

Jabri, V. (2006) 'War, Security and the Liberal State', *Security Dialogue* 37 (1): 47–64.

Jacobs, J. (1992) *The Death and Life of Great American Cities*, New York Vintage. Original edition, 1961.

James, J. (ed.) (2007) *Warfare in the American Homeland*. Durham: Duke University Press.

Jensen, E. L. and Gerber, J. (1996) 'The Civil Forfeiture of Assets and the War on Drugs: Expanding Criminal Sanctions While Reducing Due Process Protections', *Crime Delinquency* 42 (3): 421–34.

Johnson, L. B. (1968) *Public Papers of the President, 725–78*, Washington, D.C.: Government Printing Office.

Kaldor, M. (1999) *New and Old Wars. Organized Violence in a Global Era*, Stanford, California: Stanford University Press.

Kaldor, M. (2003) 'American Power: From "Compellance to Cosmopolitanism?" ' *International Affairs* 79 (1): 1–22.

Kaldor, M. and Beebe, S. D. (2010) *The Ultimate Weapon is No Weapon: Human Security and the New Rules of War and Peace*, New York: Public Affairs.

Kan, P. R. (2009) *Drugs and Contemporary Warfare*, Washington, D.C.: Potomac Books.

Kaplan, A. (2003) 'Homeland Insecurities: Reflections on Language and Space', *Radical History Review* (85): 82–93.

Kasher, A. and Yadlin, A. (2005) 'Assassination and Preventive Killing', *SAIS Review* 25 (1): 41–57.

Katyal, N. K. (2002) 'Architecture as Crime Control', *Yale Law Journal* 111 (5): 1039–139.

Keegan, J. (1993) *A History of Warfare*, New York: Vintage Books.

Kelling, G. and Coles, C. (1996) *Fixing Broken Windows: Restoring Order and Reducing Crime in Our Communities*, New York: Free Press.

Kennedy, J. F. (1961) 'Address "The President and the Press" Before the American Newspaper Publishers Association, New York City. April 27, 1961'. In *Public Papers of the Presidents of the United States: John F. Kennedy. January 20 to December 31, 1961*, Washington, D.C.: United States Government Printing Office.

Kenney, M. (2007) *From Pablo to Osama. Trafficking and Terrorist Networks, Government Bureaucracies, and Competitive Adaptation*, University Park, PA: The Pennsylvania State University Press.

Kienscherf, M. (2010) 'Plugging Cultural Knowledge into the U.S. Military Machine: The Neo-Orientalist Logic of Counterinsurgency', *Topia – Canadian Journal of Cultural Studies* (23–24): 121–43.

Kienscherf, M. (2011) 'A Programme of Global Pacification: US Counterinsurgency Doctrine and the Biopolitics of Human (In)security', *Security Dialogue* 42 (6): 517–35.

Kiersey, N. J. (2010) 'Neoliberal Political Economy and the Iraq War: A Contribution to the Debate about Global Biopolitics'. In *Security and Global Governmentality: Globalization, Governance and the State*, De Larrinaga, M. and Doucet, M. G. (eds.), London: Routledge, 61–78.

Kilcullen, D. J. (2005) 'Countering Global Insurgency', *Journal of Strategic Studies* 28 (4): 597–617.

Kilcullen, D. J. (2007a) 'Ethics, Politics, and Non-State Warfare', *Anthropology Today* 23 (3): 20–20.

Kilcullen, D. J. (2007b) 'The Urban Tourniquet – "Gated Communities" in Baghdad', *Small Wars Journal* (April 2007). Available online at: http://smallwarsjournal.com/blog/2007/04/the-urban-tourniquet-gated-com/ (accessed 1 February 2010).

Kilcullen, D. J. (2009) *The Accidental Guerrilla: Fighting Small Wars in the Midst of a Big One*, Oxford: Oxford University Press.

Kilcullen, D. J. (2010) *Counterinsurgency*, Oxford: Oxford University Press.

Kilcullen, D. and McDonald Exum, A. (2009) 'Death From Above, Outrage Down Below', *New York Times* (17 May 2009). Available online at: www.nytimes.com/2009/05/17/opinion/17exum.html?ref=opinion (accessed 1 March 2012).

Kipling, R. (1899) 'The White Man's Burden'. Available online at: http://en.wikisource.org/wiki/The_White_Man%27s_Burden (accessed 9 May 2010).

Kipp, J., Grau, L., Prinslow, K. and Smith, D. (2006) 'The Human Terrain System: A CORDS for the 21st Century', *Military Review* 86 (5): 8–15.

Kitson, F. (1971) *Low Intensity Operations: Subversion, Insurgency and Peacekeeping*, London: Faber and Faber.

Klare, M. T. (1988) 'The Interventionist Impulse: U.S. Military Doctrine for Low-Intensity Warfare'. In *Low-Intensity Warfare: Counterinsurgency, Proinsurgency, and Antiterrorism in the Eighties*, Klare, M. T. and Kornbluh, P. (eds.), New York Pantheon Books, 49–79.

Klare, M. T. and Kornbluh, P. (1988) 'The New Interventionism: Low-Intensity Warfare in the 1980s and Beyond'. In *Low-Intensity Warfare: Counterinsurgency, Proinsurgency, and Antiterrorism in the Eighties*, Klare, M. T. and Kornbluh, P. (eds.), New York: Pantheon Books, 3–20.

Knemayer, F.-L. (1980) 'Polizei', *Economy & Society* 9 (2): 172–96.

Kraska, P. B. (1999) 'Militarizing Criminal Justice: Exploring the Possibilities', *Journal of Political & Military Sociology* 27 (2): 205–15.

Kraska, P. B. and Kappeler, V. E. (1997) 'Militarizing American Police: The Rise and Normalization of Paramilitary Units', *Social Problems* 44 (1): 1–18.

Krepinevich, A. F. Jr. (1986) *The Army and Vietnam*. Baltimore: The Johns Hopkins University Press.

Kuehl, D. (2004) 'Foreword'. In *Information Operations: Warfare and the Hard Reality of Soft Power*, Armistead, L. (ed.), Washington, D.C.: Brassey's, xvii–xviii.

Kuzmarov, J. (2009) *The Myth of the Addicted Army: Vietnam and the Modern War on Drugs*. Amherst: University of Massachusetts Press.

Lahav, G. (2008) 'Mobility and Border Security: The U.S. Aviation System, the State, and the Rise of Public–Private Partnerships'. In *Politics at the Airport*, Salter, M. B. (ed.), Minneapolis: University of Minnesota Press, 77–103.

Laquement, R. A. Jr. (2010) 'Integrating Civilian and Military Activities', *Parameters: US Army War College* 40 (1): 20–33.

Laqueur, Walter (ed.) (1978) *The Guerrilla Reader. A Historical Anthology*. London: Wildwood House.

Larner, W. (2008) 'Spatial Imaginaries: Economic Globalization and the War on Terror'. In *Risk and the War on Terror*, Amoore, L. and De Goede, M. (eds.), London: Routledge, 41–56.

Larner, W., Le Heron, R. and Lewis, N. (2007) 'Co-constituting "After Neoliberalism": Political Projects and Globalising Governmentalities in Aoteara New Zealand'. In *Neo-liberalization: States, Networks, People*. England, K. and Ward, K. (eds.), London: Blackwell Publishers, 223–47.

Larner, W. and Walters, W. (eds.) (2004a) *Global Governmentality: Governing International Spaces*. London: Routledge.

Larner, W and Walters, W. (2004b) 'Globalization as Governmentality', *Alternatives: Global, Local, Political* 29 (5): 495–514.

Lemke, T. (2000) Foucault, Governmentality, and Critique. Paper read at Rethinking Marxism, September 21–24, at University of Amherst.

Light, J. S. (2002) 'Urban Security From Warfare to Welfare', *International Journal of Urban & Regional Research* 26 (3): 607–13.

Light, J. S. (2004) 'Urban Planning and Defense Planning, Past and Future', *Journal of the American Planning Association* 70 (4): 399–410.

Lind, W. S. (2004) 'Understanding Fourth Generation War', *Military Review* (September–October 2004): 12–16.

Long, A. (2006) *On "Other War": Lessons from Five Decades of RAND Counterinsurgency Research*, Santa Monica, CA: RAND Corporation.

Lyon, D. (2005) 'The Border is Everywhere: ID Cards, Surveillance and the Other'. In *Global Surveillance and Policing: Borders, Security, Identity*, Zureik, E. and Salter, M. B. (eds.), Portland, Oregon: Willan Publishing, 66–82.

Lyon, D. (2008) 'Filtering Flows, Friends, and Foes'. In *Politics at the Airport*, Salter, M. B. (ed.), Minneapolis: University of Minnesota Press, 29–49.

Lyons, W. (1999) *The Politics of Community Policing: Rearranging the Power to Punish*, Ann Arbor: The University of Michigan Press.

Madriz, E (1997) *Nothing Bad Happens to Good Girls: Fear of Crime in Women's Lives*, Berkeley: University of California Press.

Mair, J. (2003) 'The New World of Privatized Violence', *Internationale Politik und Gesellschaft (International Politics and Society)* (2). Available online at: www.fes.de/ipg/IPG2_2003/ARTMAIR.HTM (accessed 10 March 2012).

Makaremi, C. (2010) 'Utopias of Power: From Human Security to the Responsibility to Protect'. In *Contemporary States of Emergency: The Politics of Military and Humanitarian Interventions*, Fassin, D. and. Pandolfi, M. (eds.), New York: Zone Books, 107–27.

Mandeles, M. D. (2005) *The Future of War: Organizations as Weapons*, Washington, D.C.: Potomac Books.

Manwaring, M. G. (2005) 'The New Global Security Landscape: The Road Ahead'. In *Networks, Terrorism and Global Insurgency*, Bunker, R. J. (ed.), London, New York: Routledge, 20–39.

Manwaring, M. G. (2008) 'Gangs and *Coups D' Streets* in the New World Disorder: Protean Insurgents in Post-modern War'. In *Criminal-States and Criminal-Soldiers*, Bunker, R. J. (ed.), London, New York: Routledge, 176–215.

Mao, Tse-tung (1954) *On Protracted War*, Beijing: People's Publishing House.

Mao, Tse-tung. (1961) *On Guerilla Warfare*; trans. S. B. Griffith, Champaign, IL: University of Illinois.

Mao, Tse-tung. (1978) 'The Three Stages of Protracted War'. In *The Guerrilla Reader. A Historical Anthology*, Laqueur, W. (ed.), London: Wildwood House, 189–97.

Maple, J. and Mitchell, C. (1999) *The Crime Fighter: How You Can Make Your Community Crime-Free*, New York: Broadway Books.

Marshall, A. (2010) 'Imperial Nostalgia, the Liberal Lie, and the Perils of Postmodern Counterinsurgency', *Small Wars & Insurgencies* 21 (2): 233–58.

Marshall, J. (1987) 'Drugs and United States Foreign Policy'. In *Dealing with Drugs*, Hamowy, R. (ed.), Lexington, Mass.: D. C. Heath and Co, 137–76.

Marx, G. T. (2005) 'Some Conceptual Issues in the Study of Borders and Surveillance'. In *Global Surveillance and Policing: Borders, Security, Identity*, Zureik, E. and Salter, M. B. (eds.), Portland, Oregon: Willan Publishing, 11–35.

Matulich, P. (2012) 'Why COIN Principles Don't Fly with Drones', *Small Wars Journal*

(24 February 2012). Available online at: http://smallwarsjournal.com/jrnl/art/why-coin-principles-dont-fly-with-drones (accessed 1 March 2012).

Mayer, J. (2005) 'Outsourcing Torture: the Secret History of America's "Extraordinary Rendition" Program', *The New Yorker* (14 February 2005).

Mbembe, A. and Meintjes, L. (2003) 'Necropolitics', *Public Culture* 15 (1): 11–40.

McClintock, M. (1992) *Instruments of Statecraft: U.S. Guerrilla Warfare, Counter-Insurgency, and Counter-Terrorism, 1940–1990*, New York: Pantheon Books.

McCoy, A. W. (2003) *The Politics of Heroin: CIA Complicity in the Global Drug Trade.* Chicago: Lawrence Hill Books.

McCuen, Lt. Col. John J. (1966) *The Art of Counter-Revolutionary War: The Strategy of Counter-Insurgency*, Harrisburg, Penn.: Stackpole Books.

McFalls, L. (2010) 'Benevolent Dictatorship: The Formal Logic of Humanitarian Government'. In *Contemporary States of Emergency: The Politics of Military and Humanitarian Interventions*, Fassin, D. and Pandolfi, M. (eds.), New York: Zone Books, 317–33.

McFate, M. (2004) 'ONR Conference Makes Case for Study of Cultures', *Office of Naval Research.* Available online at: http://fellowships.aaas.org/PDFs/2004_1210_ORIG-conf.pdf (accessed 18 November 2008).

McFate, M. (2005a) 'Anthropology and Counterinsurgency: The Strange Story of Their Curious Relationship', *Military Review* 85 (2): 24–38.

McFate, M. (2005b) 'The Military Utility of Understanding Adversary Culture', *JFQ: Joint Force Quarterly* (38): 42–48.

McFate, M. (2007) 'Building Bridges or Burning Heretics?' *Anthropology Today* 23 (3): 21.

McFate, M. and Jackson, A. (2005) 'An Organizational Solution for DOD's Cultural Knowledge Needs', *Military Review* 85 (4): 18–21.

McFate, M and Jackson, A. (2006) 'The Object Beyond War: Counterinsurgency and the Four Tools of Political Competition', *Military Review* (January–February 2006): 56–69.

Medovoi, L. (2007) 'Global Society Must Be Defended', *Social Text* 25 (2 91): 53–79.

Meisler, S. (1989) 'Nothing Works', *Los Angeles Times Magazine*, 3 April, 1989.

Merlingen, M. (2008) 'Monster Studies', *International Political Sociology* 2 (3): 272–74.

Miller, G. (2010) 'Muslim Cleric Aulaqi is 1st U.S. Citizen on List of Those CIA is Allowed to Kill', *Washington Post* (7 April 2010). Available online at: www.washingtonpost.com/wp-dyn/content/article/2010/04/06/AR2010040604121.html (accessed 1 March 2012).

Miller, P. and Rose, N. (2008) *Governing the Present: Administering Economic, Social and Personal Life*, Cambridge: Polity Press.

Milward, H. B. and Raab, J. (2006) 'Dark Networks as Organizational Problems: Elements of a Theory 1', *International Public Management Journal* 9 (3):333–60.

Moore, M. H. (1990) 'Problem-solving and community policing'. In *Modern Policing*, Morris, N. and Tonry, M. (eds.), Chicago: University of Chicago Press, 99–158.

Moore, M. H. and Trojanowicz, R. C. (1988) *Policing and the Fear of Crime: Perspectives on Policing*, Washington D.C.: National Institute of Justice.

Morales, W. Q. (1989) 'The War on Drugs: a New US National Security Doctrine?' *Third World Quarterly* 11 (3): 147–69.

Mouffe, C. (2005) *The Return of The Political*, London: Verso.

Muller, B. J. (2005) 'Borders, Bodies and Biometrics: Towards Identity Management'. In *Global Surveillance and Policing: Borders, Security, Identity*, Zureik, E. and Salter, M. B. (eds.), Portland, Oregon: Willan Publishing, 83–96.

Nadelmann, E. A. (1993) *Cops Across Borders: The Internationalization of U.S. Criminal Law Enforcement*, University Park, PA: The Pennsylvania State University Press.

Nagl, J. A. (2005) *Learning to Eat Soup with a Knife. Counterinsurgency Lessons from Malaya and Vietnam*, Chicago: University of Chicago Press.

Nagl, J. A. (2007) 'Foreword to the University of Chicago Press Edition'. In *The U.S. Army/Marine Corps Counterinsurgency Field Manual*, Department of the Army, Chicago: University of Chicago Press, xii–xx.

Naím, M. (2003) 'The Five Wars of Globalization', *Foreign Policy* (1 January 2003). Available online at: www.foreignpolicy.com/articles/2003/01/01/five_wars_of_globalization?page=full (accessed 9 March 2012).

Neal, A. W. (2004) 'Cutting Off the King's Head: Foucault's Society Must be Defended and the Problem of Sovereignty', *Alternatives* 29 (4): 373–98.

Neal, A. W. (2006) 'Foucault in Guantanamo: Towards an Archaeology of the Exception', *Security Dialogue* 37 (1): 31–46.

Neocleous, M. (2000) *The Fabrication of Social Order: A Critical Theory of State Power*, London: Pluto Press.

Neocleous, M. (2006a) 'From Social to National Security: On the Fabrication of Economic Order', *Security Dialogue* 37 (3): 363–84.

Neocleous, M. (2006b) 'The Problem with Normality: Taking Exception to "Permanent Emergency."', *Alternatives: Global, Local, Political* 31 (2): 191–213.

Neocleous, M. (2007) 'Whatever Happened to Martial Law? Detainees and the Logic of Emergency', *Radical Philosophy* 143 (May/June 2007): 13–22.

Neocleous, M. (2008) *Critique of Security*, Edinburgh: Edinburgh University Press.

Neocleous, M. (2011) ' "A Brighter and Nicer New Life": Security as Pacification', *Social & Legal Studies* 29 (2): 191–208.

Newman, O. (1972) *Defensible Space: Crime Prevention through Urban Design*, New York: Macmillan.

Newman, O. (1996) *Creating Defensible Space*, Washington D.C.: U.S. Department of Housing and Urban Development Office of Policy Development and Research.

Nixon, R. M. (1969) 'Text of Nixon Message on Plan to Attack Drugs Abuse'. In *Congressional Quarterly Almanac*, Washington D.C.: CQ Press.

Nixon, R. M. (1973) 'Message to the Congress Transmitting Reorganization Plan 2 of 1973 Establishing the Drug Enforcement Administration', (28 March 1973). Available online at: www.presidency.ucsb.edu/ws/index.php?pid=4159#axzz1gz1kkZSw (accessed 19 December 2011).

North, A. (2012) 'Will Afghan Koran Row Prove Nato's Tipping Point?' *BBC News* (23 February 2012). Available online at: www.bbc.co.uk/news/world-asia-17140569 (accessed 24 February 2012).

Norton, R. J. (2003) 'Feral Cities', *U.S. Naval War College Review* (Autumn 2003). Available online at: www.usnwc.edu/Publications/Naval-War-College-Review/2003--Autumn.aspx (accessed 25 September 2010).

Norton, R. J. (2010) 'Feral Cities: Problems Today, Battlefields Tomorrow', *Marine Corps University Journal* (1). Available online at: www.marines.mil/news/publications/Documents/Marine%20Corps%20University%20Journal%20Vol%201,%20No%201%20PCN%2010600001400.pdf (accessed 5 February 2012).

Obama, B. (2009) 'Remarks by the President in Address to the Nation on the Way Forward in Afghanistan and Pakistan at Eisenhower Hall Theatre, United States Military Academy at West Point, West Point, New York', (1 December 2009). Available online at: www.whitehouse.gov/the-press-office/remarks-president-address-nation-way-forward-afghanistan-and-pakistan (accessed 6 May 2010).

Olson, M. Jr. (1963) 'Rapid Growth as a Destabilizing Force', *Journal of Economic History* 23 (4): 529–52.

Parenti, C. (1999) *Lockdown America: Police and Prisons in the Age of Crisis*, London: Verso.

Parenti, C. (2005) 'New Orleans: Raze or Rebuild?' *The Nation* (26 September 2005). Available online at: www.thenation.com/article/new-orleans-raze-or-rebuild (accessed 6 September 2010).

Parnaby, P. F. (2006) 'Crime Prevention through Environmental Design: Discourses of Risk, Social Control, and a Neo-liberal Context', *Canadian Journal of Criminology & Criminal Justice* 48 (1): 1–29.

Pasquino, P. (1993) 'Political Theory of War and Peace – Foucault and the History of Modern Political Theory', *Economy and Society* 22 (1): 77–88.

Peck, J. (2003) 'Geography and Public Policy: Mapping the Penal State', *Progress in Human Geography* 27 (2): 222–32.

Peters, R. (1994) 'The New Warrior Class', *Parameters: US Army War College* (Summer 1994). Available online at: www.carlisle.army.mil/usawc/parameters/Articles/1994/peters.htm (accessed 2 June 2010).

Peters, R. (2000) 'The Human Terrain of Urban Operations', *Parameters: US Army War College* 30 (122): 4–12.

Peters, R. (2007) 'Progress and Peril: New Counterinsurgency Manual Cheats on the History Exam', *Armed Forces Journal International* (February 2007). Available online at: www.afji.com/2007/02/2456854/ (accessed 11 May 2010).

Petraeus, D. H. (2010) 'COMISAF's Counterinsurgency Guidance', (1 August 2010). Available online at: http://usacac.army.mil/blog/blogs/coin/archive/2010/07/28/general-petraeus-issues-new-comisaf-coin-guidance.aspx (accessed 3 August 2010).

Petraeus, D. H. and Amos, J. F. (2007) 'Foreword'. In *The U.S Army/Marine Corps Counterinsurgency Field Manual*, Department of the Army, Chicago: University of Chicago Press, xlv–xlvi.

Price, D. (2007) 'Pilfered Scholarship Devastates General Petraeus's *Counterinsurgency Manual*', *Counterpunch* (30 October 2007). Available online at: www.counterpunch.org/price10302007.html (accessed 11 March 2010).

Price, D. (2009) 'Faking Scholarship: Domestic Propaganda and the Republication of the *Counterinsurgency Field Manual*'. In *The Counter-Counterinsurgency Manual or, Notes on Demilitarizing American Society*, Network of Concerned Anthropologists (eds.), Chicago: Prickly Paradigm Press, 59–76.

Prozorov, S. (2006) 'Liberal Enmity: The Figure of the Foe in the Political Ontology of Liberalism', *Millennium-Journal of International Studies* 35 (1): 75–99.

Purdham, T. S. (1993) 'Giuliani Campaign's Theme: Dinkins Isn't up to the Job', *New York Times* 24 October.

Quiao, L. and Xiangsui, W. (1999) 'Unrestricted Warfare'. Available online at: www.terrorism.com/documents/TRC-Analysis/unrestricted.pdf (accessed 21 October 2009).

Raab, J. and Milward, H. B. (2003) 'Dark Networks as Problems', *Journal of Public Administration Research and Theory* 13 (4): 413–39.

Reagan, R. (1986) 'Remarks on Signing the Anti-Drug Abuse Act of 1986'. In *Ronald Reagan. Public Papers of the Presidents of the United States*, Washington, D.C.: U.S. Government Printing Office.

Reid, J. (2005) 'The Biopolitics of the War on Terror: A Critique of the "Return of Imperialism" Thesis in International Relations', *Third World Quarterly* 26 (2): 237–52.

Reid, J. (2006) *The Biopolitics of the War on Terror. Life Struggles, Liberal Modernity, and the Defence of Logistical Societies*, Manchester: Manchester University Press.

Rejali, D. (2007). *Torture and Democracy*, Princeton, NJ: Princeton University Press.

Renzi, F. (2006) 'NETWORKS: Terra Incognita and the Case for Ethnographic Intelligence', *Military Review* 86 (5): 16–22.

Rice, C. (2005) 'The Promise of Democratic Peace: Why Promoting Freedom is the Only Realistic Path to Security', *The Washington Post* (11 December 2005).

Robertson, G. (1999) *Crimes Against Humanity: The Struggle for Global Justice*, London: Penguin.

Rose, N. and Miller, P. (1992) 'Political Power Beyond the State – Problematics of Government', *British Journal of Sociology* 43 (2): 173–205.

Roston, A. (2009) 'How the US Funds the Taliban', *The Nation* (30 November 2009). Available online at: www.thenation.com/article/how-us-funds-taliban (accessed 15 August 2010).

Roston, A. (2010) 'Congressional Investigation Confirms: US Military Funds Afghan Warlords', *The Nation* (21 June 2010). Available online at: www.thenation.com/article/36493/congressional-investigation-confirms-us-military-funds-afghan-warlords (accessed 12 August 2010).

Rudziak, N. D. (1966) 'Police–Military Relations in a Revolutionary Environment', *The Police Chief* (September 1966).

Russell, K. (1998) *The Color of Crime*, New York: New York University Press.

Sadd, S. and Grinc, R. (1994) 'Innovative Neighborhood Oriented Policing: an Evaluation of Community Policing Programs in Eight Cities'. In *The Challenges of Community Policing: Testing the Promises*, Rosenbaum, D. (ed.), Thousand Oaks, CA: Sage Publications, 27–52.

Sageman, M. (2004) *Understanding Terror Networks*, Philadelphia: University of Pennsylvania Press.

Sageman, M. (2008) *Leaderless Jihad: Terror Networks in the Twenty-first Century*, Philadelphia: University of Pennsylvania Press.

Sahlins, M. (2009) 'Preface'. In *The Counter-Counterinsurgency Manual or, Notes on Demilitarizing American Society*, Network of Concerned Anthropologists (eds.) Chicago: Prickly Paradigm Press, i–vii.

Said, Edward (1979) *Orientalism*, New York: Vintage Books.

Salter, Mark B. (2005) 'At the Threshold of Security: a Theory of International Borders'. In *Global Surveillance and Policing: Borders, Security, Identity*, Zureik, E. and Salter, M. B. (eds.), Portland, Oregon: Willan Publishing, 36–50.

Salter, Mark B. (2008a) 'Introduction: Airport Assemblage'. In *Politics at the Airport*, Salter, M. B. (ed.), Minneapolis: University of Minnesota Press, ix–xix.

Salter, Mark B. (2008b) 'The Global Aiport: Managing Space, Speed, and Security'. In *Politics at the Airport*, Salter, M. B. (ed.), Minneapolis: University of Minnesota Press, 1–28.

Scahill, J. (2007) *Blackwater. The Rise of the World's Most Powerful Mercenary Army*, New York: Nation Books.

Scahill, J. (2009a) 'Blackwater Still Armed in Iraq', *The Nation* (14 August 2009). Available online at: www.thenation.com/article/blackwater-still-armed-iraq (accessed 2 September 2010).

Scahill, J. (2009b) 'Blackwater: CIA Assassins?' *The Nation* (20 August 2009). Available online at: www.thenation.com/article/blackwater-cia-assassins (accessed 2 September 2010).

Scahill, J. (2009c) 'The Secret US War in Pakistan', *The Nation* (2 December 2009). Available online at: www.thenation.com/article/secret-us-war-pakistan-0 (accessed 2 September 2010).

Scahill, J. (2010) 'Obama Administration Keeping Blackwater Armed and Dangerous in Afghanistan', *The Nation* (19 June 2010). Available online at: www.thenation.com/blog/36444/obama-administration-keeping-blackwater-armed-and-dangerous-afghanistan (accessed 2 September 2009).

Scheider, M. and Chapman, R. (2003) 'Community Policing and Terrorism', *Homeland Security Institute*. Available online at: www.homelandsecurity.org/journal/articles/Scheider-Chapman.html (accessed 10 August 2009).

Schinkel, W. (2009) 'Illegal Aliens and the State, or: Bare Bodies vs. the Zombie', *International Sociology* 24 (6): 779–806.

Schlesinger, A. M. Jr. (1965) *A Thousand Days*, London: Andre Deutsch.

Schmitt, C. (1985) *Political Theology*, Cambridge, MA: MIT Press. Original edition, 1922.

Schmitt, C. (1996) *The Concept of the Political*, Chicago: University of Chicago Press.

Schneider, R. H. and Kitchen, T. (2002) *Planning for Crime Prevention: A Transatlantic Perspective*, New York: Routledge.

Scott, J. C. (2005) 'Afterword to "Moral Economies, State Spaces, and Categorical Violence"', *American Anthropologist* 107 (3): 395–402.

Sellars, K. (1999) 'The Tyranny of Human Rights', *Spectator* (28 August 1999): 11–12.

Sewall, S. (2007) 'Introduction to the University of Chicago Press Edition'. In *The U.S. Army/Marines Counterinsurgency Field Manual*, Department of the Army Chicago: University of Chicago Press, xxi-xliii.

Shafer, M. D. (1988) *Deadly Paradigms. The Failure of U.S. Counterinsurgency Policy*, Princeton: Princeton University Press.

Shapiro, M. J. (2009) 'Managing Urban Security: City Walls and Urban Metis', *Security Dialogue* 40 (4–5): 443–61.

Shaw, M. (1994) *Global Society and International Relations: Sociological Concepts and Political Perspectives*, Cambridge: Polity Press.

Sherry, M. S. (1995) *In the Shadow of War. The United States since the 1930s*, New Haven: Yale University Press.

Shils, E. (1958) 'The Concentration and Dispersion of Charisma', *World Politics* 11 (1).

Silverman, E. B. and Della-Guistina, J.-A. (2001) 'Urban Policing and the Fear of Crime', *Urban Studies* 38 (5–6): 941–57.

Simon, J. (1993) 'From Confinement to Waste Management: the Post-Modernization of Social Control', *Focus on Law Studies* 8 (2): 4–8.

Simon, J. (1998) 'Refugees in a Carceral Age: The Rebirth of Immigration Prisons in the United States', *Public Culture* 10 (3): 577–607.

Simon, J. (1999) 'Paramilitary features of contemporary penality', *Journal of Political & Military Sociology* 27 (2): 279–90.

Simon, J. (2000) 'The "Society of Captives" in the Era of Hyper-Incarceration', *Theoretical Criminology* 4 (3): 285–308.

Simon, J. (2007) *Governing through Crime: How the War on Crime Transformed American Democracy and Created a Culture of Fear*, Oxford: Oxford University Press.

Singer, P. W. (2003) *Corporate Warriors. The Rise of the Privatized Military Industry*, Ithaca: Cornell University Press.

Singer, P. W. (2007) 'Can't Win With 'Em, Can't Go To War Without 'Em: Private Military Contractors and Counterinsurgency', *Brookings Institution Foreign Policy Papers* (September 2007). Available online at: www.brookings.edu/papers/2007/0927militaryc ontractors.aspx (accessed 6 September 2010).

Slim, H. (2004) 'With or Against? Humanitarian Agencies and Coalition Counter-Insurgency', *Centre for Humanitarian Dialogue* (July 2004). Available online at: www.hdcentre.org/files/With%20or%20Against%20.pdf (accessed 16 February 2010).

Solnit, R. (2010) 'Reconstructing the Story: Hurricane Katrina at Five', *The Nation* (26 August 2010). Available online at: www.thenation.com/article/154168/reconstructing-story-storm-hurricane-katrina-five (accessed 6 September 2010).

Sontag, S. (1989) *AIDS and Its Metaphors*, New York: Farrar, Straus and Giroux.

Sorenson, T. (1965) *Kennedy*, New York: Harper and Row.

Sparke, M. B. (2006) 'A Neoliberal Nexus: Economy, Security and the Biopolitics of Citizenship on the Border', *Political Geography* 25 (2): 151–80.

Sparke, M. B. (2008) 'Fast Capitalism/Slow Terror: Cushy Cosmopolitanism and its Extraordinary Others'. In *Risk and the War on Terror*, Amoore, L. and De Goede, M. (eds.), London: Routledge, 133–57.

Stamper, N. (2011) 'Paramilitary Policing From Seattle to Occupy Wall Street', *The Nation* (9 November 2011). Available online at: www.thenation.com/article/164501/ paramilitary-policing-seattle-occupy-wall-street (accessed 25 January 2012).

Statman, D. (2004) 'Targeted Killing', *Theoretical Inquiries in Law* 5 (1): 179–98.

Stern, M. and Ojendal, J. (2010) 'Mapping the Security–Development Nexus: Conflict, Complexity, Cacophony, Convergence?' *Security Dialogue* 41 (1): 5–29.

Stevens, J. (2010) 'America's Secret ICE Castles', *The Nation* (4 January 2010): 13–17.

Stokes, D. (2005) *America's Other War: Terrorizing Colombia*. New York: Zed Books.

Sullivan, J. P. (1997) 'Generation Street Gangs: Turf, Cartels and NetWarriors', *Crime & Justice International* (10). Available online at: www.cjimagazine.com/archives/cji673a. html?issn=10&vol=13&pub=International (accessed 27 June 2010).

Sullivan, J. P. (2000) 'Urban Gangs Evolving as Criminal Netwar Actors', *Small Wars & Insurgencies* 11 (1): 82–96.

Sullivan, J. P. (2005) 'Terrorism, Crime and Private Armies'. In *Networks, Terrorism and Global Insurgency*, Bunker, R. J. (ed.), London, New York: Routledge, 69–83.

Sullivan, J. P. (2008) 'Maras Morphing: Revisiting Third Generation Gangs'. In *Criminal-States and Criminal-Soldiers*, Bunker, R. J. (ed.), London, New York: Routledge, 159–76.

Sullivan, J. P. and Bunker, R. J. (2011) 'Rethinking Insurgency: Criminality, Spirituality, and Societal Warfare in the Americas', *Small Wars & Insurgencies* 22 (5): 742–63.

Summers, H. (1982) *On Strategy: A Critical Analysis of the Vietnam War*, Novato, CA: Presidio Press.

Taw, J. and Hoffman, B. (1994) 'The Urbanization of Insurgency: The Potential Challenges to US Army Operations', *RAND Monograph Report*. Available online at: www. rand.org/pubs/monograph_reports/MR398/ (accessed 28 September 2010).

Thompson, R. (2005) *Defeating Communist Insurgency*, St. Petersburg, FL: Hailer Publishing. Original edition, 1966.

Thruelsen, P. D. (2010) 'The Taliban in Southern Afghanistan: a Localised Insurgency with a Local Objective', *Small Wars & Insurgencies* 21 (2):259–76.

Tierney, J. F. (ed.) (2010) *Warlord, Inc.: Extortion Along the U.S. Supply Chain in Afghanistan. Report of the Majority Staff*. Washington, D.C.: Subcommittee on National Security and Foreign Affairs, Committee on Oversight and Government Reform.

Tilly, C. (1985) 'War Making and State Making as Organized Crime'. Available online at: https://netfiles.uiuc.edu/rohloff/www/war%20making%20and%20state%20making. pdf (accessed 23 November 2008).

Tilly, C. (1992) *Coercion, Capital, and European States, AD 999–1992*, Oxford: Blackwell.

Townshend, C. (1986) *Britain's Civil Wars: Counterinsurgency in the Twentieth Century*, London: Faber and Faber.

Trinquier, R. (1964) *Modern Warfare: A French View of Counterinsurgency*, New York: Praeger.

Tucker, D. (1998) 'Fighting Barbarians', *Parameters: US Army War College* (Summer 1998). Available online at: www.carlisle.army.mil/usawc/parameters/Articles/98summer/ tucker.htm (accessed 2 June 2010).

Tyner, J. (2009) *War, Violence, and Population: Making the Body Count*, New York: The Guilford Press.

Ucko, D. H. (2009) *The New Counterinsurgency Era: Transforming the U.S. Military for Modern Wars*, Washington D.C.: Georgetown University Press.

United Nations (1945) 'Chapter 1 Purposes and Principles', *Charter of the United Nations* (Article 2). Available online at: www.un.org/en/documents/charter/chapter1.shtml (accessed 24 September 2010).

United Nations (1999) *UNHCR Revised Guidelines on Applicable Criteria and Standards Relating to the Detention of Asylum Seekers*, Geneva: Office of the UNHCR.

United Nations (2003) 'Human Security Now', *United Nations Commission on Human Security*. Available online at: www.humansecurity-chs.org/finalreport/index.html (accessed 20 May 2010).

United States Customs and Border Protection (2009) 'NEXUS Program Description'. Available online at: www.cbp.gov/xp/cgov/travel/trusted_traveler/nexus_prog/nexus. xml (accessed 27 January 2010).

United States Government (1961a) 'National Security Action Memorandum Number 2: Development of Counter-guerrilla Forces', *John F. Kennedy Presidential Library and Museum.* Available online at: www.jfklibrary.org/Asset+Tree/Asset+Viewers/ Image+Asset+Viewer.htm?guid={9D435253–7A2A-4B26–8712–94F6AD7C15F7}&ty pe=Image (accessed 11 December 2008).

United States Government (1961b) 'National Security Action Memorandum No. 119: Civic Action', *John F. Kennedy Presidential Library and Museum.* Available online at: www.jfklibrary.org/Asset+Tree/Asset+Viewers/Image+Asset+Viewer.htm?guid= {0B85A9A1-F374–443D-8B2E-E9EFA1D6D2CA}&type=Image (accessed 19 December 2008).

United States Government (1962a) 'National Security Action Memorandum No. 124: Establishment of the Special Group (Counter-Insurgency)'. In *The Pentagon Papers. The Defense Departments History of United States Decisionmaking on Vietnam Vol. II*, Boston: Beacon.

United States Government (1962b) 'United States Overseas Internal Defense Policy', (September 1962). Available online at: http://drworley.org/NSPcommon/OIDP/OIDP. pdf (accessed 15 December 2008).

United SZtates Government (1967) *Report of the National Advisory Commission on Civil Disorders*, New York: Bantham Books.

United States Government (2002) 'The National Security Strategy of the United States of America', (September 2002). Available online at: http://merln.ndu.edu/whitepapers/ USnss2002.pdf (accessed 1 February 2012).

United States Joint Forces Command (2008) 'The Joint Operating Environment 2008: Challenges and Implications for the Future Joint Forces'. Available online at: www. jfcom.mil/newslink/storyarchive/2008/JOE2008.pdf (accessed 8 February 2010).

United States Senate, (1976) 'COINTELPRO: The FBI's Covert Action Programs Against American Citizens', *Select Committee to Study Governmental Relations with respect to Intelligence Activities*. Available online at: www.archive.org/stream/ finalreportofsel03unit#page/n3/mode/2up (accessed 16 December 2011).

Urquhart, B. (2000) 'In the Name of Humanity', *New York Review of Books* XLVII (27 April): 19–22.

Valverde, M. (2003) 'Targeted Governance and the Problem of Desire'. In *Risk and Morality*, Ericson, R. and Doyle, A. (ed.), Toronto: University of Toronto Press, 438–58.

Valverde, M. and Mopas, M. (2004) 'Insecurity and the Dream of Targeted Governance'. In *Global Governmentality: Governing International Spaces*, Larner, W. and Walters, W. (eds.), London: Routledge, 233–50.

Van Creveld, M. (1991) *The Transformation of War*, New York: The Free Press.

Van Creveld, M. (2006) *The Changing Face of War: Lessons of Combat from the Marne to Iraq*, New York: Ballantine Books.

Van Creveld, M. (2008) 'The Fate of the State Revisited'. In *Criminal-States and Criminal-Soldiers*, Bunker, R. J. (ed.), London, New York: Routledge, 1–36.

Van Konynenberg, M. (1997) 'The Urban Century: Developing World Urban Trends and Possible Factors Affecting Military Operations', *Defense Intelligence Reference Document. Marine Corps Intelligence Agency* (November 1997).

Virilio, P. (1989) *War and Cinema. The Logistics of Perception*; trans. P. Camiller, London: Verso. Original edition, 1984.

Voelkner, N. (2010) 'Governmentalizing the State: the Disciplinary Logic of Human Security'. In *Security And Global Governmentality: Globalization, Governance and the State*, De Larrinaga, M. and Doucet, M. G. (eds.), London: Routledge, 132–49.

Von Clausewitz, C. (1976) *On War*, Princeton, NJ: Princeton University Press.

Wacquant, L. (2001a) 'The Advent of the Penal State is Not a Destiny', *Social Justice* 28 (3): 81–87.

Wacquant, L. (2001b) 'Deadly Symbiosis: When Ghetto and Prison Meet and Mesh', *Punishment and Society* 3 (1): 95–134.

Wacquant, L. (2008) 'The Militarization of Urban Marginality: Lessons from the Brazilian Metropolis', *International Political Sociology* 2 (1): 56–74.

Wacquant, L. (2009a) 'The Body, the Ghetto and the Penal State', *Qualitative Sociology* 32 (1): 101–29.

Wacquant, L. (2009b) *Punishing the Poor: The Neoliberal Government of Social Insecurity*, Durham: Duke University Press.

Walker, R. B. J. (1990) 'Security, Sovereignty, and the Challenge of World Politics', *Alternatives* 15 (1): 3–27.

Walker, R. B. J. (1993) *Inside/outside: International Relations as Political Theory*, Cambridge: Cambridge University Press.

Walker R. B. J. (1997) 'The Subject of Security'. In *Critical Security Studies*, Krause, K. and Williams, M. C. (eds.), Minneapolis: University of Minnesota Press, 61–81.

Walsh, D., Addley, E. and MacAskill, E. (2011) '40 minutes of Fighting, and Then Two Fatal Shots', *Guardian* (3 May 2011). Available online at: www.guardian.co.uk/ world/2011/may/02/osama-bin-laden-killed-abbottabad-raid?intcmp=239 (accessed 1 March 2012).

Walters, W. (2004) 'Secure Borders, Safe Haven, Domopolitics', *Citizenship Studies* 8 (3): 237–60.

Warren, R. (2002) 'Situating the City and September 11th: Military Urban Doctrine, "Pop-up Armies" and Spatial Chess', *International Journal of Urban & Regional Research* 26 (3): 614–19.

Warren, R. (2004) 'City Streets – The War Zones of Globalization: Democracy and Military Operations on Urban Terrain in the Early Twenty-First Century'. In *Cities, War, and Terrorism. Towards an Urban Geopolitics*, Graham, S. (ed.), Oxford: Blackwell, 214–30.

Watson, J. (2005) 'Oil Wars, or Extrastate Conflict "Beyond the Line": Schmitt's Nomos, Deleuze's War Machine, and the New Order of the Earth', *South Atlantic Quarterly* 104 (2): 349–57.

Weber, M. (1919) 'Politics as a Vocation'. Available online at: www.ne.jp/asahi/moriy-uki/abukuma/weber/lecture/politics_vocation.html (accessed 29 July 2008).

Weizman, E. (2007) *Hollow land: Israel's architecture of occupation*, London: Verso.

Welch, M. and Schuster, L. (2005a) 'Detention of Asylum Seekers in the UK and USA: Deciphering Noisy and Quiet Constructions', *Punishment Society* 7 (4): 397–417.

Welch, M and Schuster, L. (2005b) 'Detention of Asylum Seekers in the US, UK, France, Germany, and Italy: A Critical View of the Globalizing Culture of Control', *Criminal Justice* 5 (4): 331–55.

Wikileaks (2010) 'Kabul War Diary'. Available online at: http://wardiary.wikileaks.org/ (accessed 23 August 2010).

Wilder, A. (2009a) 'Losing Hearts and Minds in Afghanistan', *Viewpoints Special Edition: Afghanistan, 1979–2009: In the Grip of Conflict* (2 December 2009). Available online at: www.mei.edu/Publications/WebPublications/Viewpoints/ViewpointsArchive/tabid/541/ctl/Detail/mid/1623/xmid/831/xmfid/11/Default.aspx (accessed 25 June 2010).

Wilder, A. (2009b) 'A "weapons system" based on wishful thinking', *The Boston Globe* (16 September 2009). Available online at: www.boston.com/bostonglobe/editorial_opinion/oped/articles/2009/09/16/a_weapons_system_based_on_wishful_thinking/?s_campaign=8315 (accessed 25 June 2010).

Williams, M. C. (1998) 'Identity and the Politics of Security', *European Journal of International Relations* 4 (2): 204–25.

Williams, M. C. (2005) 'What is the National Interest? The Neoconservative Challenge in IR Theory', *European Journal of International Relations* 11 (3): 307–37.

Williams, M. C. (2007) *Culture and Security: Symbolic Power and the Politics of International Security* London: Routledge.

Wilson, J. and Kelling, G. (1982) 'Broken Windows: the Police and Neighborhood Safety', *Atlantic Monthly* Available online at: www.theatlantic.com/magazine/archive/1982/03/broken-windows/4465/ (accessed 30 January 2012).

Wilson, S. and Kamen, A. (2009) ' "Global War On Terror" Is Given New Name', *Washington Post* (25 March 2009). Available online at: www.washingtonpost.com/wp-dyn/content/article/2009/03/24/AR2009032402818.html (accessed 11 May 2010).

Zureik, E. and Salter, M. B. (2005) 'Global Surveillance and Policing: Borders, Security, Identity – Introduction'. In *Global Surveillance and Policing: Borders, Security, Identity*, Zureik, E. and Salter, M. B. (eds.), Portland, Oregon: Willan Publishing, 1–10.

Index

insecurity, contemporary problematizations of
146–8
inside/outside dichotomy 16–17
institutional firewalls 112
insurgency, definition 36, 51
interdiction 85–6
international drug trade, complicity of US
security agencies 147
international law 132–3
intervention 17, 46, 51, 85, 129, 131–3, 137–8,
141–2
Intifada 41
irregular warfare, close links between drug
trafficking and 146–7
ISAF (International Security Assistance Force)
139–40

Jabri, V. 21, 31
Jacobs, J. 93
Johnson, Lyndon B. 62
JPATS (Justice Prisoner and Alien
Transportation System) 104
JSOC (Joint Special Operations Command)
103

Kaldor, M. 130
Kan, P. R. 146–7
Kappeler, V. E. 76
Katrina, Hurricane 118–19
Katyal, N. K. 94
Kelling, G. 74, 96
Kennedy, John F. 36, 43–4, 58, 123
Kenney, M. 71
Kerner Commission on Civil Disturbances 78
Khrushchev, Nikita 37
Kilcullen, D. J. 56, 88, 138
kingpin strategy 71
Kipling, R. 32
Klare, M. T. 51
Komer, Robert 49–50
Kornbluh, P. 51
Kraska, P. B. 76
Krome Detention Centre 100
Ku Klux Klan 66

Laos 37
LAPD (Los Angeles Police Department) 68, 76
L.A. Riots 72
law, zone of indistinction between violence and
17
'Law Enforcement Faces the Revolutionary-
Guerrilla Criminal' (Hoover) 79
LEAA (Law Enforcement Assistance
Administration) 61–3
legal fetishism 153
Leonhart, Michele M. 65
liberal governmentalities of security 24, 26, 31,
129, 148–9
liberalism: Dean's observations 22; double
standards 92; Foucauldian perspective 22–3;

Schmitt's critique 24; supposed risks to 17;
the two most fundamental illiberal
assemblages of 25
liberal rule, Dean on the persistence of
authoritarian features in 25
liberal security, governmentalities and agents of
33–4
liberal way of development 27, 136
liberal way of rule 27
liberal way of war 26–7, 136
Libya 52
LIC (Low Intensity Conflict) doctrine 51–2, 61,
89
Light, J. S. 84
Lind, W. S. 101
Lockheed 83–4

Malaya 49
management of unease 34
Manichaeism 149
Mao Tse-tung 41–3, 57
Maple, J. 75
Mariel boatlift 100
McChrystal, Stanley 60, 139
McClintock, M. 45, 52
McCuen, John J. 44
McFate, M. 53, 123–4, 127
metaphorical warfare 29–30, 111
Mexico 91, 109–10
The Militarization of the U.S.-Mexico Border
(Dunn) 89
Military Aid Program 46
Military-Industrial Complex 84
Military Review 123
MOUT (Military Operations on Urbanized
Terrain) doctrine 113
My Lai 63–4

NAFTA (North American Free Trade
Agreement) 91
Nagl, J. A. 49–50, 53
narco-delinquency 64
narco-insurgency 109–10
National Defence Authorization Act 71
National Guard 84
Nation of Islam 66
NATO 140–1
Negri, A. 28–9, 56, 81, 133
Neocleous, M. 18, 31–2, 153
netwar 28, 111–12
network-centric warfare 106–8
Newman, O. 93–4
New York Times 102, 119
NEXUS 91–2
Nisour Square Massacre 119
Nixon, Richard 63
no-knock entries 63, 65, 76, 80
non-intervention 132
non-trinitarian war 28
Norton, R. 147–8